Missing Links

JOHN READER

Missing Links

The hunt for earliest man

LITTLE, BROWN AND COMPANY
Boston   Toronto

LIBRARY OF CONGRESS CATALOG CARD NO. 80-84642

First American Edition

PRINTED IN ITALY

FRONTISPIECE *The Neanderthal skullcap*

HOMO noſce Te ipſum.

Carolus Linnaeus
Systema Naturae, 1735

Foreword

JOHN READER'S book is a substantial and solid piece of work, and also a very timely one. In a field that is beginning to overflow with new texts, John's unique approach fills what ecologists would call an 'empty niche'. His photographs are superb, every one reflecting the care and artistry we have come to expect of his work. But as an added bonus we have a text which could quite easily stand on its own without illustrations as a fascinating account of the history of paleoanthropology. The book brings new information and insights to the early phases of the story, and in addition gives us detailed coverage of the contemporary history of paleoanthropology up to 1980. Contemporary history is always the most difficult kind to write, and inevitably more controversial. I think this is a successful attempt, demonstrating as it does the continuity of paleoanthropological discourse over more than a century, and the extent to which many apparently quite new problems are not in fact new. I do not agree with everything John has written; on balance, though, the contemporary events I know about seem accurately and soundly recorded.

The story told is a fascinating one. The book concentrates throughout on the stars of the field – the anthropologists who made or first interpreted major discoveries, and on the objects – the fossils. As the story comes closer to the present we see that scientists pay more attention to context: how old a fossil is and how accurate is its dating; what kind of environment existed at the time, and what part of the habitat a particular human ancestor might have exploited.

Early on the accounts of human evolution were fossil-free, or essentially so. They had to be, because Darwin, Haeckel, Huxley and the other mid-nineteenth-century theorizers had either no or few fossils. Yet they still managed to devise plausible schemes: plausible both to many of their contemporaries and as judged in the light of a century of subsequent fossil discoveries. I suppose the crux of the subject and of this book is, why have the schemes been so durable, so robust? Is it because those nineteenth-century great men were so prescient, because the story really was rather simple and straightforward? Or is something more subtle and unexpected going on? Could we be partly fooling ourselves in letting an incomplete and ambiguous record be moulded by theoretical assumptions that have remained essentially unaffected by the actual fossil record?

Careful historical research can help answer that question.

Human fossils were found infrequently in the early days, but by the early twentieth century enough were known to flesh out the evolutionary stories with real characters: Pithecanthropus, Neanderthal, Piltdown. Most authorities agreed that the human brain and its tremendous growth were of great importance in understanding the apparently inexorable rise of modern humans. There were differences of opinion about the speed of the process, how old modern humans were, exactly how many extinct side branches there had been, and so forth. But there was general agreement that the brain was important, had led the way, and that aberrant branches of the human evolutionary tree represented failed attempts at becoming human. (Of course there were always minority opinions, and Haeckel's theoretical proposal of the 1860s that bipedalism preceded brain expansion remained 'available' as a potential evolutionary framework.)

A relatively minor controversy erupted in 1925 over the first australopithecine from Taung in South Africa, only to die down when these strange small-brained creatures could be explained away as odd apes. The 1930s and 1940s provided a major injection of new fossils, mainly from China and South Africa. Those from Asia clarified the nature of Pithecanthropus, or *Homo erectus* as it became known. The African fossils revived and then resolved one of the major controversies of human origins: they greatly expanded our knowledge of the australopithecines and established virtually beyond doubt that upright walking preceded brain expansion in human evolution. With that clarified, the basic outlines of the human evolutionary story as most of us now see it were cast. Since the 1950s we have added many more fossils, but our basic schemes have hardly changed.

Along with the new fossils of the last two decades came new kinds of sophisticated evolutionary and ecological thinking, and new kinds of data, made possible by our asking new questions. We now actively seek information about context – time and habitat – when planning an expedition. Perhaps 'planning' is the key word here. Along with the growth of multidisciplinary projects has come, slowly, a different way of approaching research, by defining problems and asking questions, and then by searching for the data to answer those questions. Fossil hominids are of course still the main objects of the quest, but rather as the bearers of information than as objects in their own right. At least, this is how the current generation of practitioners likes to view its work!

Yet the fossils remain glamorous, the centre of attention certainly for the non-professional public, frequently for those paleoanthropologists who are not the actual 'hunters', and often – perhaps not surprisingly – for the hunters themselves. So the point is worth emphasizing that the fossils are important not in themselves but because of what they tell us: yet what they tell us is highly ambiguous. Interpretations, schemes, and stories vary from one authority to the other, and evolve and reemerge through time. Why? Because inferences, or conclusions, or speculations, are derived in a complicated way, depending on one's theoretical stance, implicit and explicit assumptions, and on the way in which particular items are selected to be 'facts' (for example, a tooth length is considered a useful fact while colour usually isn't). The inferential process itself is affected by assumptions, theoretical frameworks, the particular facts collected, and so forth. The facts chosen, and the inferences drawn, are heavily dependent upon theoretical background assumptions many of which are either not acknowledged or not even recognized.

If you read technical papers on human evolution today you will often find them full of quantitative techniques and the jargon of hypothesis testing: formalism, objectivity, quantification, and rigour have finally come to the field. More and more of our students spend time learning methodology, reading about it and writing about it: learning to behave like 'real' scientists. Our science, we learn, is empirical and involves the collection of facts; when enough are collected we should be able to derive, by a process of induction, theories to explain the facts. From the theories we then invent hypotheses which are tested experimentally or observationally by collecting more facts, enabling us to reject or modify those hypotheses.

Actually, just as paleoanthropology has hit its 'philosophical' phase the emphasis elsewhere in science has begun to shift, or expand, to look more closely at the history of science, to see what actually did happen in the development of an idea rather than what ideally ought to have happened. Hence the timeliness of John Reader's book, because it helps explain how discoveries were made, both the finding of the fossils and, infinitely more importantly, the invention of the concepts which are built upon or sometimes exist in spite of the fossils. The book tells us what happened, not only in the past but up to the present too, and it tells us a little of why things happened: through a blend of 'ideas in the air at the time', a little sociology, a dash of ideology, a touch of individual psychology, and some good or bad luck.

There are some surprises for the reader in the book. A new hero, or rather perhaps a forgotten one, emerges: Robert Broom, who did more than any man to establish the australopithecines as hominids and therefore as creatures central to our understanding of human evolution. I think there were some surprises for the author too. John has stumbled on the fact that scientists (or at least paleoanthropologists) don't behave as scientists are supposed to behave: as fact-grinding, theory-generating, objective automata. He finds that 'Science' is often subjective and untidy. Nowhere is the dependence of fact on theory, or the existence of pre-conceptions, or the importance of emotional commitment, more clearly demonstrated than in the case of Piltdown; or in the controversy over the KBS tuff; or in the debate over *Australopithecus afarensis*. They are 'sloppy', 'untidy', 'personal', yes. But that is because they involve scientists who are also people and because much is at stake, for there are glittering prizes in the form of fame and publicity. And there is more general pressure too for answers to cosmic questions, a hunger that sometimes makes paleoanthropologists priests of a new kind of secular theology.

Yet we should not despair. Progress has been made. Out of the KBS tuff-dating debate came general advances in methodology and approach, and a much deeper understanding of the chronology of that time period. Although the human evolutionary story remains ambiguous we now have many more data – fossils, and contextual information – than we did even ten years ago. There is a new realism enabling us to narrow our quest to answerable problems, and to devise ingenious new ways of reopening apparently unanswerable questions. Despite our obsession with methodology our science is becoming more mature. As far as explanations can go it is beginning to look as though the old story of human evolution, one dominated by a brain expanding in response to elaboration of culture and tools, tells only a fraction of the story. Upright stance came long before brain enlargement, probably in response to changes in mainly vegetable foods that were being eaten. Food and how it is obtained and eaten are now considered of prime importance in the evolution of other kinds of animals, and these seem now increasingly important in telling the story of human evolution. This realigns us with 'nature', by involving the same determining factors in both human and non human evolution.

John Reader's book describes some of what has gone into the process of understanding our past, and demonstrates that what is said about that past can reveal much of how we perceive ourselves today. It shows the humanism of the science of human evolution, and does it with skill, care, and beauty.

David Pilbeam Yale University 19 iv 1980

Contents

Introduction

ON THE MORNING of 2 August 1978 Mary Leakey joined her research team clearing the surface of a solidified volcanic ash-bed at Laetoli Site G, in north-eastern Tanzania. Assistants were deployed around the perimeter while Mary Leakey worked for three hours on a small patch near the centre. She used a dental pick, a soft brush and great care. Time passed slowly: there was little conversation or apparent purpose and the uninitiated might have been struck by the incongruity of the scene – seven adults on their knees tediously sweeping back a tiny patch of wilderness in the company of giraffes and antelopes.

Then, at 10.45, Mary Leakey straightened up abruptly. She lit a cigar, leant forward again, scrutinized the excavation before her and announced: 'Now this really is something to put on the mantelpiece'.

She had uncovered a human-like footprint fossilized in the ash. It was not the first to be found that season, but it was certainly the clearest so far – heel, toes and arch were all well defined. 'This *must* be Homo,' said Mary Leakey. In 1976 geochronologists had reported that the Laetoli ash surface was 3.6 million years old, so the footprint Mary Leakey had found was, in effect, the earliest indisputable evidence of mankind's bipedal gait – an outstanding discovery. While she knelt, the rest of the team gathered round to congratulate her and admire the discovery. But for everyone it was a private moment whose import was not easily shared. The sight of footprints left by an ancestor so long ago combines the commonplace and the miraculous in a manner that language cannot accommodate. It strikes a chord that words distort – especially superlatives.

As the assistants returned to their own work in search of their own discoveries, Mary Leakey, still on her knees, still puffing at her cigar and still gazing at the footprint, said quietly: 'Ah, it is pretty'.

It should be noted that mantelpieces are more a part of Mary Leakey's cultural heritage than of her present lifestyle and the footprints will *never* be removed from Laetoli. But even so, the Laetoli expedition in itself and the moment of discovery that morning demonstrate very well both the fascination and the frustration that attend the study of fossil man. The evidence is rarer than diamonds, and the study is therefore an intriguing mixture of science and treasure hunt.

The study aspires to discover the origins of mankind and define the course of human evolution. But these objectives are concealed by a breadth of time we can barely comprehend. The Laetoli evidence shows that more than 3.6 million years ago some ape-like creature must have stumbled on to the evolutionary path that has led to modern man, but we know very little of the events that determined the route and we have not identified the ancestor who pre-determined the result. Yet the mystery intrigues everyone. Where did we come from, how, why? For many generations religious explanations of one sort or another sufficed to answer these questions, but during the latter half of the nineteenth century the theory of evolution added a biological dimension to the mystery. And ever since scientists have endeavoured to explain the origins of mankind in evolutionary terms.

The best evidence of human evolution, they believed, would be found in fossils linking modern man and extinct ancestor. Accordingly, scientists have scoured the globe for such 'missing links' during the past 120 years. Some remarkable finds have been unearthed: strange and fragile relics that evoke fascinating images of the men who lived long ago, but leave the story of human evolution tantalizingly incomplete. The trouble is that the evolutionary significance of the fossils found so far is not easily determined, and the specimens are pitifully few. One modern scientist describes attempts to decipher the course of human evolution from the fossil evidence presently available as 'rather like trying to follow the story of *War and Peace* from twelve pages torn at random from the book'.

The ideal fossil evidence would be a sequence of complete fossil skeletons spanning a known period of time – this would enable scientists to trace evolutionary development with exemplary precision. But the arbitrary nature of the fossilization process virtually eliminates all chance that such an ideal could ever be achieved or even approached. Far from the ideal, the study of fossil man has been restricted to a slowly accumulating collection of diverse specimens. In the first fifty years only five were discovered, another twenty-five years passed before a dozen were known and even today the significant specimens could all be accumulating collection of diverse specimens. In the first fifty years only the Far East and Africa; they span over three million years; but their clues to the mystery of human evolution represent a minute fraction of mankind's potential ancestry during that time. It has been calculated that the ten skulls from East Turkana in Kenya (an exceptional collection covering over one million years), for example, represent only one individual in every one hundred million – which means that their evidence is no more valid than any two living Americans are today representative of the entire population of the United States.

Such severe shortage of evidence is problem enough, but there are other difficulties too. Uncertain geological age, for instance, means that differing features cannot be placed in chronological order and, most important of all, the fragmentary condition of many fossils means that unequivocal interpretation of their significance is rarely possible. Fossils are often so broken, distorted or incomplete that different authorities may stress different features with equal validity, and the points distinguishing their interpretations may be so slight or unclear that each depends as much upon the proponent's preconceived notions as upon the evidence of the fossil.

Preconceived notions have played a fundamental role in the study of fossil man. Indeed, the science itself was not founded upon the evidence of fossils that needed explanation, but upon the notion that if mankind had evolved then fossils would provide the evidence of links between modern and ancestral forms. Thus scientists have sought evidence to prove an idea. But fossil evidence is rare, and a variety of ideas about human evolution have developed in the long gaps between discoveries, when interpretative speculation inevitably became a predominant activity of the science. Different theories about the origin of mankind were formulated, theories that accommodated the existing evidence and created a preconceived notion of what fossils ought to be found next. And it is remarkable how often the first interpretations of new evidence have confirmed the preconceptions of its discoverer.

Throughout the study of fossil man, the related elements of interpretation, theory and preconception have always been firmly connected with the personality and persuasive ability of their proposer. Thus the science has been dominated by ambitious individuals and has advanced as much by the force of argument as by the strength of the evidence, and as much by the lure of the treasure hunt as by the discipline of science.

Knowledge is the ultimate goal of all science, though evidence occasionally has its own intrinsic appeal. In the study of fossil man, however, both knowledge and evidence are uniquely appealing. The knowledge sought is the ancestry of a supremely important animal – *Homo sapiens*. The evidence consists of rare and mysterious fossils.

Fossils are objects of inestimable value because they are so few, and of highest promise because of the secrets they may reveal. Some are objects of beauty as well, but above all, each is an object of wonder. They are the tangible evidence of our ancestors' existence, and affirm mankind's ancient presence of earth. Scientists say fossils can help us define the

Mary Leakey with 3.6 million-year-old fossil footprint
at Laetoli site G, 2 August 1978

course of human evolution, but everyone – including scientists – is subject to a more emotive response while handling, or even just looking at, a fossil. And the discovery of a fossil is the epitome of this sensation – a sublime moment that quite transcends any knowledge the fossil may afford.

'You must love the fossils,' says Ralph von Koenigswald, who found some important specimens in Java. 'If you love them,' he says, 'then they will come to you.'

The footprints at Laetoli are the latest discovery in a saga that blends the discipline of science with the romance of a treasure hunt and the vagaries of human nature. The saga is far from finished, but it began over 120 years ago when the discovery of Neanderthal Man coincided with the publication of Darwin's theory of evolution.

Chapter One

Neanderthal Man
(1857)

THE THEORY of evolution implied that man was simply a product of life on earth, not its ultimate purpose; it suggested that his origins were shared by the animals of the jungle. An outrageous idea. But if it were true, then the proof would be found in the fossilized remains of early man, which would link man to an earlier form. And since the theory of evolution proposed that man and the apes shared a common ancestor, then the link could be expected to bear some attributes of both. So began the search for the Missing Link, pursued with equal zeal by evolutionist and anti-evolutionist alike – the former seeking the incontrovertible evidence that would establish his theory as fact, and the latter anxious to prove that the link was indeed missing, thus reconfirming his belief that the human form had remained unchanged since the day of creation.

It soon became apparent that conclusive evidence – one way or the other – was exceptionally hard to find. A fossilized vertebral column and other parts which the Swiss naturalist Johann Scheuchzer (1672–1733) had claimed were the remains of a pre-diluvian man were shown by Cuvier a century later to be those of a large salamander.[1] A skeleton from Guadaloupe, found aboard a French ship captured by a British naval vessel and described by the British Museum in 1814 as 'the first known example of the bones of man in a fossil state',[2] later proved to be less than two hundred years old and not fossil at all. And here is a fundamental problem of paleontology: how can it be determined whether or not the bones are fossilized?

Even today, the fossilization process is not fully understood. But the effect is that instead of breaking down into its chemical components after death, a bone (or plant, or insect) is buried and infiltrated by minerals from the soil which replace it, molecule by molecule, until, where organic material existed before, stone remains, exactly preserving the form of the original.

Fossil remains of marine creatures, extinct elephants and so forth, are unmistakable. Human fossils, on the other hand, are found only in geologically recent – and therefore comparatively shallow – deposits, where they may easily be confused with historically recent burials. And how can fossilized and unfossilized bone be distinguished one from the other? In the early nineteenth century the 'tongue test' was a method commonly used – the idea being that bone or fossil adhered to the tongue to a greater or lesser extent depending upon the amount of collagen it contained. However, the tongue test was occasionally contradicted by the hydrochloric acid test – which sometimes revealed large quantities of collagen where the tongue test had shown it to be absent.[3] In view of these factors, geological circumstances were always the best indication of antiquity – were the remains found above, below or among the bones of extinct animals? But such circumstances are always susceptible to sub-jective interpretation, and this in turn could cast doubt upon the validity of the discovery. Which probably explains why a series of early discoveries was largely ignored.

Even the fossils found by Baron von Schlottheim in 1820 near Koestritz, Upper Saxony, nearly two metres below the remains of extinct hyenas and rhinoceros, attracted little attention, although he insisted that 'these human bones from the nature of the soil could not have been buried there, nor have fallen into fissures during battles of ancient times'.[4] And then again, as the concept of evolution filtered from the confines of science into the public consciousness, there were people who sought to hide evidence accidentally encountered.

In 1852 a man chasing rabbits on a French hillside near Aurignac thrust his arm down a hole after his prey and, instead of a rabbit, drew out a large bone. He dug deeper and eventually discovered a cave filled with human remains. Together with most of the local populace the mayor, Dr Amiel, was attracted to the scene; and, once the learned gentleman had satisfied his curiosity to the extent of establishing that the bones had belonged to seventeen individuals of both sexes and all ages, he arranged for their prompt Christian burial in the parish cemetery. Eight years later the sexton professed complete ignorance of the burial site when the paleontologist Edouard Lartet inquired after them in the hopes of adding something to the study of human evolution.[5]

The idea of evolution probably did not reach many people in any comprehensive, or even comprehensible form, during the first part of the nineteenth century; but in 1844 it appeared in a form that was available to all – in a book called *Vestiges of the Natural History of Creation*. It was written by Robert Chambers (1802–71), a journalist of scientific bent. It was very successful, selling out four editions in seven months and more than 20,000 copies before Darwin's *The Origin of Species* appeared fifteen years later.[6]

Vestiges was published anonymously to protect Chambers's business interests and thus, writing for a popular audience and free from the constraints of precise scientific presentation, he could afford to be bold in presenting what he called 'the first attempt to connect the natural sciences into a history of creation'. He drew together all available scientific evidence and hypothesis to describe how the universe is arranged, and how the earth is composed of matter condensed from 'vaporiform chaos'. Calling upon (and occasionally misinterpreting) the evidence of biology and paleontology he told how organic creation and the proliferation of life was the result of natural law, rather than divine intent. 'The simplest and the most primitive type . . . gave birth to the type next above it, . . . this again produced the next higher, and so on to the very highest'.[7] There was a principle of *development* involved, he said, that had operated over a vast space of time. All animals were variations of the same basic skeletal plan; they were, in fact, 'merely modifications of that plan to suit particular conditions' and 'the whole train of animated beings, from the simplest and oldest, up to the highest and most recent [should] be regarded as a series of advances of the principle of development'.[8]

Chambers did not stress the point, but his development hypothesis clearly made man an immediate descendant of the apes (albeit fossil apes then still undiscovered), retaining a 'strong affinity' to the preceding form, just like every other animal. And, of course, 'the development hypothesis would demand . . . that the original seat of the human race should be in a region where the quadrumana [i.e. apes and monkeys] are rife'.[9] It may be tempting to think of *Vestiges* as a brilliant forerunner of Darwin's evolutionary theory, lacking only the principle of Natural Selection to make the hypothesis complete. But it lacked other elements too. Darwin himself remarked that the book displayed 'little accurate knowledge and a great want of scientific caution'; even so, he praised the 'powerful and brilliant style', and considered that the book had 'done excellent service . . . in calling attention to the subject, in removing prejudice, and in thus preparing the ground for the reception of analogous views'.[10]

A charitable thought. It is possible that with *Vestiges* having drawn the fire, so to speak, the attack on Darwin's work was less fierce than it might have been. But it is equally possible that *Vestiges* awakened a broader spectrum of prejudice than would otherwise have been the case and, furthermore, that the book was regarded as a popular version of evolutionary theory upon the basis of which Darwin's work could be attacked without the necessity of reading his more knowledgeable and cautiously scientific book.

As public opinion gradually became aware of the evolutionary theory, it was most anxious about the proposition that man was an animal who shared a common ancestor with the apes. It was at this level that anxiety turned to heated debate wherein science appeared to oppose religion – as popular records monotonously continue to recite. But serious debate is rarely as straightforward as that. There was much more to evolutionary theory than the question of man's place in nature. The pulpit may well have been the most outspoken and inflammatory source of opposition, but there also were scientists who disagreed with the theory of evolution and, although they may have held religious views, scientists were obliged to call upon science, before religion, to support their arguments. And at this level the debate inspired a great deal of earnest endeavour as scientists attempted to reconcile the new facts their colleagues had glimpsed with the old truths they still believed.

In Britain the scientific opposition was led by the distinguished anatomist and paleontologist Richard Owen (1804–92) who energetically applied his indisputable talents to the search for an alternative explanation of the evolutionary phenomena. In 1848 he published his concept of an archetypal vertebrate skeleton.[11] The skeleton did not represent a creature that had ever existed; it was a structural idea, he said, of which all actual vertebrates were functionally diverse embodiments – arisen without any direct evolutionary association. And later, in 1855, Owen used his anatomical expertise in an attempt to disprove the theory of evolution at its most controversial point – man's link with the apes.

The occasion was an evening meeting of the Royal Institution of Great Britain. Owen discussed the structure of the apes as compared to man, referring in particular to 'the last link in the chain of changes – from Quadrumana to Bimana proposed in the hypothesis that specific characters can be so far modified by external influences, operating on successive generations, as to produce a new and higher species of animal, and that thus there had been a gradual progression from the monad up to man'.[12] Beginning and ending with his customarily disparaging remarks on those who proposed the evolutionary theory, Owen endeavoured to show that although ape and man are structurally very similar, the differences between them are much more relevant. He mentioned especially the differences that are not subject to external influences, and therefore should be passed from generation to generation without modification, appearing exactly alike in ancestor and descendant. Owen cited the gorilla's prominent eyebrow ridge as an example of such a feature. There is no muscle attached to it, he pointed out, nor is there any aspect of the gorilla's behaviour which suggests that the prominent ridge could be lost or gained by external causes operating on successive generations. Therefore the ridges must have occurred in the gorilla's ancestors, said Owen, and should occur in all that ancestor's descendants. It followed that if man and gorilla shared a common ancestor, they should also share the prominent eyebrow ridge. But ridges rarely – and then only feebly – occur in man, he pointed out; therefore man and gorilla could not have an ancestor in common. Thus, Owen concluded, the notion that man had evolved from the apes was disproved.

The gorilla's eyebrow ridges were not the only evidence Owen offered in support of his contentions that evening, nor was this the only occasion on which he argued against the common ancestry of man and ape. Nonetheless, it is an extraordinary coincidence that the first fossil to be accepted as evidence of early man's physical form, Neanderthal Man, should have presented prominent eyebrow ridges as its most distinctive feature. Since 1857, when the Neanderthal remains were found, the prominent ridges above its eyes, which Owen claimed were an exclusively ape-like feature, have become symbolic of early man.

Neanderthal Man was found by limestone quarrymen clearing a cave in the deep and narrow ravine known as the Neander valley, through which the Düssel river flows, a short distance from its confluence with the Rhine at Düsseldorf. The cave was quite large but could be entered only with difficulty, the entrance being just a metre or so high and situated twenty metres up a precipitous cliff. The bones were found among the one and a half metres of mud that was dug from the cave floor. It is quite likely that the entire skeleton was present, but the bones were not immediately recognized as human and were unceremoniously dumped with the quarry debris. Several weeks passed before they came to the attention of Dr Fuhlrott, a teacher from Elberfeld, some six or seven kilometres distant, and by then only the skullcap and some limb bones could be found. No faunal fossils – extinct or otherwise – were found with the remains; and because they were in a cave deposit, no stratigraphic position of any relevance could be determined. Consequently, Neanderthal Man could not be placed on the geological scale of relative ages, and the evidence of the fossil's antiquity lay solely in its physical appearance.

Dr Fuhlrott promptly showed the remains to an anatomist, Professor Schaaffhausen, who presented them to the world of science at a meeting of the Lower Rhine Medical and Natural History Society held in Bonn on 4 February 1857 – nearly three years before the publication of *The Origin of Species*. Schaaffhausen was convinced that the remains were ancient and human; but the limb bones were exceptionally thick, he remarked, with pronounced muscle attachments denoting an extremely powerful individual. The strange shape of the skull was due to natural conformation, said Schaaffhausen, but was quite unlike any modern race, even the most barbarous. The prominent eyebrow ridges – 'characteristic of the facial conformation of the large apes' – must have been typical of the Neanderthal race, he suggested, giving them a savage and brutal aspect. He concluded that the remains must have belonged to one of the original wild races of north-western Europe; a barbarous lot whose 'aspect and flashing of their eyes' had terrified even the Roman armies.[13] Some listeners challenged Schaaffhausen's views (mostly contending that the remains were not human at all), but controversy did not assume significant proportions until his paper appeared in the Natural History Review of April 1861. It was translated by George Busk (1807–86), then Professor of Anatomy at the Royal College of Surgeons, who appended some remarks of his own, drawing particular attention to the Neanderthal skull's overall resemblance to that of the gorilla and chimpanzee. Shortly thereafter the recently knighted geologist, Sir Charles Lyell, acquired a plaster cast and some photographs of the original specimen which were examined and described by the biologist Thomas Huxley (1825–95), and before very long Neanderthal Man became the nub of an argument that was distinguished by its vigour, imagination and unintended humour.

Broadly speaking there were two points of view. The physical peculiarities of Neanderthal Man represented either an early stage of human evolution linking man to an ape-like ancestor, or pathological deformities of modern man more gross than any medical science had ever encountered. Because their antiquity could be neither proved nor disproved, the fossils themselves were the only evidence and, as was to be expected, interpretation of the evidence was decidedly coloured by preconceptions concerning the theory of evolution in general. Those willing to accept the theory believed the remains were very old and freely discussed their primitive, 'barbarous' and ape-like characteristics in evolutionary terms. Those opposed to the theory of evolution, on the other hand, believed the remains were of modern man and sought a modern, medical explanation for their peculiarities.

As it happened, the first thorough descriptions of the fossils were compiled by evolutionists and, while the fossils and casts remained unavailable for general inspection, these reports constituted the evidence

OVERLEAF *The original remains of Neanderthal Man*

itself. Which no doubt added the suspicion of bias and misrepresentation to every anti-evolutionist stance. Add the clashing personalities of very ambitious individuals to this already volatile mixture of inconclusive evidence and preconceived belief, and the result is a very lively brew. The protagonists were 'in danger of allowing the wanderings of imagination to take the place of scientific deduction, and to lead us far away from sober fact', as the *Medical Times and Gazette*, Britain's leading medical journal of the day, commented in an editorial reviewing the evidence of 'Homo Antiquus',[14]

Taken out of context, this remark seems the essence of moderation and good sense, but the context reveals how preconceptions may rule in the absence of conclusive evidence. Professor Schaaffhausen's description of the Neanderthal fossils 'strongly reminds one of Sir Walter Scott's Black Dwarf,' wrote the editors, 'a theory of rickets and idiocy would . . . go some way towards unravelling the mystery,' they said, and concluded that '. . . this skull belonged to some poor idiotic hermit whose remains were found in the cave where he died'.

There is a salutary observation to be made here, which applies to virtually every discovery that has added new knowledge to the story of human evolution. Where the evidence is not sufficient to prove interpretations based on current beliefs right or wrong, any speculation is permissible and the acceptance that speculation achieves is more a measure of the proposer's standing than of its validity. Some speculation of course turns out to be correct but corroborative evidence is always required to show that it is so and, until that evidence is found, speculative argument continues.

For many years idiocy and rickets remained the anti-evolutionists' best explanation of Neanderthal Man's physical peculiarities.[15] The theme was developed and expounded most forcefully by F. Mayer, Professor of Anatomy at Bonn University. Mayer had the advantage of having examined the original fossils. He dismissed the significance of the prominent eyebrow ridges and remarked instead upon the absence of a sagittal crest (i.e. the ridge of bone running along the top of an ape's skull to which the chewing muscles are affixed). 'Show me a human fossil skull with a sagittal crest, and I will acknowledge the descent of man from an ape-like ancestor,' he said.[16]

Mayer was convinced that the remains had belonged to a modern individual. In the skull he saw similarities with some Mongolian, and even some Caucasian specimens that he had examined but, nevertheless, Neanderthal Man had been a degraded creature in his view, and one who had probably suffered from rickets as a child – the disease being common, he pointed out, among those who lived in wet houses and ate nothing but potatoes. Thus rickets might explain the distinctly bent legs of Neanderthal Man. But bow-legs are also common among those who spend a lifetime in the saddle, Mayer observed. And so turning to the evidence of history, the anatomist offered his interpretation of Neanderthal Man: a Cossack army under General Tchernitcheff had camped in the vicinity prior to their advance across the Rhine on 14 January 1814, and he believed that the bones in the Neanderthal cave must have belonged to an ailing Cossack deserter who had hidden and died there.

Thomas Huxley, the evolutionists' most ardent champion, dismissed Mayer's conclusions as a work 'laden with numerous jocosities of small size, but great ponderosity, directed against Mr Darwin and his doctrine . . .'. He also noted that Professor Mayer had failed to explain how the dying man had managed to climb a precipice twenty metres high and bury himself after death; and wondered why the man would have removed all his clothes and equipment before performing these wonderful feats.[17]

On a more serious plane, Huxley meanwhile had defined the evolutionist view concisely in three essays published together under the title *Man's Place in Nature* in 1863. Here he described the natural history of the apes, defined man's relationship with the lower animals and presented the first thorough and detailed comparative description of the Neanderthal remains. Huxley concluded that although the skull was the most ape-like yet known, it did not represent a being that was intermediate between the apes and man; at most it showed some reversion from the modern human skull towards that of an ape-like ancestor. The determining factor, Huxley said, was the size of the brain. The cranial capacity of the Neanderthal skull was well within the modern human range and twice that of the largest ape. And so, with these remarks, Huxley effectively set brain size as the definitive characteristic of the genus *Homo*.

The assessment of Neanderthal Man's brain size raised the interesting question of his mental abilities. Could a creature of such ape-like appearance think like a man? The anti-evolutionists, of course, said no, he had been an idiot; and even among the evolutionists some were unwilling to accept the creature as sapient man. William King, for instance, Professor of Geology at Queens College Galway, believed that Neanderthal Man had stood next to 'benightedness' with 'thoughts and desires . . . which never soared beyond those of the brute'. In fact, King felt so strongly about Neanderthal Man's mental deficiencies that he proposed his exclusion from the human species (*Homo sapiens*). He would have liked to exclude him from the genus *Homo* altogether, he said, but in the absence of facial bones and the base of the skull he appreciated that this 'would be clearly overstepping the limits of inductive reasoning'. So King settled for a new species: *Homo neanderthalensis.*[18] This was a startling development, suggesting that formal zoological distinction could be given to the fossils of ancestral man. Since then naming new species on man's evolutionary path has become common practice, as we shall see.

Given the liveliness of the Neanderthal debate it was inevitable that corroborative, or dismissive, evidence would eventually be found. It arrived just a matter of weeks after King had created the new species: a skull that, though missing some parts, possessed everything the Neanderthal skull had lacked – the entire face, the upper jaw and most of the teeth. Furthermore, it was strikingly similar to the Neanderthal specimen, especially in respect of the eyebrow ridges. In short, the new skull was just what King had required to complete his inductive reasoning; but it would not have helped him relegate Neanderthal from the genus *Homo.* On the contrary, it might well have persuaded him that the specimen did not deserve specific distinction, for its general aspect confirmed Huxley's assessment.

The new skull had been found during the construction of military fortifications in Gibraltar. When and by whom is not known. The first mention of the relic appears in the minutes of the Gibraltar Scientific Society for 3 March 1848, where it is recorded that the secretary 'presented a human skull from the Forbes Quarry, North Front'. In other words, the discovery pre-dated Neanderthal by at least eight years, but the Gibraltar specimen did not attract attention until much later. It was consigned to the 'small museum of natural curiosities which at one time existed in Gibraltar', where it languished while the museum was 'allowed to fall into a state of confusion and neglect' until 1863 when 'its extraordinary peculiarities fortunately struck the notice of Dr Hodgkin', an ethnologist on a visit to Gibraltar who then arranged for its dispatch to George Busk.[19]

Busk, of course, having translated Schaaffhausen's Neanderthal paper, immediately recognized the importance of the new and more complete specimen, not only in its own right, but also for the corroborative evidence it brought to the Neanderthal case. The Gibraltar skull 'adds immensely to the scientific value of the Neanderthal specimen', he wrote in the *Reader* a few days after receiving the skull, 'showing that the latter does not represent . . . a mere individual peculiarity, but that it may have been characteristic of a race extending from the Rhine to the Pillars of Hercules; for . . . even Professor Mayer will hardly suppose that

George Busk and the Gibraltar skull

a ricketty Cossack engaged in the campaign of 1814 had crept into a sealed fissure in the Rock of Gibraltar'.[20]

Busk exhibited the skull at the meeting of the British Association for the Advancement of Science held in Bath during September 1864. He spoke of its general appearance and compared it with the skulls of modern races, but primarily stressed how it matched and complemented the Neanderthal specimen.[21] In a letter discussing the forthcoming meeting, the paleontologist Hugh Falconer had suggested that Busk should name the fossil *Homo calpicus*, from Calpe, the ancient name for the Rock of Gibraltar. Falconer also composed an advertisement that would introduce the new species to science: 'Walk up! and see Professor Busk's Grand Priscan, Pithecoid, Mesocephalous, Prognathous, Agrioblemmatous, Platycnemic, wild *Homo calpicus* of Gibraltar'. Falconer was particularly pleased with Agrioblemmatous, feeling that the Greek combination happily united 'the truculence of the eye and the savagery of the face' which he was certain must have characterized the man on the Rock of Gibraltar.[22]

Curiously, despite its undoubted significance, the Gibraltar skull inspired very little comment. Today it has virtually disappeared from the literature, and its corroborative evidence was ignored by the eminent pathologist Rudolf Virchow in 1872, when he added his views to the Neanderthal debate. Virchow (1821–1902) was a highly respected medical academician. He had been the first to describe the breakdown of the cell that marks the onset of disease, and the science of pathology was built upon his discoveries. He was also the founder and president of Germany's Institute of Anthropology; and, while his fierce opposition to the theory of evolution predicated his conclusions on the Neanderthal remains, his twin interests – pathology and anthropology – characterized their substance.

On the evidence of pathology Virchow decided that the bones had belonged to a very old man who had suffered from rickets as a child, severe head injuries in middle age, and from crippling arthritis for many years before he died. Thus the physical peculiarities were accounted for. To show that Neanderthal Man had died in the recent past and was not, therefore, an ancestor of man, Virchow called upon the evidence of anthropology. Such an ill and crippled individual could not have survived to old age in one of the nomadic hunter-gatherer groups that characterized the earliest stages of human social development, he said; therefore the man must have lived in an agricultural society of much more recent times, when people were settled and able to care for their sick and aged relatives.[23]

Virchow's pronouncements on the Neanderthal remains were the last to be made by an eminent scientist reared and educated in the years before Darwin presented the first comprehensive theory of evolution; in effect they were the last words of the pre-evolutionists, and they present yet another example of a scientist struggling to reconcile new evidence with his old beliefs. But of course the debate concerning human evolution did not end with Virchow. Subsequently the search for more conclusive fossil evidence became intense and some spectacular discoveries were made. Two complete skeletons were found in a cave near Spy in Belgium during 1887; another was found near La Chapelle-aux-Saints in France during 1908 and several more came from La Ferrassie in 1909, and from La Quina in 1911. The most striking feature of these remarkably complete finds was their overall similarity to the Neanderthal specimens; clearly they all represented a race that had populated Europe from Belgium to Gibraltar.

Had he seen the new evidence, Virchow might have felt obliged to revise his diagnosis of head injuries and arthritis. But now the discoveries were examined by a new generation of investigators: a generation born and educated in the post-Darwinian era, but one which was nonetheless subject to serious and erroneous preconceptions of its own. And it is ironic that although fundamental beliefs had changed so radically, the conclusions of Virchow and the new investigators were essentially the same – both excluded Neanderthal from the family of man.

Marcellin Boule (1861–1942) was perhaps the most authoritative of the post-Darwinian investigators. He eventually became Director of Human Paleontology at the French National Museum of Natural History, and for more than fifty years commanded the respect of both science and the interested public, especially after the First World War had cast German science into disfavour and disarray. Boule wrote extensively on the fossils of early man.[24] His views and preconceptions are very largely responsible for the image – which is still with us today – of Neanderthal Man as a shambling, frowning brute of low intelligence. By the turn of the century, virtually all active scientists accepted the great antiquity of the earth, the theory of evolution and the inevitable conclusion that man had evolved from an ancestor in common with the apes. There was no question that Neanderthal Man *had* evolved from some primitive stock – but could such a creature represent the ancestor of modern man? This was a question that Boule and his fellow thinkers barely deigned to contemplate.

Boule's judgement was based on his extremely thorough studies of the skeleton from La Chapelle-aux-Saints.[25] Neanderthal Man, he pointed out, was quite different from modern man in physical form, yet very close in time; and he concluded that the process of evolution could not have effected so much change in so few generations. Neanderthal Man had divergent toes like the apes, Boule said; he had walked on the outer edges of his feet like the orang-utan; he could not have straightened his knees; he lacked the convex spine essential for upright posture; he had the head slung forward with jutting jaw; and possessed only the most rudimentary psychic nature and articulate language.

Of those who endorsed Boule's conclusions, Grafton Elliott Smith, the distinguished Professor of Anatomy at the University of London, was among the most influential. In his book *The Evolution of Man*, published in 1924, Elliott Smith described Boule's reconstruction of the La Chapelle-aux-Saints skeleton as

> a clear-cut picture of the uncouth and repellent Neanderthal Man. His short, thick-set and coarsely built body was carried in a half-stooping slouch upon short, powerful and half-flexed legs of peculiarly ungraceful form. His thick neck sloped forward from the broad shoulders to support the massive flattened head, which protruded forward, so as to form an unbroken curve of neck and back, in place of the alternation of curves which is one of the graces of the truly erect *Homo sapiens*. The heavy overhanging eyebrow-ridges and retreating forehead, the great coarse face with its large eye-sockets, broad nose, and receding chin, combined to complete the picture of unattractiveness, which it is more probable than not was still further emphasized by a shaggy covering of hair over most of the body. The arms were relatively short, and the exceptionally large hands lacked the delicacy and the nicely balanced co-operation of thumb and fingers which is regarded as one of the most distinctive of human characteristics. . . . The contemplation of all these features emphasizes the reality of the fact that the Neanderthal Man belongs to some other species than *Homo sapiens*.[26]

The views of Boule and Elliott Smith are a mirror image of those expressed fifty years before – the same evidence called to support diametrically opposed conclusions. Mayer and Virchow had claimed that the Neanderthal fossils were of a modern man who was not related to the apes; now Boule and Elliott Smith claimed that Neanderthal Man was a descendant of the apes who was not related to modern man. In both cases the evidence lay in the physical peculiarities of the fossils and, in the interpretation of this evidence, Boule and Elliott Smith were no

The bent limbs and arthritic vertebral column of this fossil skeleton from La Chapelle-aux-Saints led Marcellin Boule to conclude that Neanderthal Man had been a degenerate race.

less guilty than their predecessors of allowing preconception to cloud conclusion. Mayer and Virchow had stressed the pathological aspects that supported the conclusions they preferred; Boule and Elliott Smith ignored the pathological aspects that would have refuted their conclusions.

In both cases the pathological evidence was exactly the same – severe arthritis. It was first noted by Camille Arambourg in 1955 and precisely defined in 1957 by Straus and Cave.[27] They complained about Boule's fanciful reconstruction of the La Chapelle-aux-Saints skeleton (the centre of gravity was placed so far forward, they said, that the man would have fallen flat on his face before taking a step). Straus and Cave expressed surprise that Boule had not noticed the 'severity of the osteo-arthritis deformens affecting the vertebral column'. There was 'no valid reason for assuming that the posture of Neanderthal Man differed significantly from that of present day man', they said. Given a bath, a collar and tie, he would have passed unnoticed in a New York subway.

The Straus and Cave interpretations found support and added impetus to the Single Species Hypothesis (which suggests that all man-like fossils should be assigned to one species),[28] but it did not end the argument about Neanderthal Man's position on the family tree. Modern estimates suggest he lived between one hundred thousand and forty thousand years ago; some scientists maintain that he is blended in the gene pool of modern man,[29] others that he became extinct. The reasons given for his extinction are various. Some suggest that his rugged specialized adaptation to the Ice Age did not fit him for survival during the easier times that followed.[30] Other authorities consider it more likely that the 'classic' Neanderthals were gradually supplanted by less rugged types found in the Middle East.[31]

But of course these theories were developed with the benefit of further fossil evidence. Though still controversial, the Neanderthals are now the best represented example of fossil man. For thirty years after the first discovery, however, Neanderthal Man was the *only* fossil that provided clues to human evolution. From the 1860s to the 1890s (when the next new evidence was found) great minds were free to speculate upon the mystery. Theory abounded; and firm notions emerged of the sort of fossils that needed to be found.

Chapter Two

Java Man
(1891)

In 1865, six years after *The Origin of Species* first appeared, and six years before Darwin published *The Descent of Man*, the eminent German zoologist Ernst Haeckel (1834–1919) published a book called *Generelle Morphologie*. In it he treated evolution as fact and ventured to speculate upon the yet deeper mysteries of life and natural order to which Darwin's theory might be applied. Haeckel subsequently expanded and developed his ideas in *The History of Creation*, an extremely popular book which caused Darwin to write: '. . . if *History of Creation* had appeared before my essay [*The Descent of Man*] had been written, I should probably never have completed it. Almost all the conclusions at which I have arrived I find confirmed by the naturalist, whose knowledge on many points is much fuller than mine'.[1]

Ernst Haeckel was a perceptive and energetic scientist who created several of the words and images by which the natural sciences are now defined ('ecology' is one worthy of mention). In *The History of Creation* he constructed the first of the now commonplace ancestral trees, depicting the evolution of life from 'living creatures of the simplest kind imaginable, organisms without organs',[2] through twenty-one stages of development to modern man – the twenty-second and final stage. Within this general scheme of things, Haeckel created the concept of the *Phylum*, that is the 'stem', to accommodate all organisms descended from a common form, and the word *Phylogeny* to describe their evolutionary development from common form to distinct species. Within each species, Haeckel suggested that *Ontogeny* should describe the development of the individual from conception to maturity and, recognizing the parallels that exist between the evolution of a species and the development of an individual, proposed his 'fundamental biogenetic law' – Ontogeny recapitulates Phylogeny.

In principle, Haeckel's law synthesized the observation that an organism seemed to pass through all the stages of its species's evolution

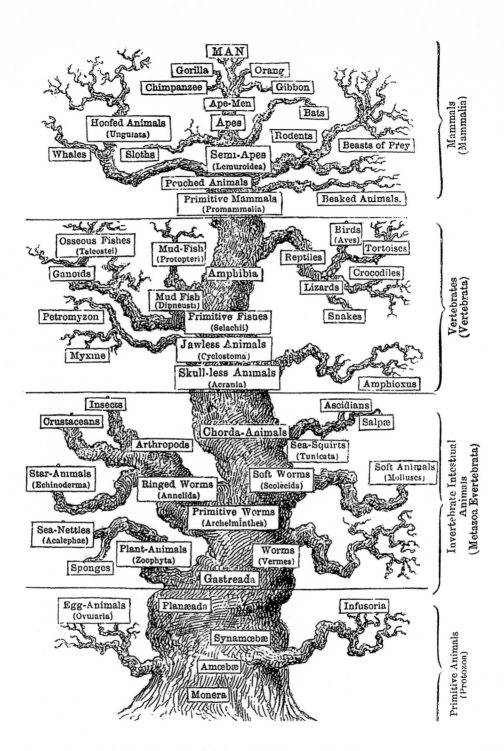

Ancestral tree devised by Ernst Haeckel, from The History of Creation

as it grew from egg to mature individual. During nine months in the
womb the human embryo could be said to recapitulate man's entire
evolutionary history, and as it grew the important stages of development
could be recognized. To begin with the foetus had only the internal
organs of the simplest creatures. Later the gill-arches of the fish appeared,
followed by the backbone of the vertebrates and finally the placenta of
the mammals. An important corollary of Haeckel's observation was that,
at certain stages, the embryos of quite different creatures should reveal
the identical form of their common ancestor. And indeed, in *The History
of Creation* Haeckel presented illustrations which he believed showed
that at four weeks, for example, there was little to choose between the
embryos of man, dog and tortoise; differentiation between the embryos
of man and ape came very much later.[3]

Thus Haeckel found the theory of evolution proved to his satisfaction
in the science of embryology. There were several awkward anomalies,
it is true – some organs appeared in the embryo out of the evolutionary
sequence, for instance, and some vestigial features were retained while
other, once important features scarcely showed at all. But Haeckel
created a new term for each anomaly – caenogenesis, dysteleology,
heterochronism – and regarded them as mysterious puzzles rather than
negative evidence. A similarly creative attitude characterized much of
Haeckel's work. Where no scientific evidence was available he used his
own persuasive logic to fill the gap. The 'Chain of the Animal Ancestors
of Man' he devised is a case in point, particularly relevant here because
its twenty-first link is believed to have inspired the discovery of some
important fossil human remains.

Haeckel's chain began with 'structureless and formless little lumps of
mucous or albuminous matter' – that is, protoplasm, spontaneously
generated, and proceeded via the sack worms (eighth stage) the mud fish
(twelfth stage), the tailed amphibians (fourteenth stage) to the tailed ape
(nineteenth stage). The twentieth stage in the chain comprised the man-
like apes (Anthropoides) – the orang-utan, the gibbon, chimpanzee and
gorilla. But were the man-like apes the ancestors of man? 'There do not
exist direct human ancestors among the Anthropoides of the present
day,' reasoned Haeckel, 'but they certainly existed among the unknown
extinct Human Apes of the miocene period.' And how did he know?
'The certain proof of their former existence is furnished by the comparative anatomy of Manlike Apes and Man,' he wrote.

In fact, Haeckel considered the man-like apes to be so much like man
that his chain hardly required an intermediate stage connecting the two.
But there was one behavioural characteristic that merited distinction in

Haeckel's opinion – articulate speech. This important human attribute was not shared by the apes, and could not have been acquired in just one stage of the Chain, he reasoned, so there must have been some sort of speechless primeval man between the apes and Genuine Man. He proposed the Ape-like Man (*Pithecanthropi*) as 'this intermediate link and twenty-first stage of his Chain of the Animal Ancestors of Man. 'The certain proof that such Primeval Man without the power of speech, or Ape-like Man, must have preceded men possessing speech is the result arrived at by an inquiring mind,' he wrote.

> We as yet know of no fossil remains of the hypothetical primeval man who developed out of the anthropoid apes, but considering the extraordinary resemblance between the lowest woolly-haired men, and the highest man-like apes, which still exists at the present day it requires but a slight stretch of the imagination to conceive an intermediate form connecting the two, and to see in it an approximate likeness to the supposed primeval men, or ape-like men. The form of their skull was probably very long, with slanting teeth; . . . their arms comparatively longer and stronger; . . . their legs, on the other hand, knock-kneed, shorter and thinner, with entirely undeveloped calves; their walk but half erect.[4]

And where might this chain of man's ancestry have been wrought? Haeckel said a continent now sunk below the Indian Ocean was the most likely place. Such a landmass had been postulated by other scientists on the basis of plant and animal distributions; it was called Lemuria, after the ancestral primates (the lemurs) that would have characterized the fauna of the ancient continent. In Haeckel's scheme, Lemuria embraced what is now Madagascar and India, and extended from Africa across the Indian Ocean to Indonesia and the Philippines. From this 'so-called Paradise, the cradle of the human race',[5] the ancestor Haeckel called *Pithecanthropus alalus* (speechless ape-man) would have spread and populated the world. Westward to Africa, north westward to the Middle East and Europe, northward to Asia and over the landbridge to the Americas, eastward via Java to Australasia and Polynesia.

Of course, the best proof of Haeckel's contentions would be a series of fossils representing each of the links in his chain, but Haeckel was fully aware that fossil collecting was in imprecise affair – it is 'ridiculous to expect paleontology to furnish an unbroken series of positive data,' he once wrote.[6] And besides, for Haeckel, logic and reason supplied ample proof of evolutionary theory. 'The descent of man from an extinct series of primates is not a vague hypothesis' to be proved, he said, 'but an historical fact', and therefore as incapable of exact scientific proof as the fact that Aristotle, Caesar and King Alfred once lived.[7]

The History of Creation was translated into a dozen languages and remained in print for many years. Haeckel's ideas were well known by students of the immediate post-Darwinian era, and among those whom they inspired was Eugene Dubois (1858–1940), the eldest son of a devout Dutch Catholic family who collected fossils as a boy and entered medical school in 1877 at the age of nineteen.

The impressionable, formative years of Dubois' generation of medical students coincided with the period during which evolutionary thinking filled the biological sciences with new vigour. Scientists were exploring the new horizons revealed by Darwin's work, formulating new hypotheses to answer old questions – creating new beliefs. It was a period of unhesitating consolidation, but while medical school introduced Dubois to the persuasive excitement of a revolutionary discipline, at home he was subject to the intractability of the old faith. And from these irreconcilable influences of his youth, Dubois emerged as an ambitious, determined and intractable believer in evolution.

Dubois completed his medical studies in 1884 and seemed poised for a successful academic career. He taught anatomy, and might have succeeded Max Fürbringer as Professor of the Department had he not angered the gentleman excessively in 1886 by publishing, under his own name, a paper on the larynx of the platypus which Fürbringer thought should have carried *his* name. This may have been only a contributory factor, but in any event, the matter of his status became the subject of increasingly heated conversations with senior colleagues thereafter, and Dubois finally decided that he would much rather look for fossils of early man than become a professor of anatomy. In 1887 he resigned his lectureship, leaving behind only the rumour that he had promised to return with the 'Missing Link'.

As an anatomist acquainted with both geology and paleontology, Dubois was well equipped for the search. And, indeed, the circumstances of the day were especially auspicious: Darwin's theory was established; Huxley and Haeckel had shown that man's ancestry lay among the extinct apes; Haeckel had proposed *Pithecanthropus* as a likely link, and the East Indies as an early stage in man's dispersal from Lemuria, 'the cradle of mankind'. Furthermore, Emil Selenka had recently shown that certain human embryological features were closer to those of the orang-utan and gibbon than to those of the African apes. The orang and gibbon live only in the East Indies, and the East Indies were a colony of Holland. Where better could a Dutchman search for the fossil evidence of early man? Getting there, however, was another matter. His attempts to raise finance for a private expedition failed completely, so as a last resort, we are told, Eugene Dubois signed on for eight years in the Medical Corps of the Dutch East Indian Army. With wife and infant daughter, he sailed for Sumatra in the autumn of 1887.

Such a long spell of military service might seem a desperate choice for a medical man in search of man's ancestors, but if Dubois had not arranged a degree of official connivance at his real ambition before leaving Holland, he certainly managed to do so within a few months of arriving in the East Indies. First his immediate colleagues, then his commanding officer, then some senior administrators were all persuaded to lighten his duties and allow him to explore the fossil-bearing deposits as often as possible. Later, Dubois honoured two of the gentlemen concerned by naming a new fossil antelope and fossil tiger after them.

Finally, Dubois won the support of the Dutch East Indian Government itself. During 1889 he persuaded the relevant officials that a comprehensive paleontological survey should be conducted under his full time supervision. Second Lieutenant Eugene Dubois was placed on active reserve, inactive duty with instructions to pursue scientific investigations as he saw fit, and in March 1890 he moved to Java, where convict labour awaited his deployment under the direction of sergeants Kriele and de Winter.

Dubois made his base at Tulungagang, in the south of eastern Java. Immediately to the north stood Mount Willis, one of the many volcanoes that form the spine of the Malay Archipelago (another is Krakatoa, which had killed 36,417 people seven years before). The region was well endowed with promising limestone caves and volcanic sedimentary deposits. Dubois had a predilection for the former, not only because of boyhood discoveries in such places, but also because all the remains of early man known in Europe had been found in caves and rock shelters. So his Java search began near Wadjak where, in fact, some fossil human skull bones had been found the previous year by a Dutchman looking for workable marble deposits. Marble is usually associated with limestone caves. By May 1890 Dubois' team had recovered a skull, some teeth and other fragments from the same site but, like the earlier find, they all proved to be of recent origin. Soon thereafter Dubois abandoned the caves and turned to the sediments.

Dubois' proposal to the Government had called for a systematic, widespread survey and indeed he did travel extensively on his preliminary explorations; but before long his attention was almost exclusively devoted to the Kendeng deposits at the foot of Mount Lawu, an occasionally active volcano standing about thirty-two kilometres west of Mount Willis. In trial excavations throughout the Kendeng deposits his workmen found many vertebrate fossils, some in quite large accumulations, which led Dubois to believe that the animals had been killed simultaneously by volcanic action, and their bodies and bones swept together by flood waters down ancient rivers, to be deposited in calm pools and on sharp bends. The quantity and variety of the fossil fauna Dubois' expedition recovered from the Kendeng is most impressive. It includes fish and reptiles, elephants, rhinoceros, hippopotamus and tapir, deer, cats and a giant pangolin. In all more than twelve thousand fossils were collected, filling more than four hundred cases when they were shipped back to Holland and holding a wealth of information on the fauna and environment of prehistoric Java. But Dubois' consuming interest was fossils that would shed light on the ancestry of man, and these remains were very few.

The first appeared in November 1890. It was a fragment of a primate's chin unearthed at Kedung Brubus. The first right pre-molar was still in place, and the socket of the canine tooth next to it could be seen. Dubois mentioned the specimen in his regular quarterly report.[8] It was man-like, he said, but 'of another and probably lower type than those existing and the extinct diluvial species'. His judgement was based on the manner by which the digastric muscle appeared to have been attached to the bone – Dubois felt the attachment was incompatible with the functioning of the tongue for normal articulate speech.

Kedung Brubus specimen

The Kendeng deposits are transected by the Solo river. On a bend in the river near a village called Trinil, a sequence of sandstone and volcanic deposits fifteen metres thick attracted Dubois' attention. He decided to concentrate his efforts there for a while, and began excavations in August 1891, less than three months before the seasonal rains would flood the Solo. Once Dubois had outlined how excavations should proceed, he left day to day management to Kriele and de Winter while he continued to reconnoitre or returned to Tulungagang. Every few weeks the sergeants packed the newly-found fossils in teak leaves and sent them to Dubois, together with progress reports which were frequently little more than complaints about the weather and the workmen. The fossils accumulated on Dubois' verandah as he endeavoured to discover their affinities with fossils from other parts of the world. Ultimately he concluded that the Kendeng fauna corresponded in age with some from the Siwalik deposits in India. While not exactly confirming the existence of Lemuria, this certainly affirmed the existence of a landbridge between India and Java across which animals could have mingled.

The Trinil excavation was roughly circular, about twelve metres in diameter. Up to fifty convicts laboured in the pit, each of them assigned a specific portion of the deposit to remove each day. Fossils characteristic of the Kendeng fauna were frequently encountered as the excavation floor progressed below the highwater mark. Within a month the workers had reached the low water mark, fifteen metres below the surface, and here they struck a lapilli formation – a bed of compacted tuff containing numerous fragments of volcanic rock. The lapilli bed was a metre or so thick, beneath it was a layer of conglomerate and beneath that a bedrock of marine origin extending beneath the river itself. Fossils were most numerous in the lapilli bed, and removing them from the hard material was arduous, especially as the approaching monsoon heightened humidity. The rains finally brought excavations to a halt sometime around the end of October.

During the course of these excavations, two very important fossils were discovered. It is generally assumed that Dubois personally witnessed the discoveries, but there is no evidence of this. Indeed, the absence of any such assertion from his reports on the discoveries, and the lack of dates and precise detail, make it seem more likely that he first encountered the fossils on his verandah at Tulungagang. This point subsequently became very important when the position of one fossil in relation to another became crucial to its interpretation. Then Dubois found himself most embarrassed: if he had been present at the time of discovery, he was guilty of not recording the details carefully enough; if he had not been

present, then he had to admit that the sergeants' reports were open to question.

The fossils were a tooth, found in September, and a skull cap found in October. It was immediately clear that both specimens had belonged to a primate, but which genus and species of primate was far from clear, and Eugene Dubois was the first to demonstrate the uncertainty of their affinities. He did so not by indecision, nor by emphasizing the ambiguous and inconclusive nature of the evidence they offered – on the contrary, Dubois consistently expressed the most confident opinions on his discoveries; but they changed with his needs. In the beginning Dubois decided that the tooth and skullcap had both belonged to a chimpanzee. In the *Mining Bulletin* for the fourth quarter of 1891 he wrote, 'The Pleistocene fauna of Java which in September of this year was augmented by a molar of a chimpanzee, was much further enriched a month later. Close to the site on the left bank where the molar had been found, a beautiful skullcap was excavated which without any doubt, like the molar belongs to the genus *Anthropopithecus* (troglodytes).'[9] (Anthro-

ABOVE *Dubois' original annotated photograph of the Trinil site on the Solo river*

popithecus was the scientific name of the chimpanzee then in use and means 'man-like ape'.) However, a fossil found the following year caused him to revise this assessment.

Weather and water level did not permit the resumption of excavations at Trinil until May 1892. Then the convicts began digging a trench twenty-four metres long and eight metres wide upstream from the 1891 excavations. In August a fossil thighbone was discovered, man-like in every respect. The fossil was found in the same lapilli bed that had held the 'chimpanzee' tooth and skullcap, but some distance away. No accurate record was made at the time, but on various occasions Dubois later asserted that the femur had been found ten, twelve and fifteen metres away from the skull. In any event, Dubois was convinced that thighbone, skullcap and tooth had all belonged to the same individual. But was it a chimpanzee? The thighbone suggested not, because it quite obviously had belonged to a creature with an habitual upright stance. But Dubois resolved that problem by blending his evidence into a new species of upright chimpanzee, which he called *Anthropopithecus erectus* ('upright man-like ape'). The creature was announced in the *Mining Bulletin* for the third quarter of 1892, where Dubois claimed 'through each of the three recovered skeletal parts, and especially by the thighbone, the *Anthropopithecus erectus* (Eugene Dubois) approaches closer to man than any other anthropoid'.[10]

In October 1892, another tooth was picked up two or three metres from the spot where the skullcap had been found. No more primate remains were discovered that year, nor during 1893 when the excavations were doubled, nor during subsequent years when more than ten thousand cubic metres of sediments were removed from around the site of the original discoveries. With the exception of a few thighbone fragments found among the four hundred cases of vertebrate fossils when they were examined during 1932, Dubois' collection was complete at the end of the 1892 season – a scrap of jawbone, two teeth, one skullcap and one thighbone.

While preparing a monograph[11] on the fossils during 1893, Dubois revised their attribution once again. In this he was entirely justified, for *Anthropopithecus erectus* would have been very difficult to support with the meagre evidence he held. It was inconclusive; the thighbone was too human, and the skullcap too large for an ape – even a fossil man-like ape. So what could the creature have been? In truth, the evidence was too scanty, and the current state of knowledge too slight, for any specific attribution at all. But an absence of evidence encourages speculation; and Dubois was free to reach the conclusion which became a point of faith (and argument) dominating the rest of his life. He decided the bones had belonged to an ape-like man. In other words, he reversed the earlier attribution and *Anthropopithecus* became *Pithecanthropus*, though he retained the species name. *Pithecanthropus erectus* – upright ape-man. The generic name, *Pithecanthropus*, acknowledges the hypothetical form Haeckel had created for the twenty-first stage on the Chain of the Animal Ancestors of Man. On the basis of the chin fragment which Dubois had earlier described as having belonged to a 'speechless lower type of man', we may ask why Dubois did not call the Trinil fossils *Pithecanthropus alalus* – the speechless ape-man that Haeckel had proposed. But, of course, the chin fragment afforded only weak evidence of an inability to speak, while the thighbone presented strong evidence of an erect posture, and Dubois needed to emphasize the stronger elements of his evidence rather than draw attention to the less substantial. Later he wrote: 'this was the man-like animal which clearly forms such a link between man and his nearest known mammalian relatives as the theory of development supposes . . . the transition form which in accordance with the teachings of evolution must have existed between man and the anthropoids.'[12]

Dubois believed he had discovered the Missing Link, and telegraphed the news to Holland. He followed in August 1895, eight years of military service completed. *Pithecanthropus erectus* was presented at the Third International Congress of Zoology held in Leiden that same year, at a meeting presided over by Rudolf Virchow. The fossils were greeted by unanimous recognition of their great importance – up to that time only four other examples of fossil man were known – but Dubois' interpretation was questioned. Virchow did not believe the fossils had belonged to one individual; others felt they were more ape than man, while another group said they were more man than ape. A minority agreed with Dubois that the creature represented an intermediate stage. Among them was Ernst Haeckel, certain that the fossils confirmed his prediction of a Missing Link, but astute enough to remark: 'Unfortunately, the fossil remains of the creature are very scanty: the skullcap, a femur, and two teeth. It is obviously impossible to form from these scanty remains a complete and satisfactory reconstruction of this remarkable Pliocene Primate.'[13]

The reaction at Leiden was repeated at meetings in Liege, Brussels, Paris, London, Dublin, Edinburgh, Berlin, Jena. Everywhere, Dubois' discoveries were applauded and his interpretations doubted. Dubois became increasingly impatient and angry with his critics; as Sir Arthur Keith wrote, 'he attributed their opposition to ignorance, or to personal animosity, rather than to a desire to reach the truth.'[14]

The points of contention were quite straightforward. If the remains had belonged to one individual, as Dubois claimed, then they represented an ape, a man, or the intermediate ape-man that Dubois proposed. But not everyone agreed that the fossils had belonged to one individual, which considerably increased the number of interpretations; and the question could never be proved one way or the other. It was a more a matter of probability than of fact, and in considering it, the protagonists were free to choose the facts they thought more probable. Dubois, for example, ignored his own assertion that the Kendeng fossil accumulations were the jumbled remains of many volcano victims, while his critics ignored the observation that the four fossils were the only primate remains among thousands of fossils recovered from the lapilli bed, which Dubois felt was enough to prove their association. But, while the question of provenance could never be proved, Dubois was certain that the proof of status lay in the fossils themselves, and he thoroughly re-examined the scanty evidence they presented. He compared the thighbone with more than one thousand modern specimens. He removed the compacted sediment from the interior of the skullcap, made a cast of the braincase thus revealed and estimated the cranial capacity. He could do no more, but from this limited amount of information Dubois drew conclusions which he believed were enough to convince everyone that *Pithecanthropus erectus* was the Missing Link.

Presenting his conclusions at the Fourth International Congress of Zoology, held at Cambridge in August 1898, Dubois announced that the thighbone was significantly different from that of modern man, suggesting that although *Pithecanthropus* had stood erect and walked on two legs, it retained some ape-like characteristics. And turning to the evidence of the braincast, Dubois produced an 'index of cephalization' and attempted to prove the intermediate, ape-man status of *Pithecanthropus* by disproving the contentions that it was either ape or man. Applying the brain size/ body weight ratio of modern apes to the fossils, Dubois pointed out that an ape with *Pithecanthropus*' cranial capacity of 855 cubic centimetres would have weighed 230 kilogrammes, while a man with so small a brain would have weighed only nineteen kilogrammes. Both propositions failed the test of logic in Dubois' view and he concluded his Cambridge address: 'From all these considerations it follows that *Pithecanthropus erectus* undoubtedly is an intermediate form between man and the apes . . . a most venerable ape-man, representing a stage in our phylogeny.'[15]

Approaching the problem of interpretation from another direction, it could have been shown that a modern man with a thighbone the size

of the Java specimen would have weighed about seventy kilogrammes and, with a cranial capacity of 855 cubic centimetres, would have made a perfect candidate for man's immediate ancestry. In other words, not an ape, or an ape-man, but a slightly less brainy man; and there the arguments might have ended. But Dubois was absolutely committed to his belief. He is not known to have made any converts at the Cambridge congress, though he may have earned an apologist or two; nonetheless, his conclusions invited comment and scientists travelled to Holland to examine the fossils and discuss their interpretation. But Dubois found these visits increasingly tiresome, especially as so few of the visitors shared his views. Science had honoured him with gold medals, diplomas and honorary degrees in recognition of his work, but it would not give him what he most wanted – general agreement with his belief that *Pithecanthropus erectus* was neither ape nor man but a link between the two. Finally Dubois retaliated by severely restricting access to the fossils.

By thus alienating the sympathizers as well as his critics, and by withdrawing himself, as well as the fossils, from the international

ABOVE *Eugene Dubois (standing centre), and Arthur Keith (standing left) with other scientists attending Cambridge meetings, 1898*

scientific community, Dubois probably harmed himself more than he affected scientific opinion. If he had been able to change his mind instead of closing it with the fossils, the remaining forty years of his life might have been less difficult.

The fact is, at the turn of the century Dubois' circumstances were not suited to a man of his refractory nature. Science rejected his views, and at home in Holland his work was even less appreciated than elsewhere. The Church reviled him from the pulpit and the academic establishment showed him very little respect. In 1898 he was appointed Assistant Professor of Crystallography, Mineralogy, Geology and Paleontology at the University of Amsterdam, but it was not a prestigious post. The salary was less than he had earned as a lecturer in anatomy ten years before.

During the years of seclusion Dubois described the Wadjak skulls found in 1889 and 1890 as those of a proto-Australian[16] and published a number of papers on the geology and hydrology of Holland. He also refined his Law of Phylogenetic Cephalization, postulating a 'coefficient of cephalization' and publishing a series of papers which culminated in a formula whereby all mammals could be placed in an evolutionary sequence in respect of brain size and body weight. The sequence was a geometric progression, with one convenient gap. 'Putting the cephalization of Man equal to 1,' wrote Dubois,[17] 'we find exactly $\frac{1}{4}$ for the *Anthropomorphae* inclusive Gibbons; about $\frac{1}{8}$ for the majority of our large Mammals: Ruminants, Cats, Dogs etc.; about $\frac{1}{16}$ for Kanchils, Civet-Cats, Hares, Large Bats (*Megachiroptera*) etc.; about $\frac{1}{32}$ for Mice, Moles, Leaf-nosed Bats (*Phyllostomidae*) etc.; about $\frac{1}{64}$ for Shrews, common Small Bats (*Microchiroptera*) etc.

'The only real void space in the series,' Dubois observed, 'is between Man and the anthropomorphous Apes (incl. Gibbons). This void marks the place of *Pithecanthropus*,' he concluded, the fossil having twice the cephalization of the apes and half that of man – according to Dubois' computations.

For a time it was rumoured that Dubois had abandoned his belief in evolution and returned to the Catholic faith, destroying the fossils in expiation of his sins and in remorse for the pain he had caused his sister, who was a nun. But it was only a rumour.

The fossils appeared again in 1923, when discreet but persistent representations finally found favour with Dubois and some distinguished scientists were invited to examine them. Dr Ales Hrdlicka of the Smithsonian Institution and Professor H. H. McGregor of Columbia University were among the first. They were given every facility and courtesy, but

The original skull of Pithecanthropus erectus *rests on Dubois' own photographs of the specimen (annotated with his printing instructions) beside photographs of Dubois as a young man, in middle age and shortly before he died.*

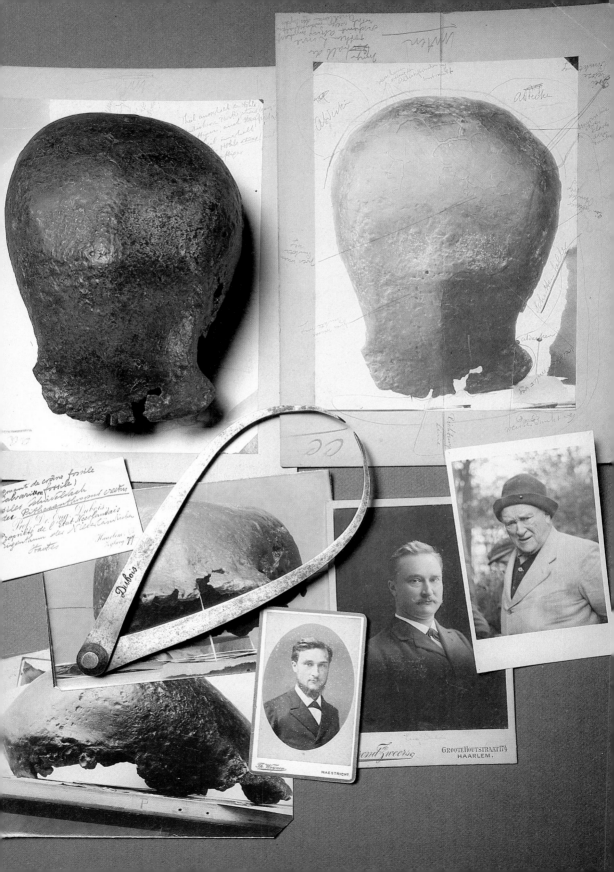

their conclusions still differed from Dubois'. The Java fossils had belonged to an early form of man, they said, not an ape or an ape-man.

By now it must have been abundantly clear to everyone except Dubois that the amount of controversy surrounding his fossils reflected a severe lack of definitive evidence. He spent the greater part of his life trying to wring from those few scraps of bone the proof they could never provide – not simply because their evidence was too fragmentary for unequivocal interpretation, but also because the judgement Dubois wished to impose upon them was wrong. It is a sad tale – if the fossils had been more complete Dubois could not have avoided the truth; less complete and he could not have built any serious claims upon them.

The argument lingered on, while others searched for the more complete fossils that would either corroborate or confound the theories and beliefs of its protagonists. Eventually new evidence was found, the first in 1929, when Dubois was over seventy years old. It was a skull from Peking, with undeniable similarities to the Java specimen, but Dubois dismissed its significance entirely. The Peking skull was just another example of the Neanderthal race, he said.[18]

Then came a stream of discoveries from Java – a skull from the banks of the Solo River at Ngandong, not far from Trinil, and others from Sangiran, about seventy-five kilometres away. In all a dozen fine Java specimens were recovered, most of them under the direction of the German paleontologist Ralph von Koenigswald, who called the Sangiran specimens *Pithecanthropus*.

As the evidence of affinity between Dubois' fossils and the new specimens became increasingly difficult to resist, so Dubois' effort became more desperate. In 1935 he attempted to show that *Pithecanthropus* was in fact a very large ape of gibbon-like appearance, weighing about 104 kilogrammes.[19] In 1940 he claimed the new skulls variously resembled the Neanderthals of Europe and the Proto-Australians he had discovered from Wadjak.[20] But by then events had overtaken Dubois and his interpretation.

In 1938 von Koenigswald described a superb skull from Sangiran as *Pithecanthropus*[21] and in 1939 he collaborated with Franz Weidenreich, then working in Peking, to define the precise relationship between the Java and the Peking fossils.[22] The similarities far exceeded the differences that Dubois would have stressed. The new specimens matched what there was of Dubois' fossils, and supplied enough of what was missing to satisfy everyone that the Java and Peking fossils all represented an early form of man, with almost nothing of the ape about him. *Pithecanthropus erectus* was not an ape-man. (Subsequently, in fact, the name was

Dubois' full size reconstruction of Pithecanthropus, *made in 1899, now resides in the basement of the Natural History Museum, Leiden.*

changed to *Homo erectus*.)[23]

Needless to say, these conclusions did not satisfy Dubois. In his eighty-third year he embarked on a tedious attempt to challenge the evidence von Koenigswald and Weidenreich had presented. These papers were the last he published, and they reflect the acrimony of a weary old man. There is a touch of irony too, in the very last paragraph:

> 'It is most regrettable, that for the interpretation of the important discoveries of human fossils in China and Java, Weidenreich, von Koenigswald and Weinert were thus guided by preconceived opinions, and consequently did not contribute to, on the contrary they impeded, the advance of knowledge of man's place in nature ... Real advance appears to depend on obtaining material data in an unbiassed way, such as the *Pithecanthropus* fossil remains ...'.[24]

Eugene Dubois suffered a heart attack and died sixteen days after delivering those words. In an obituary, Sir Arthur Keith wrote: 'He was an idealist, his ideas being so firmly held that his mind tended to bend facts rather than alter his ideas to fit them.'[25]

Chapter Three

Piltdown Man
(1912)

ARTHUR KEITH (1866–1955), anatomist, was one of a British scientific triumvirate whose beliefs and work profoundly affected investigations into the evolution of man for nearly fifty years. His associates were Arthur Smith Woodward (1864–1944), paleontologist and Keeper of Geology at the British Museum of Natural History, and Grafton Elliot Smith (1871–1937), an anatomist whose speciality was the study of the brain. All three gentlemen were knighted for their contributions to science, and their talents were memorably displayed in discussions concerned with the significance of alleged fossil human remains found at Piltdown, Sussex, between 1908 and 1915.

In an autobiography written late in life, Keith remarked that 'the ideas which a man devotes his life to exploring are, for the greater part, those which come to him in the first tide of his inquiries'.[1] The observation is certainly sustained by the facts of Arthur Keith's career. In the first year of his medical studies, Keith was awarded a copy of *The Origin of Species* for his distinctive work in the anatomy class. While working as medical officer to a mining company in Siam immediately after he qualified, Keith dissected monkeys in the hope of determining whether or not the animals shared the affliction of malaria that plagued the human population and discovered an absorbing interest in comparative anatomy as the means of elucidating the evolutionary development of mankind. Within a year he dissected thirty-two assorted primates, and on returning to England in 1892 arranged to receive and dissect primate carcasses from the London Zoo. He dissected human foetuses as well, and the comparative anatomy of the ligamentous structure of the feet and hands of monkeys and human babies became both the subject of his doctoral dissertation and the basis of his views on the evolution of man's erect posture.[2] At home in Scotland Keith performed cerebral dissections on farmyard cats of all ages to clarify his understanding of the development of the individual brain, and in London he studied primate

skulls at the Royal College of Surgeons and at the British Museum of
Natural History. He carefully noted about 150 observations on each of
over 200 skulls and it was here, in the winter of 1894, Keith writes[3] that
he learned 'the alphabet by which we spell out the long-past history of
man and ape' from the evidence of fragmentary fossils.

In 1895 Keith met Dubois; he made a reconstruction of the Java skull
and wrote an article on the specimen for a popular journal (concluding
the specimen was essentially human, but of a lowly kind). Thereafter he
wrote frequently on the subject of human ancestry and, on his appointment as Hunterian Professor of Anatomy at the Royal College of
Surgeons in 1908, vowed to uncover and write 'the anthropological
history of the British'.[4]

In *The Descent of Man*, Charles Darwin had implied that the early
forerunners of man probably retained some characteristics of the ancestor
they shared with the apes. Males were probably furnished with great
canine teeth at one time, he said, but as they acquired the habit of using
stones, clubs and other weapons for fighting they would have used their
jaws less and less, with consequent decrease in the size of the canines
and some restructuring of the jaw.[5] Scientists of the day drew several
important conclusions from Darwin's observation. Reshaping the jaw
would have provided the space essential for the movement of the tongue
in articulate speech; the ability to handle stones and clubs presumed an
erect posture; both speech and erect posture require a considerable
development of the mental abilities – and thus the crucial developments
on mankind's evolutionary path were clearly defined. But which came
first? Development of the brain? The erect posture? Or the ability to
speak? Darwin hardly commented upon the question but, as the slowly
accumulating fossil remains inspired competing interpretations of their
imprecise evidence, it was clear that some idea of the manner in which
human evolution had proceeded would help by suggesting the features
that fossils ought to possess. If man had walked before he could talk,
then fossils could be expected to demonstrate the fact.

As a result of his work on the feet and hands of apes and human babies,
Arthur Keith believed erect posture was an ancient attribute and the
large brain mankind's most recent acquisition.[6] An opposing view was
ardently championed by Grafton Elliot Smith, whose important and
pioneering work on the function and evolution of the vertebrate brain
had convinced him that 'the brain led the way'. At its most primitive, the
brain had discerned little more than the sensation of smell, he said.
Later, vision had been acquired and then 'an arboreal mode of life
started man's ancestors on the way to pre-eminence' for, while they

avoided the fierce comp   size and supremacy waged among
carnivores and ungulate   n tl earth below, 'the specialization of
the higher parts of the brain gave them [the primates] the seeing eye,
and in the course of time also the understanding ear; . . . all the rest
followed in the train of this high development of vision working on a
brain which controlled ever-increasingly agile limbs'. Thus 'the Primates
found in the branches the asylum and protection necessary for the
cultivation of brain and limbs,' he said, and the erect posture developed
when they had become 'powerful enough to hold their own and wax
great'. It was 'not the real cause of man's emergence from the Simian
stage, but . . . one of the factors made use of by the expanding brain as a
prop still further to extend its growing dominion'.[7]

Arthur Smith Woodward appears to have contributed little to the
early stages of the debate. In 1885 he remarked upon the preponderance
of 'Missing Links' in the fossil record;[8] and subsequently he stated that
'we have looked for a creature with an overgrown brain and ape-like
face',[9] missing from the chain connecting man and his primate ancestors,
but by far the greater part of his career was devoted to the study of fossil
fish rather than fossil man. In all Smith Woodward published more than
six hundred papers on fossil fish and related paleontological subjects –
more than three hundred before he became Keeper of Geology at the
British Museum in 1901 – and only thirty or so on fossil man. These
figures, of course, accurately reflect the relative abundance and otherwise
of the fossils in question.

By 1908 the fossil evidence of early man was still very slight. Specimens
from France and Belgium had confirmed the existence of a Neanderthal
race; there were the enigmatic Java discoveries, and a lower jaw found
in a sandpit near Heidelberg in 1907 suggested that mankind's late
Pleistocene ancestors had been able to talk and bore a receding chin as
evidence of their simian associations. These specimens added a measure
of information to the story of mankind's evolution in general, but of the
British anthropological history that Arthur Keith had vowed to write
there was no indisputable evidence whatsoever. Fossils had been sought
in the caves and gravels of England, Ireland, Scotland and Wales; some
remains had been found, but their antiquity was questionable and their
aspect distinctly modern. For the most part, therefore, the remains of
fossil man in Britain were granted little credence. It was believed more
likely that each was a case of recent remains interred in old deposits than a
genuine example of early man in Britain.

The Galley Hill skeleton was a case in point. The bones were found
to the east of London, in gravels deposited by the River Thames when it

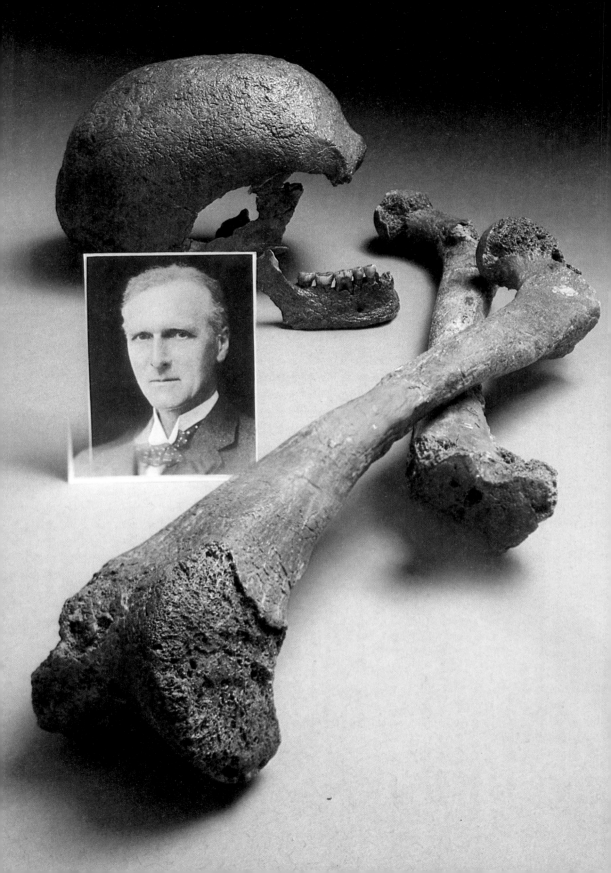

flowed one hundred feet above its present level. The deposits were considered to be of early Pleistocene age; crude stone tools found near the skeleton were similar to others found elsewhere in association with extinct fauna of the same period, so the related geological and archaeological evidence seemed to suggest that Galley Hill Man was very old indeed. The anatomical evidence, however, clearly showed that the specimen represented *Homo sapiens*. The cranial capacity (about 1400 cubic centimetres) was well within the modern range, the chin did not recede, the jaw structure was compatible with the faculty of speech and the thighbone indicated an habitual erect posture. Furthermore, the skeleton was unusually complete and had been found with its parts in close proximity. All these factors combined to convince most authorities that the Galley Hill remains were of recent origin and had been entombed by the hand of men, not nature.[10]

The Galley Hill skeleton was discovered in 1888 and soon thereafter consigned to the obscurity of a private collection in East London, where it remained until 1910, when Arthur Keith decided that the evidence merited reappraisal. Over a period of months he confirmed the skeleton's affinities with *Homo sapiens* and agreed that the remains had been buried in the ancient deposits but, whereas these factors had caused earlier investigators to reject the claims of great antiquity, Keith deduced from them that Galley Hill Man was as ancient as the deposits in which he had been buried, and the burial was not recent, but ancient. 'We hardly do justice to the men who shaped the [artefacts],' he wrote, 'if we hold them incapable of showing respect for their dead.'[11] The implications of these deductions were considerable – if large-brained, talking, walking *Homo sapiens* had existed at the beginning of the Pleistocene, as Keith claimed, then all the crucial evolutionary development of man must have taken place long before, true men had remained unchanged for a very long time, and the Neanderthal and Java fossils represented not the ancestors of man, but a 'degenerate cousin'.

Geologists, in particular, did not agree that true man could be so ancient. But Keith claimed this was because they had grown up with a belief in the recent origin of man and therefore expected to see a sequence of anatomical change marking the evolution of man.[12] In fact the geologists' views simply conformed with the rationale of their paleontological training, which taught that the long and absolute lack of evolutionary change Keith proposed would be unique among the higher vertebrates, and therefore unlikely. But Keith, the anatomist, was untroubled by these niceties of paleontology and quite prepared to believe that mankind is unique. Thereafter his concept of true man's

Arthur Keith and the Galley Hill specimen

exceptional antiquity becam.   oint of faith. He called upon it to
explain the anomaly of app   itly modern human remains found
beneath ancient deposits at   ch[13] and, at a meeting of the British
Association for the Advancem nt of Science held at Dundee in 1912,
Arthur Keith offered perhaps the first full and authoritative exposition
of the belief that mankind had acquired both large brain and erect
stature a very long time ago and has remained relatively unchanged ever
since.

xemarking upon the Neanderthal and Java fossils, Keith told his
distinguished audience: 'thus we have a knowledge – a very imperfect
knowledge – of only two human individuals near the beginning of the
istocene period. The one was brutal in aspect, the other certainly low
in intellect.' If these are the ancestors of modern man, he said, then we
have to accept 'that in the early part of the Pleistocene, within a comparatively short space of time, the human brain developed at an astound-
ing and almost incredible rate'. To Keith it seemed more reasonable to
reject Neanderthal and Java from man's ancestry and assume they were
simply contemporaries and cousins of true man's large-brained ancestor,
whose evolutionary development had occurred long before. 'Is it then
possible,' he asked, 'that a human being, shaped and endowed as we are,
may have existed so early as the Pliocene?' Briefly reviewing the evidence
he had presented, Keith concluded that it was. 'The picture I wish to leave
in your minds,' he said, 'is that in the distant past there was not one kind
but a number of very different kinds of men in existence, all of which
have become extinct except that branch which has given origin to
modern man. On the imperfect knowledge at present at our disposal it
seems highly probable that man as we know him now took on his
human characters near the beginning of the Pliocene period.'[14] At
the same meetings, Grafton Elliot Smith confidently extended the
pedigree of man's ancestors back to the Eocene, explaining how the
'steady and uniform development of the brain along a well-defined course
throughout the Primates right up to Man . . . gives us the fundamental
reason for "Man's emergence and ascent" '.[15]

Thus the leading anatomists of the day expounded the theories of
human evolution that they hoped paleontologists might one day substantiate with the evidence of fossil human remains. Just a few months
later, in December 1912, Arthur Smith Woodward, perhaps the leading
paleontologist of the day, unveiled Piltdown Man and thus presented
the anatomists with a conundrum in which the expectation of theory and
the logic of observed fact were wonderfully counterpoised.

Though he was responsible for the reconstruction and presentation of

Piltdown Man, Smith Woodward had not discovered the remains. The first pieces of fossil skullbones were brought to him by Charles Dawson, an amateur geologist who had already contributed important paleontological specimens to the British Museum collections. Dawson (1864–1916) was a solicitor practising at Uckfield in Sussex, a position which left time for a wide range of other activities (in 1909 he published *A History of Hastings Castle* in two volumes and at the onset of his terminal illness was investigating a case of incipient horns on the head of a carthorse) but geology and paleontology were the interests he pursued most energetically. In 1885 – at the age of twenty-one – Dawson was elected a fellow of the Geological Society for his contributions to the science, though little appeared in the literature under his own name. 'He preferred to hand over his specimens to experts who have made a special study of the groups to which they belonged,' an obituary recounts,[16] rather than describe them himself, and Smith Woodward was surely rewarding this respectful deference to greater knowledge when he named Piltdown Man *Eoanthropus dawsoni* (Dawson's Dawn Man), made Dawson principal author of their joint paper[17] and let him present the geological and archaeological evidence of the discovery while he, paleontologist Smith Woodward, spoke first on the anatomy of the specimen and *then* on the significance of the faunal remains found in the same deposit.

The details of Dawson's initial discovery are imprecise; not even the exact year is known. In the paper read at a meeting of the Geological Society on 18 December 1912, Dawson told how he had been attracted to the site 'several years' before when he traced some unusual brown flints found on a farm near Fletching to a small gravel pit on a farm adjacent to Piltdown Common, Sussex. He asked the labourers who occasionally worked there to keep any fossils they might encounter, and on a subsequent visit, they presented him with a small, concave, tabular object. It was part of a coconut shell, the men said, which they had found and broken in the course of their digging. They had kept one piece for Dawson and discarded the rest. Dawson, however, realized that the object was part of a fossil human skull. Thereafter he visited the site frequently and 'some years later – in the autumn of 1911' – he found another fragment of the same skull among the spoil heaps. Believing the pieces might match the proportions of the Heidelberg jaw, in May 1912 Dawson took his finds to the British Museum for more accurate assessment. Smith Woodward was impressed with the importance of the discovery and joined Dawson in the search for more remains that summer – though only as a private, weekend holiday affair, and without the

OVERLEAF *Artist's portrayal of Piltdown Man with the original specimens and some of Dawson's many letters to Smith Woodward*

A DISCOVERY OF SUPREME IMPORTANCE TO A

A RECONSTRUCTION BY OUR SPECIAL ARTIST,

THE OLD LODGE
LEWES

31. Jan? 1913

My dear Woodward,

Thank you for the newspapers from Ireland. Clement Reid has that the thrust the God

very annoyed

it.

Sussex Daily News people just rang me up have referred them as I do not know at cause you wish —adopt. Perhaps no better be said till the soc: meeting but you know best.

I expect to be at the museum with my brother either tomorrow or Thursday

Yn sincerely,
Charles Dawson

RECONSTRUCTED FROM A PART OF THE JAW AND A PORTION OF THE SKULL: THE

To quote the special article given on another page of this issue: "A discovery of supreme importance to all who are interested in the history of the human race was

INTERESTED IN THE HISTORY OF THE HUMAN RACE.

(See Article and other Illustrations Elsewhere.)

involvement of any British Museum resources. Apparently they wished to keep the discovery wholly to themselves. At first, just one labourer was employed to do the heavy digging in the small pit, but later they were joined by Father Teilhard de Chardin and a colleague, both French priests then studying at the Jesuit College near Hastings. Teilhard de Chardin shared Dawson's amateur interest in fossils and geology: they had met by chance in their rambles about the Sussex countryside. In later years Teilhard de Chardin became an authority on the fossil evidence of early man.

During the summer of 1912 solicitor, paleontologist and priests scrutinized every spadeful dug from the pit and sifted through all the spoil heaps of previous years. In one heap they found three pieces of the right parietal bone from the skull – one piece on each of three successive days – and later Smith Woodward found another fragment which fitted the broken edge of the occipital and connected with the left parietal found by Dawson. 'Finally, on a warm summer evening after an afternoon's vain search,' Smith Woodward recounts,[18] 'Mr Dawson was exploring some untouched remnants of the original gravel at the bottom of the pit, when we both saw half of the human lower jaw fly out in front of the pick-shaped end of the hammer he was using. Thus was recovered the most remarkable portion of the fossil which we were collecting.' In addition the pit supplied three artefacts, fragments of an elephant tooth, some beaver teeth and one much-rolled fragment of a mastodon tooth, while on the surface of an adjacent field the party found a piece of red deer antler and a horse's tooth – both fossilized and both presumed to have been thrown over the hedge by the workmen. In all, a remarkably comprehensive haul.

According to Dawson's determination, the Piltdown gravel bed lay about eighty feet above the level of the River Ouse, deposited there before the river began excising the valley through which it presently flows. The gravel bed could be divided into four distinct strata, he said, and the fossils had come from the third, which lay about three and a half feet below the land surface and was distinguished by a dark ferruginous appearance and the presence of ironstone. The fossil fauna from the pit were of early Pleistocene – even Pliocene – age, and the flint artefacts appeared to be similarly ancient – all of which strongly implied that the human remains found in the same deposit represented the earliest known example of true man.

Arthur Smith Woodward completed an anatomical reconstruction of the remains sometime during the autumn of 1912. He worked alone, apparently without the advice, assistance or even knowledge of his colleagues at the British Museum.[19] He made a cast of the interior of the reconstructed skull and invited Grafton Elliot Smith to comment upon the brain of Piltdown Man when the specimen was unveiled at the Geological Society in December, but Elliot Smith has made it clear that he did not help with the reconstruction of the skull.[20]

The audience that packed the Geological Society's lecture room on 18 December 1912 was larger than any before, and the Piltdown skull they had come to see perfectly fulfilled the expectations of many who attended. Smith Woodward's reconstruction had produced a creature with the jaw of an ape, the skull of a man and a cranial capacity (1070 cubic centimetres) appropriate to an intermediate stage between man and ape. A small minority thought the combination of ape and human characteristics was just a little too good to be true, and Smith Woodward himself accurately defined the point when he told the meeting: 'while the skull, indeed, is essentially human, only approaching a lower grade in certain characters of the brain [as described in Elliot Smith's contribution to the same meeting] . . . the mandible appears to be almost precisely that of the ape'.[21] Elliot Smith, however, did not find the combination beyond the bounds of reason. The Piltdown brain was the most primitive and the most simian so far recorded, he said, and its association with an ape-like jaw was not surprising to anyone familiar with recent research into the process by which the human brain had evolved from the brain of the ape.[22]

Arthur Keith, on the other hand, was among those who had misgivings. He was jealous that the remains had been given to a paleontologist at the British Museum and not him, an anatomist known to be specially interested in the anthropological history of the British. But then he knew that Smith Woodward regarded his belief in the antiquity of *Homo sapiens* as 'an amusing evolutionary heresy'.[23] At the Geological Society meeting, Keith hailed Piltdown as perhaps the most important discovery of fossil human remains ever made, but took exception to some aspects of the reconstruction. The chin region and the form of the front teeth were too much like the chimpanzee, he said.[24]

The arguments concerning the association of jaw and skull, and the form of the reconstruction, would never have arisen if the remains had been more complete. But the problem was, of course, that the anatomical features capable of proving or confounding the association of jaw and skull were exactly those missing from the original specimens – the chin region of the jaw which would have clearly demonstrated the form of the canines; and the articular knob which would have shown the form of the skull joint. In June 1913 Arthur Keith acquired casts of the remains and

made his own reconstruction of the Piltdown skull, one which assembled
the available parts in accordance with anatomical principles and supplied
the missing parts in accordance with his belief in the antiquity of *Homo
sapiens*. The chin and front teeth were entirely human and the cranial
capacity was 1500 cubic centimetres – greater than the average for
modern man. A few weeks later the conflicting interpretations of anatomist and paleontologist were reviewed by the participants at an
International Congress of Medicine held in London during August.
At the British Museum the distinguished gentlemen of medical science
viewed Smith Woodward's anatomical reconstruction of the original
remains, and at the Royal College of Surgeons Arthur Keith showed them
where the paleontologist had gone wrong.

Because of a misconceived notion of the nature of the jaws and teeth
in fossil man, Smith Woodward had fitted a chimpanzee palate and jaw
on a skull that could not possibly carry them, Keith said, with the result
that the upper joints of the backbone were so close to the palate that there
was no room for windpipe or gullet and Piltdown man would have been
unable to either eat or breathe. The Smith Woodward reconstruction
was anatomically impossible, he said.[25] If skull and jaw truly belonged
together then the skull must be large enough to accommodate the massive
jaw and the front teeth must be human enough to match the articular
capacity.

In the course of the ensuing discussions Grafton Elliot Smith lent his
support to the paleontologist's reconstruction, but Smith Woodward
did not respond publicly to Keith's challenge until 16 September 1913,
when he told a meeting of the British Association for the Advancement of
Science assembled in Birmingham of further discoveries at Piltdown.

> Fortunately, Mr Dawson has continued his diggings during the past
> summer,' he said, 'and, on August 30, Father P. Teilhard, who was
> working with him, picked up the canine tooth which obviously
> belong to the half of the mandible originally discovered. In shape
> it corresponds exactly with that of an ape, and its worn face shows
> that it worked upon the upper canine in the true ape-fashion. It
> only differs from the canine of my published restoration in being
> slightly smaller, more pointed, and a little more upright in the
> mouth. Hence, we have now definite proof that the front teeth of
> *Eoanthropus* resembled those of an ape, and my original determina-
> tion is justified.[26]

The Piltdown canine settled the argument about the chin so conclu-

The Piltdown canine rests on an Illustrated London News *photograph of Dawson (left)
and Smith Woodward at the Piltdown excavation*

Right Lower Canine of
Eoanthropus
dawsoni, A.S.W.

Form...

Loc.: Pilt...ssex.
Des. & fig. Q. Jo... Soc.
vol. 70 (1914), p.87, pl. X, figs. 2, 3.
Presented by
Charles Dawson, Esq.
Sept. 1915.   E.611.
Brit. Mus. Geol. Dept...

sively in Smith Woodward's favour that Arthur Keith was forced to concede an important point of his belief in the antiquity of *Homo sapiens*. Despite the evidence of Galley Hill and Ipswich, it seemed that some of man's ancestors in the early Pleistocene had displayed distinctly ape-like characteristics after all. But the argument about the size of the Piltdown brain-case was still unresolved. Smith Woodward believed it must have been small because, in his view, the association of the primitive jaw with a *large* brain-case would be a most improbable combination of primitive and modern features. Keith, on the other hand, insisted that the brain must have been large because the association of a large jaw with a *small* brain-case was anatomically impossible. The 300 cubic centimetres separating the estimates of anatomist and paleontologist soon became a subject of heated debate in the pages of *Nature* and elsewhere. But Smith Woodward was only slightly involved; in his stead, Grafton Elliot Smith promoted the smaller estimate and thus the paleontologist was able to remain a passive observer while the merits of his Piltdown reconstruction were argued by two anatomists. In Keith's view the anatomical errors responsible for the small brain-case were manifest and glaringly obvious; he was surprised and irritated by Elliot Smith's refusal to acknowledge them. Acrimony developed between the two men and, although Keith eventually came to terms with most of the colleagues with whom he argued during his career, he and Elliot Smith were never friends again.

The difference in the estimates of the Piltdown brain size resulted solely from the manner in which the existing fragments were assembled and their curves projected to delineate the parts missing in between. A large area of the forehead, and the roof of the skull were among the important missing pieces, as Keith pointed out in a letter to *Nature*,[27] but he believed it was possible to reconstruct a complete skull from what remained of it by applying the principle of symmetry. 'The right and left halves of the mammalian head and skull are approximately alike,' he continued, but Dr Smith Woodward's reconstruction showed a 'great discrepancy between the right and left halves',[28] the extent of which was largely responsible for Smith Woodward's low estimate of brain size – if the symmetry of the paleontologist's reconstruction was restored by adding to the right side of the skull, then the cranial capacity was sub-stantially increased.

In reply, Elliot Smith stressed the position of the middle line of the skull as the most important factor in reconstructing a skull, and attributed Keith's alleged misplacement of this feature to his having worked from casts of the Piltdown fragments without reference to the original specimens.[29] He made little mention of the asymmetry of the skull, though it is interesting to note that such a feature was fundamental to his subsequent theory that the left- or right-handedness of a person is shown in the relative sizes of certain parts of the left and right hemispheres of the brain.[30] A few weeks later Keith pointed out that Elliot Smith's remarks did less than justice to Mr F. O. Barlow, who had made the casts, and even reflected badly upon the conduct of Dr Smith Woodward who, he wrote, had permitted 'the freest access to the specimens', even to those who like himself 'regarded the original reconstruction of the skull and brain cast as fundamentally erroneous'.[31]

Keith championed his views in *The Times* and challenged Grafton Elliot Smith's conclusion at a memorable meeting of the Royal Society where he claims to have earned the reputation of a brawler; but behind the public controversy he was, by his own admission,[32] beginning to have private doubts about the validity of the argument. The problem he saw was quite simple: can a skull *ever* be reconstructed accurately from just a few fragments of the original? Such skills obviously were essential to anyone aspiring to study the progress of human evolution because most of the evidence was contained in fragmentary fossil remains. Several authorities claimed to possess the skills needed to reassemble such fragments, but in the case of Piltdown Man, their differing results begged the question: is there, or is there not, a *science* of fossil reconstruction?

To test his own skills scientifically, Keith arranged that some colleagues should cut fragments exactly duplicating the Piltdown remains from a modern skull in their possession, which he would then reconstruct according to his anatomical principles and afterwards compare with a cast of the original. The results were close enough to restore Keith's confidence in his skills and re-confirm his belief that Piltdown Man had possessed a large brain; the experiment was described at a meeting of the Royal Anthropological Institute and published in a scientific manner.[33] But nevertheless, the reconstruction was wrong in one important respect: Keith failed to reproduce the proper form of the forehead, of which there was almost no evidence at all among the Piltdown remains.

While the deliberations concerning the form and size of the Piltdown skull were exercising the skills of the experts in London, Charles Dawson continued the search for more remains. The gravel pit seemed to have been worked out, and in wandering further afield, he examined newly ploughed land and the heaps of stones raked from the fields. His endeavours were attended by extraordinary good fortune. Sometime before 20 January 1915, in a field about two miles from the site of the original discovery,

Dawson found a fragment of fossil bone which, he was certain, had belonged to a second Piltdown Man. The fragment was a piece of the forehead, retaining a portion of the eyebrow ridge and the root of the nose. In July 1915 he found a molar tooth at the same site; and on another occasion a piece of the back of the skull.

Unhappily, Dawson became seriously ill with anaemia in the autumn of 1915. The condition worsened and turned to septicaemia, of which he died in August 1916. His last discoveries were presented before the Geological Society by Arthur Smith Woodward in February 1917, where it was concluded that the new evidence must support the contention that *Eoanthropus dawsoni* was a definite and distinct form of early man, as originally supposed, for, as Smith Woodward pointed out, the occurrence of the same type of bone with the same type of molars in two separate localities must add to the probability that they belonged to one and the same species.[34] The frontal bone revealed the form of only a small area of the interior surface, and one devoid of obtrusive features, but nonetheless Grafton Elliot Smith found that its evidence corroborated his opinion that the Piltdown skull presented features 'more distinctly primitive and ape-like than those of any other member of the human family at present available for examination'.[35] Arthur Keith attended the meeting too, and in the ensuing discussion effectively abandoned his opposition to the specimen. He never accepted the small brain Smith Woodward postulated, but he succumbed to the persuasive logic of the amazing discoveries and their presentation. The new Piltdown finds 'established beyond any doubt that *Eoanthropus* was a very clearly differentiated type of being', Keith said; adding that the frontal bone was particularly valuable because it cleared up any doubt as to the contour of the forehead.[36]

The triumvirate of British paleoanthropological science was now united in its belief that the Piltdown remains represented the earliest known ancestor of *Homo sapiens*, a unique link between mankind and the ape-like creatures from which he had evolved. And did their knighthoods (Sir Arthur Keith 1921; Sir Arthur Smith Woodward 1924; Sir Grafton Elliot Smith 1934) reflect a shade of patriotic pride colouring this conviction that the ancestor of man was an Englishman?

But while the three experts were gathering around Piltdown Man, the creature was still under attack from other quarters. And the attacks were concerned not simply with the size of the skull, but with the more fundamental question of whether or not the jaw and skull belonged together. Arthur Smith Woodward, it will be remembered, had drawn attention to this problem when the remains were first presented to science; and, at that same meeting, Professor Waterston had remarked that it was very difficult to believe that the two specimens could have come from the same individual.[37] Later Waterston strengthened his opinion; in a letter to *Nature* he wrote: 'it seems to me to be as inconsequent to refer the mandible and the cranium to the same individual as it would be to articulate a chimpanzee foot with the bones of an essentially human thigh and leg.'[38]

Similar views were voiced elsewhere. In America Gerrit Miller compared casts of the Piltdown fossils (he never saw the originals) with the corresponding parts of twenty-two chimpanzees, twenty-three gorillas, seventy-five orang utans and a series of human skulls, concluding that 'a single individual cannot be supposed to have carried this jaw and skull' without assuming 'the existence of a primate combining braincase and nasal bones possessing the exact characters of a genus belonging to one family, with a mandible, two lower molars and an upper canine possessing the exact characters of another' without any blending of their distinctive characteristics. Miller concluded that the remains must represent two individuals despite the amazing coincidence of their discovery in such close proximity, and created a completely new species of chimpanzee *(Pan vetus)* to accommodate the peculiarities of the Piltdown jaw.[39]

In 1921 the French authority on fossil man, Marcellin Boule, approached 'the paradoxical association of an essentially human skull with an essentially simian jaw' with the question: 'Is *Eoanthropus* an Artificial and Composite Creature?' Boule considered the evidence and concluded that Piltdown Man was at least composite (if not artificial). The jaw had come from a chimpanzee, he said, and the skull was human but had belonged to a race of men quite distinct from the Neanderthals and closely related to the ancestry of modern man.[40]

Many authorities in America and France supported the views put forward by Miller and Boule; objections to the paradoxical association of ape jaw and human skull were also raised in Italy and Germany. In all the anatomical evidence seemed so strong as to be incontrovertible; indeed, if the jaw and skull had been discovered in separate excavations no expert would have dreamt of suggesting they belong to the same species, but at Piltdown the scientific evidence of anatomy collapsed against the circumstantial evidence of paleontology. The first remains had lain within feet of each other on the same geological level (or so it was said) and therefore *must* belong together; and the discovery of matching remains some distance away supported the conclusion. As Grafton Elliot Smith remarked: there was no reason to assume 'that

Nature had played the amazing trick of depositing in the same bed of gravel the brain-case (*without* the jaw) of a hitherto unknown type of early Pleistocene Man displaying unique, simian traits, alongside the jaw (*without* the brain-case) of an equally unknown Pleistocene Ape displaying human traits unknown in any Ape'.[41] Rational minds found it much more likely that jaw and skull belonged together – especially since the creature thus formed so closely resembled the form of man many authorities believed had existed at that stage of human evolution.

In 1922 Elliot Smith, in conjunction with a colleague, made another reconstruction of the skull, supplementing those by Keith and Smith Woodward. The cranial capacity was 1200 cubic centimetres, its form was more in keeping with the structure of the jaw and Marcellin Boule, for example, found Elliot Smith's contribution persuasive. The new facts should eliminate or at least lessen the 'anatomical paradox', he wrote; expressing the view that the balance of the argument now inclined more towards Smith Woodward's theory. Boule was glad of this, he said, for he esteemed 'both the knowledge and the personal attributes of this scientist'.[42]

There can be no doubt that the prestige and status of Arthur Smith Woodward were very largely responsible for the degree of acceptance that Piltdown Man achieved. His pronouncements on the fossils constituted a very small part of his work, as we have seen, but they carried the ring of conviction. Sir Arthur Keith has remarked that Smith Woodward liked to set a puzzling specimen on a table where the light from a window caught it at all hours of the day, so that as he passed and re-passed it in the course of his work, a chance glance might reveal aspects he had not seen before and the significance of the fossil would gradually become clear. The Piltdown specimens were afforded this treatment,[43] so we must assume the paleontologist was satisfied with what he saw.

In the early stages of the debate Elliot Smith had said examination of the originals was essential to correct interpretation. Indeed opposition stemmed mainly from those who had dealt with casts only, and several sceptics who subsequently handled the originals are known to have changed their minds. The American-based anthropologist, Ales Hrdlicka, was one of these. Having examined the originals extensively he remarked on the great difference that exists between the study of a cast and its original. 'It is very probable,' he reported, 'that . . . some of the conclusions arrived at by some authors would not have been made had they been able to study the jaw itself.' Hrdlicka accepted Smith Woodward's designation of the remains as 'a being from the dawn of the human period'.[44]

One Sunday morning in July 1921 another sceptic, Henry Fairfield Osborn, President of the American Museum of Natural History, spent two hours after church examining the Piltdown remains. He concluded that 'paradoxical as it had appeared to the sceptical comparative anatomists, the chinless Piltdown jaw, shaped exactly like that of a chimpanzee . . . does belong with the Piltdown skull, with its relatively high, well-formed forehead and relatively capacious brain case.'[45]

But behind the controversy, it must be noted, there was unanimous agreement among the experts on a point which had a most pervasive effect, particularly in respect of the beliefs and predispositions that were presented to the anthropology students of the day. The experts may have disputed the association of the Piltdown jaw and skull, they may have argued about the absolute size of the brain, but of one thing they were all certain: the Piltdown remains proved beyond doubt that mankind had already developed a remarkably large brain by the beginning of the Pleistocene. And the implications of this were very important – firstly, a brain so large at that time must have begun its development long before, which implied that true man was very ancient indeed; and secondly, since the Piltdown remains of this 'true man' were older (as it was believed) than the Java and Neanderthal fossils, they firmly dismissed those small-brained, 'brutish' creatures from the human line to the status of 'aberrant offshoots' – evolutionary experiments that led to extinction – cousins of mankind perhaps, but not ancestors.

Thus Piltdown Man contributed to the intellectual climate of the 1920s and 1930s when some significant discoveries were scorned because they did not conform with accepted beliefs, while others, less accurately founded, were welcomed because they conformed only too well. Regardless of the continuing controversy over their details, the Piltdown remains became a standard requiring mention in related literature, and a measure against which subsequent discoveries had to be compared. This Piltdown effect, as it might be called, is well demonstrated in the work of Louis Leakey (1903–1972), who studied anthropology at Cambridge during the 1920s and was an admiring disciple of Sir Arthur Keith.

In 1934 Leakey published a popular book on fossil man called *Adam's Ancestors*. In it he supported Keith's appraisal of the Galley Hill remains and described Piltdown Man as a good candidate for the ancestry of man (he took care to explain why the specimen had not been presented in the preceding chapter on 'Our Stone Age Cousins'). 'The Piltdown skull is probably very much more nearly related to *Homo sapiens* than to any other yet known type,' Leakey wrote, and would have granted the specimen full ancestral status if it had been 'vastly more ancient' than the

Kanam mandible he had recently found in East Africa and which, he believed, must represent the oldest ancestor of true man.[46]

We have concentrated so far on the anatomists' and paleontologists' views of Piltdown Man, but a third approach was available to science – geology – and it was from this direction that the riddle eventually was solved. Charles Dawson had said that the remains were found in a gravel bed lying about eighty feet above the level of the River Ouse. This implied an antiquity not much less than that of other river terraces in Britain and Europe, and indeed, on the evidence of the extinct fauna they were said to contain the Piltdown gravels could hardly have been younger. Thereafter Dawson's estimate was repeated as fact by other authorities and, in particular, gained considerable respect from the support of W. J. Sollas, Professor of Geology at Oxford – who even improved upon the Dawson estimate.

In his book, *Ancient Hunters* (1924), Sollas converted eighty feet to twenty-five metres, bracketed twenty-five with thirty and thus correlated the Piltdown gravels with those lying on terraces thirty metres above other rivers (the Thames for instance), concluding that the Piltdown remains must, therefore, date from the early Pleistocene. Thereafter, Sollas's assessment became the most authoritative reference on the geology and age of the Piltdown deposits. 'Thirty metres' was frequently converted to 'one hundred feet' and in turn offered to support a contention that the fossils might be even older than originally thought, perhaps even of Pliocene age – though the only Pliocene deposits known from that part of England were of marine origin and above the five hundred-foot contour. All of which undoubtedly helped to obscure the fact that Dawson's original estimate was based on an erroneous assumption.

Dawson had claimed the Piltdown gravels were part of a plateau lying above the one hundred-foot contour line, and he had calculated their height in relation to these features. But the gravels are actually part of a larger, well-defined terrace which maintains a constant height of fifty feet above the River Ouse throughout its extent. The portion in which the fossils were found is no exception, as was clearly revealed on the six inch to one mile Ordnance Survey map of the district published in 1911. If this had been noted in 1913, and the stratigraphy of the area accurately ascertained, it may have seemed more correct to correlate the Piltdown gravels with the fifty-foot terraces of the River Thames rather than with anything older, in which case the Piltdown fossils could only have been of Late, not Early Pleistocene. In such a scenario interest in the remains probably would have evaporated very quickly – the fossils might have seemed odd and anomalous, but no one could have claimed any great antiquity for them, especially since Smith Woodward had always said that the skull was the same age as the deposit in which it had been found.

But the error was not noted in 1913; and it drew no comment in 1926 when a map giving the correct elevation appeared in a Geological Survey publication with text repeating Dawson's estimate.[47] In fact, the error and its significance was first mentioned only in 1935, when the attributes of the Piltdown skull seemed difficult to reconcile with those of another skull found at Swanscombe. The Swanscombe specimen came from gravels of the one hundred-foot terrace of the River Thames itself, and when the problem of its correlation with the Piltdown remains arose at a meeting of the British Association at Norwich, Kenneth Oakley, a geologist at the British Museum, challenged Sollas's assertion that the Piltdown gravels were part of the thirty-metre terrace. He draw attention to the 1926 map of the area and its author's observation that the deposits more satisfactorily corresponded with those of the fifty-foot terrace.

The Swanscombe remains were found by Alvan T. Marston, a dentist with an interest in fossils, in a gravel pit not far from the site of the Galley Hill discovery. They comprise the rear half of a skull; there is no clue whatsoever to the form of the face, the jaw or the forehead. The cranial capacity was estimated to be 1325 cubic centimetres and comparative anatomists could find little to distinguish the specimen from *Homo sapiens*. Yet the Swanscombe skull had come from deposits no younger than those at Piltdown, and the Piltdown skull was held to be so old and so distinct from *Homo sapiens* as to merit the creation of a new genus, *Eoanthropus*. Clearly something was amiss. The geology at Swanscombe was well documented, and the Swanscombe skull's affinities were well defined, so Marston concluded that the fault must lie with the Piltdown specimen. The jaw must have belonged to an ape, he said, and the skull must have belonged to a man more recent than even the Swanscombe remains – whatever the circumstances of the discovery. Marston summarized the problem in 1937: 'that the Swanscombe skull had to be considered in its relations to the Piltdown was inevitable, and once this was embarked upon the gross inconsistencies of the large-brained, Pliocene, ape-jawed, eolithic medley became apparent. The relegation of the Piltdown skull to a later date will remove the disharmony which has occasioned so much difficulty for those who have tried to describe it as an early Pleistocene type.'[48]

By the 1930s, fossil evidence accumulating from other parts of the world seemed to suggest that the brain had not led the way in the evolution of mankind. Fossils of no less antiquity than was proposed for Piltdown Man revealed distinctly man-like jaws and teeth, while the brain remained relatively small, so that it became increasingly difficult to reconcile the large brain and ape-like jaw of Piltdown Man with a reasonable interpretation of mankind's evolution as suggested by the new evidence. Scientific papers repeatedly drew attention to the differences rather than the similarities between Piltdown and the new fossils. The triumvirate of British anthropology (they became two with the death of Sir Grafton Elliot Smith in 1937) remained convinced of the specimen's validity, and regarded the new evidence as proof of the theory that two lines (at least) of hominid evolution had once co-existed, the surviving line represented by modern man, Piltdown and little else, while all the new discoveries represented lines that had led to extinction. To other authorities, however, Piltdown simply did not fit; the specimen was a chimaera, a once-intriguing riddle about which there seemed little more to be said.

But the truth – if discernible at all – must be contained in the evidence. The question was: could it ever be extracted? Oakley actually had begun to answer this question in 1935 when he had referred to the observation that Dawson had estimated the height of the Piltdown gravels incorrectly. The implications of Dawson's error were clear: the age of Piltdown Man was derived solely from its association with extinct fauna of the early Pleistocene found in the same pit; but if the deposits were younger than had been claimed, then the older fossils must have come from somewhere else and there could be no compelling reason to believe that *all* the Piltdown fossils were of equal antiquity. The extinct fauna was indisputably older than the deposit, but Piltdown Man could be the same age or even younger. The next question was: is there some way of determining whether or not bones found close together in a single deposit are actually the same age? This question became a subject of Kenneth Oakley's research programme after the war, and although the solution of the Piltdown riddle was not his specific interest, that was an important result of his endeavours.

Fossils absorb fluorine from the soil in which they are buried, and Oakley's research explored the observation that the amount of fluorine in a fossil steadily increases with time and therefore might give some indication of its geological age. The phenomenon had been noted by J. Middleton in 1844, who remarked that the 'accumulation of fluorine seems to involve the element of time, so interesting to geological investigations',[49] and attempted to establish a timescale based on fluorine content by which the absolute age of fossils could be determined. Taking the quantity of fluorine in a bone of an ancient Greek known to be 2000 years old as his standard, Middleton dated fossils from the Siwaliks at

7700 years, and an extinct pachyderm at 24,200 years – age estimates which even then must have seemed a trifle ungenerous. Furthermore, Middleton had overlooked that fact that, because the soil's fluorine content varies considerably from place to place, fossils found in different deposits are likely to have absorbed quite different amounts and therefore cannot be dated one against the other reliably on this basis.

Middleton's observations were not pursued, and the significance of fluorine in fossil bones slipped into obscurity until it was discovered anew by Adolf Carnot, a French mineralogist. In 1892 Carnot published tables showing the increasing amounts of fluorine in fossil bones from progressively more ancient deposits; the following year he reported on the fluorine contents of a fossil mammoth bone and a human bone from the same deposit – they were different, he said, and therefore the bones must be of different ages.[50] This observation was fundamental to the potential of fluorine content as a means of dating fossil bones. It could never provide an absolute timescale, such as Middleton had sought, but it could provide a useful relative scale and, furthermore, a means of assessing whether or not bones found together in a deposit had all been there for the same length of time. But even Carnot's work passed unnoticed; the principle of fluorine dating again slipped into obscurity, and there it remained for fifty years until it was discovered anew by Kenneth Oakley.

In 1943, while Oakley was assessing Britain's phosphate resources, a colleague working on fluorosis (another of the country's wartime problems) showed him Carnot's 1892 tables giving the fluorine content of fossil bones. Oakley realized that Carnot's work suggested a means of comparing the age of fossils within a single deposit, and for several years thereafter believed this primary observation on fluorine dating was his alone. Only after he had refined and tested his methods did he learn of Carnot's 1893 paper, and later still of Middleton's work.

The quantity of fluorine absorbed by a fossil is never large, even in the oldest bone, and measurement involves complicated chemical analysis. At the instigation of Oakley and the British Museum, preliminary trials were conducted by The Government Chemist during 1948 to establish the most satisfactory procedure, and the perfected fluorine dating method was used to assess the relative age of a fossil assemblage that same year. For this first ever test, Oakley and his colleague M. F. A. Montagu selected the Galley Hill skeleton.[51] The results profoundly contradicted Sir Arthur Keith's belief in the great antiquity of the specimen.

Briefly, Oakley and Montagu showed that the fossil fauna from the Middle Pleistocene gravels contained about two per cent fluorine, those from Upper Pleistocene deposits in the same sequence about one per cent, and the post-Pleistocene bones not more than 0.3 per cent. The Galley Hill skeleton – which, it will be recalled, had been found in the oldest gravels – contained only about 0.3 per cent fluorine. Therefore it matched the post-Pleistocene bones and cannot have been older; the skeleton must have been of recent origin, entombed in the ancient deposits by man, not nature, despite Keith's assertions to the contrary. The antiquity of the Swanscombe skull, on the other hand, was confirmed by the fluorine test; the bones contained two per cent fluorine, perfectly matching the Middle Pleistocene fauna with which it was associated.

So the antiquity of Galley Hill Man was dismissed, and of Swanscombe Man confirmed; where did that leave Piltdown Man, with his combination of 'ancient' ape-like jaw and 'recent' large brain? In October 1948 Kenneth Oakley was authorized to apply his fluorine dating method to the Piltdown material, the Keeper of Geology at the British Museum having deemed it likely that the results might help resolve the riddle of its age and association. Every available bone and tooth from the assemblage was analyzed, thirty-six specimens in all, including ten pieces of the *Eoanthropus* material, and six of the extinct fauna from which the Lower Pleistocene age of *Eoanthropus* had been derived. The fluorine content of the entire assemblage ranged from a minimum of less than 0.1 per cent to a maximum of 3.1 per cent. The higher levels all were found in the extinct fauna, confirming their antiquity; while the remains of Piltdown Man contained an average of only 0.2 per cent, clearly showing that he was not as old as the Lower Pleistocene fauna with which he was supposed to have been associated. *Eoanthropus dawsoni* – Dawson's Dawn Man – was probably no older than *Homo sapiens* from Galley Hill, it seemed.

Oakley's results were published in March 1950.[52] 'That the figures scarcely provide any differentiation between *Eoanthropus* and the recent bones requires some explanation,' he remarked, but the deeper implication of his observation was not fully realized until three years later.

Meanwhile, Oakley had simply added another twist to the riddle. The combination of jaw and skull was puzzling enough when both were believed to be of great antiquity, as we have seen, but if both stemmed from the recent past further problems arose. The skull was reasonable enough, but what about the jaw? No man could have possessed such an ape-like form at so late a stage in human evolution. This may seem to have vindicated the contention that jaw and skull represented different individuals, but this in itself presented another problem: if the jaw did not belong to the skull, obviously it came from somewhere else. But where? The great apes are totally absent from the fossil record of Britain

Reconstructed skull of Piltdown Man. The brown parts represent the fragments found at Piltdown; the remainder is plaster reconstruction

and Europe, and highly unlikely to have inhabited the region during the upheavals of the Ice Age. So Oakley provided no comfort for either side of the Piltdown controversy.

With the aging and passing of its protagonists the controversy had lost much of its impetus by 1950. Although Piltdown Man so completely contradicted the evidence of the small-brained hominid fossils with man-like jaws subsequently found in Africa and the Far East, most anthropologists were content to consign the riddle to a 'suspense account' and await clarification, rather than actively search for it.

But one evening towards the end of July 1953 a chance remark by Kenneth Oakley prompted Joseph Weiner, an anatomist working with Professor le Gros Clark at Oxford, to ponder the problem again as he drove home. In the early hours of the morning he found the key to the riddle. If Piltdown Man was not as old as had been claimed, if the strange jaw with man-like features matched no apes living or extinct, if it belonged neither to the skull nor to the deposit in which the specimens were found, then all 'natural' explanations of the Piltdown phenomenon were eliminated. Which left only an 'unnatural' alternative, reasoned Weiner. Could it be that the man-like features of the jaw were artificial, and the whole assemblage was deposited in the Piltdown gravels with the express intention of suggesting to its discoverers that man in the early Pleistocene had possessed an ape-like jaw and a large brain?

The proposition seemed outrageous, but as Weiner weighed the evidence, the case for a deliberate hoax gained strength on several counts. The discovery of the second Piltdown remains so precisely echoing the first some years before considerably lessened the likelihood of either or both being an accident. The fact that the chin region and the articular knob were missing strongly suggested that these critical diagnostic features had been deliberately removed. The pieces of the puzzle began to fall into place.

Next day, Weiner examined the casts of the Piltdown remains in the collection of the Department of Anatomy at Oxford and discussed his theory with Professor le Gros Clark. Even on the casts, the wear of the molar teeth seemed more compatible with artificial abrasion than natural; and similarly on the canine, where artificial abrasion would also explain the apparent paradox – first noted by a dentist in 1916[54] – of such excessive wear on such an immature tooth.

Weiner and le Gros Clark took their case to the British Museum, and during the autumn of 1953 the riddle of Piltdown Man was finally resolved – forty-one years after it had first arisen. The teeth confirmed Weiner and le Gros Clark's preliminary observations. Further fluorine testing revealed that the jaw was not just recent, but not long dead; the skull was slightly more ancient. The remains were all stained to match the Piltdown deposit, so too were the mammalian fossils with which they were associated. The hoax had been ingeniously planned, carefully carried out and completely unsuspected.

When the news was released in November 1953 it excited comment from many quarters. In the House of Commons a motion was put forward proposing a lack of confidence in the trustees of the British Museum 'because of the tardiness of their discovery that the skull of the Piltdown Man is partially a fake'. The proposers were angry at the 'sycophantic servility' of the museum tradition which had itself been playing a hoax on the public with this 'so-called Missing Link', they said, but the motion aroused more laughter than serious debate: Speaker – 'not sure how serious the motion is (laughter), but sure [we] have many other things to do besides examining the authenticity of a lot of old bones' (loud laughter). Lord Privy Seal – 'the government had found so many skeletons to examine when they came into office that there had not yet been time to extend the researches into skulls' (laughter).[55]

A letter to *The Times* asked: 'Sir, May we now regard the Piltdown Man as the first human being to have false teeth?'[56]

Humour may cover embarrassment satisfactorily, but it could never dispel the question: Who dunnit? Dawson, Smith Woodward, Elliot Smith, de Chardin, have all been accused by some and excused by others. Several books and many articles have been published on the subject; from time to time 'new' evidence is produced to throw new light, but so far there is no definite, incontrovertible answer. The evidence simply is not conclusive enough. A case could be made against each of the characters involved (including some not mentioned in this chapter), but none would stand serious cross-examination and judgement would depend heavily upon the predispositions of the judge.

The inconclusive nature of the Piltdown affair reflects a fundamental problem of the science as a whole, for the fossil evidence of human evolution rarely offers just one clear interpretation. At the same time, however, the Piltdown affair makes two pertinent points: firstly, accurate geological and stratigraphical determinations are essential. And secondly, when preconception is so clearly defined, so easily reproduced, so enthusiastically welcomed and so long accommodated as in the case of Piltdown Man, science reveals a disturbing predisposition towards belief before investigation – as perhaps the hoaxer was anxious to demonstrate.

Chapter Four

Australopithecus africanus
(1925)

GRAFTON ELLIOT SMITH'S contribution to the Piltdown affair was largely inspired by his belief that the imprint of the brain's fissures and convolutions on the interior of a fossil skull permitted some comparative assessment of the owner's intellectual development. His researches had shown that the significant differences in the brain development of apes and man could be recognized on casts taken from the interior of their skulls; so if the form of the ape's 'primitive' brain, and of man's 'evolved' brain was known, Elliot Smith reasoned that it should be possible to define and recognize the intermediate stages on casts taken from the fossil skulls of early man.

The idea was not universally accepted by any means, but among those with whom it found favour was Raymond Dart, a fellow Australian and senior demonstrator in anatomy at University College, London under Elliot Smith from 1919 to 1922 while the Professor was still busy with the problems of the Piltdown reconstruction. The evolution of the brain and the nervous system was Dart's own special interest, which Elliot Smith helped to supplement with an interest in the evolution of man so that by the time Dart left London in 1922, he was exceptionally well equipped to recognize the significance of certain hominid fossils that came his way a few years later.

Raymond Dart was born in a suburb of Brisbane on 4 February 1893, one of nine children. He graduated from medical school in 1917, served with the Medical Corps in France and, after a spell in London, was appointed Professor of Anatomy at the Witwatersrand University, Johannesburg, in 1922 – at the instigation of Elliot Smith and Arthur Keith.

Many might have found it flattering to be appointed a full professor at twenty-nine but, all in all, the Witwatersrand Medical School in 1922 was not the most attractive proposition for a promising young anatomist with interests in neurological research and the evolution of man. Johannesburg was still a pioneer town of tin-roofed houses and impermanent appearance. Barely fifty years old, founded on a gold-rush by the kind of people such events attract, the city was struggling to establish identity and respectability. The University had received its charter only three years before and the Chair of Anatomy was vacant only because its incumbent had been forced to resign in disgrace following his divorce. Dart was hardly a welcome replacement. He was an Australian, and the University Board did not approve of Australians much more than it approved of divorce. The Principal himself wrote expressing regret that an Australian was appointed, but presumably the choice was limited.

The medical school awaiting the new professor was an unprepossessing place – a double-storeyed building standing among exotic weeds behind an old garrison wall. The anatomy department comprised just three or four small rooms and a dissecting hall whose walls bore signs of occasional use for football and tennis practice. The department was devoid of electricity, water or gas and, apart from a few scraps of cadavers remaining from the previous course, almost entirely lacking in essential facilities. No library, no museum, no specimens, an abysmal lack of equipment. 'There wasn't a bloody thing,' says Dart, 'except what I happened to carry out with me from England.'[1] He had left England feeling more like an exile than a man elevated to a professorship[2] and for the greater part of the first two years in Johannesburg he was a very unhappy man.

The events which changed Dart's life irrevocably and introduced an important new dimension to the study of fossil man began in the early part of 1924 when Dart's sole female student, Josephine Salmons, noticed a fossil baboon skull gracing the mantelpiece of a friend's living room. She told the professor of it and he, then unaware of any fossil primates from anywhere south of the Fayoum deposits in Egypt, asked her to borrow the specimen if she could and bring it to him for examination. The skull was indeed that of a baboon, Dart confirmed the next day, possibly of a new and primitive species. It had been found in the course of lime-quarrying operations near a place called Taung, one among many such items discovered there (in fact, unbeknown to Dart, a new species of fossil baboon had been reported from the deposit in 1920[3] by a government geologist, Dr Sidney Haughton). Dart wanted more specimens if they were available, and immediately sought the advice of Dr R. B. Young, a colleague in the university's geology department. Young knew the Taung quarry and, as it happened, was due to visit the area. He agreed to look for primate fossils while he was there and to ask the quarry managers to preserve any they might discover.

The Taung fossils had been preserved in cave deposits that typically occur along valleys cut through the dolomitic rock of South Africa's inland plateau. But how were such cave deposits formed, and how did fossils accumulate in them? Dolomite is a limestone, in which caverns were initially formed when the water table of the region was so high that it covered the rock entirely. The water percolated through cracks and areas of weakness in the rock, leaching away the soluble calcium salts and thus carving out caves and tunnels. As the rivers cut valleys through the dolomite, the water table dropped with the level of the surface water. At last the caves and tunnels were left high and dry. Rain continued to percolate through rock fissures, of course, and this water leached out the soluble calcium salts as before. But instead of being washed away, these substances now accumulated within the cave system – in the form of stalagmites and stalactites.

Eventually this slow but inexorable process of deposition might fill entire caves, but frequently a rockfall or erosion would open them to the surface first; then external debris would fall in and mingle with the purer chemical deposition: animals could enter or perhaps fall in and die there, leaving their bones to fossilize among the accumulating debris in perfect alkaline conditions as the caves gradually filled. It was a continuous process of erosion and deposition that over millions of years has left the Dolomite plateau of South Africa dotted with caves and cave deposits containing fossils.[4]

Stalagmites and stalactites and such primary cave deposits consist of pure lime. Lime is an important constituent of cement and, as the South African building boom gathered momentum after the First World War, every workable deposit in the country became a valuable resource. The purer the better of course, but even those where the pure lime was surrounded and interfingered by a secondary deposit were worth exploiting. The secondary deposits of course comprised the earth and debris that had fallen in once the cave had opened to the surface; they were mixed with varying proportions of lime and compacted to rock hardness. The fossils lie within this rock, and are revealed when the limeworkers blast and quarry the deposits. The Taung quarry was an extensive operation, and it is certain that large quantities of fossil bone were shovelled into the limekilns before Dart's pronouncements on a fossil found there in 1924 brought worldwide attention to the significance of the deposits.

In a 1974 publication commemorating the fiftieth anniversary of the discovery,[5] it is said that Dr Young first saw the fossil in question on the

desk of the quarry manager where it served as a paperweight, having
been brought into the office sometime before by a workman convinced
he had found the fossilized remains of a bushman. In a newspaper report
of the day, however, Dr Young himself tells how he arrived at the Taung
quarry just after blasting operations had taken place. 'One large piece
of rock had apparently been split in two,' he says, 'embedded in the one
fragment was the "Missing Link" fossil, the face itself hidden in the
rock. The brain portion was found quite loose, but it fitted exactly into
position in the skull, each fracture corresponding. Dr Young carefully
packed the find and after returning to Johannesburg, handed it to
Professor Dart.'[6]

In his popular book *Adventures with the Missing Link*, Dart gives yet
another version of the fossil's discovery. Two large boxes of rocks,
mailed to him from the Taung limeworks on the instructions of Dr Young,
arrived while he was donning white tie and tails for a wedding to be held
at his house, Dart writes. With collar unfixed, the guests arriving and the
groom waiting, he hurriedly wrenched open the boxes. The contents of
the first were disappointing, but in the second he immediately recognized
a fossil brain cast with distinctly hominid features and, further ransacking
the boxes, also found the back of the forehead and face into which the
cast fitted. 'I stood in the shade holding the brain as greedily as any miser
hugs his gold,' he writes, 'here, I was certain, was one of the most significant finds ever made in the history of anthropology . . . These pleasant
daydreams were interrupted by the bridegroom himself tugging at my
sleeve. "My God, Ray," he said, striving to keep the nervous urgency out
of his voice, "You've got to finish dressing immediately – or I'll have to
find another best man. The bridal car should be here any moment." '

A fossil brain cast, or more correctly, an endocranial cast, is formed
when the skull cavity of the dead creature, lying undisturbed in a cave,
fills with debris – for instance, bat droppings, sand, lime – which subsequently fossilizes along with the bone. In the case of the Taung specimen, only a little more than half the skull cavity was filled, giving a cast
of the right side only and a flat surface on the left, covered with glistening
white crystals. Endocranial casts are extremely rare. Five are known
from South Africa; the Taung specimen was the first ever to be recognized.
That it was formed in the first place is remarkable enough; that it was
recovered in the course of a mining operation which, by its very nature,
is destructive, is even more remarkable – but, following such a fortuitous
chain of circumstances, that it should have found its way into the hands
of one of the three or four men in the entire world capable of recognizing
its significance, is most remarkable of all.

In the course of his pioneering work on the brain and endocranial casts, Dart's professor at University College, Grafton Elliot Smith, had identified the lunate sulcus, which is a fissure between two convolutions towards the rear of the brain, and suggested that the gap between the lunate and the parallel sulcus (another fissure close by), is an important indication of evolutionary development. In apes the sulci are close together, in man, farther apart. Dart, of course, was familiar with this work and the first glance at the Taung endocranial cast told him that the gap between its lunate and parallel sulci was about three times greater than in the living apes. In terms of cranial capacity, the cast was large for an ape, but still far, far smaller than anyone thought possible for the ancestor of man. Even so, Dart felt that 'by the sheerest good luck', the fossil had brought him 'the opportunity to provide what would probably be the ultimate answer in the . . . study of the evolution of man.'[7]

Seventy-three days later (during which Dart worked in his spare time with a variety of tools, including his wife's knitting needles, sharpened for the fine work), the matrix was removed from the rock into which the cast fitted, and the face of the Taung specimen exposed. There were no great eyebrow ridges, nor did the jaw jut forward, as in the apes. The large brain had not belonged to a large adult ape, it was revealed, but to an infant with rounded forehead, a full set of milk teeth and the first molars just emerging.

The Taung fossil had reached Dart in mid-October; by Christmas he had uncovered most of its detail; by mid-January he had written a preliminary paper on the discovery and posted it, with photographs, to *Nature* in London. During this period Dart's resources were limited. He had worked on the fossil entirely alone, without colleagues for discussion, a library for reference, or museum specimens for comparison. His most useful aid had been a book that he had brought from England which included some drawings of infant chimpanzee and gorilla skulls. In comparing these drawings with the Taung specimen, Dart saw enough to convince him that the fossil differed from both the chimpanzee and the gorilla as much as they differed from each other. And in the presentation of his findings,[8] Dart drew bold conclusions from his unavoidably limited observations.

The Taung specimen represented a creature that was advanced beyond the apes in two distinctly human characteristics, he said – its teeth and the 'improved quality' of its brain. The creature could appreciate colour, weight and form, he claimed: it knew the significance of sounds and had already passed important milestones along the road towards the acquisition of articulate speech. Furthermore, the forward position of the

The original Taung fossil, type specimen of Australopithecus africanus

foramen magnum (the hole in the base of the skull through which the spinal cord passes) suggested to Dart that the Taung skull must have balanced on the top of the vertebral column in a manner approximating that of modern man. Therefore the creature had walked upright, he concluded, with hands free to become manipulative organs and available for offence and defence – a proposal rendered all the more probable, Dart reasoned, by the absence of 'massive canines and hideous features'.

As regards the evolutionary pressures that may have given rise to this Missing Link, Dart pointed out that the creature had lived on the fringe of the Kalahari desert, two thousand miles from the easy picking of the tropical forests, at a time when, geologists proclaimed, the climate was no less harsh than in modern times. Compared with the luxuriant forests of the tropical belts, where 'nature was supplying with profligate and lavish hand an easy and sluggish solution, by adaptive specialization, of the problem of existence', Dart suggested that the relative scarcity of water and 'fierce and bitter mammalian competition' for food and with predators, made Southern Africa the perfect laboratory for sharpening the wits and quickening the intellect during the 'penultimate phase of human evolution'. Of the other candidates then proposed for the ancestry of man, Dart alluded to the chimpanzee-like features of the Piltdown jaw; and referred to Dubois' Java Man as 'a caricature of precocious hominid failure', an ape-like man destined for extinction while the Taung specimen represented 'our troglodytic forefathers' intermediate between the apes and man. He proposed a new zoological family to accommodate the phenomenon – the *Homo-simiadae* – and named the Taung child *Australopithecus africanus* as the first known genus and species of the group.

Dart has said that he prepared his preliminary report 'proudly' and with 'a sense of history'. When he sent it off to *Nature*, he fully expected some scepticism from the British scientific community, but hoped that he would be taken seriously at least. Considering the woefully inadequate facilities in Johannesburg, Dart had assembled a paper of commendable perspicacity. In some respects it tended more towards inspirational interpretation than cool scientific appraisal, and occasionally Dart lapsed into a florid style not normally encountered in *Nature*; nonetheless, the editors deemed the report important enough to merit immediate attention (no mean compliment in itself), and pre-publication review by four of Britain's most distinguished anthropologists – Sir Arthur Keith, Sir Arthur Smith Woodward, Grafton Elliot Smith and Dr W. L. H. Duckworth – the triumvirate and one other. These gentlemen received proofs of the report on 3 February 1925, but hardly had time to collect their thoughts before Fleet Street descended upon them for comment on that morning's cables from Johannesburg announcing that the Missing Link had been found there by Professor Dart. The next day, and indeed for several days thereafter, the news occupied much space in the papers. Sir Arthur Keith endeavoured to instil a note of scientific calm with the comment that 'we have a rumour of this kind three or four times a year', but his efforts had little effect. 'Missing Link 5,000,000 years old', 'Ape-Man of African had commonsense', 'Missing Link that could speak', 'Birth of Mankind', 'Missing Link 500,000 (sic) years old', . . . ran headlines around the world above stories in which Dart expounded variously and at length upon the aspect and talents of the ancestor he believed was represented by the fossil from Taung.

In the first days of his thirty-third year, Raymond Dart became a celebrity. Press enquiries and congratulatory cables inundated him, publishers offered book contracts, General Smuts and the University principal who disliked Australians both congratulated him; then, on 14 February, the first serious scientific comment appeared, when *Nature* published the reports of the four experts they had asked to review the paper.[9] Although all four saw more immediate affinities with the apes than with man, the reports were sympathetic. They all emphasized the difficulty of assessing a fossil – especially a juvenile fossil – from a preliminary report and a few photographs. To judge the claims Dart had made they needed more materials, and looked forward to receiving full-size photographs, casts of the fossils and the monograph Dart had promised. Of the four, Sir Arthur Smith Woodward was the least complimentary. He concluded his report with an expression of regret that Dart had chosen such a 'barbarous' combination of Latin and Greek in naming the specimen *Australopithecus africanus*.

Australopithecus africanus was intended to be descriptive. It means 'the southern ape of Africa' and its form follows the precedent set in 1922 by *Hesperopithecus*, the 'western ape' whom we shall meet in chapter 5. (Of course, '*Australopithecus*' is also akin to the name of Dart's homeland; but he always expresses the utmost surprise should anyone suggest that he chose the name to reflect his own origins.)

Names apart, the most important requirement during the months following the announcement of the discovery was that Dart should publish a thorough description of the remains, and make casts of it available to his senior colleagues with the same dispatch as he had preliminarily described it. The scientific establishment was not impressed with his extravagant speculations in the popular press, nor by the popular acclaim he had achieved. Dart may have been disappointed that

Daily Chronicle 6·2·25.

APE-MAN OF AFRICA
HAD COMMON SENSE!

On the Way to Speech, says Finder
Telling Where Darwin Was Right!

LONDON WAITS BEFORE ACCEPTING
THE 500,000-YEAR-OLD LINK.

Professor Dart, the discoverer of the so-called " Missing Link " skull
between Mafeking and Kimberley, proposes to christen its class
" Homo-simidæ," or man-apes.

**He thinks the six-year-old child of countless ages ago had
a brain in advance of the present-day apeish, and had such
common sense as indicated a milestone on the way to articulate
speech. So Darwin was right in fixing the birthplace of Man in
Africa!**

But Professor G. Elliot Smith, of London, says there are not yet enough
data to prove that the skull is other than that of an anthropoid.

WALKED HALF-UPRIGHT.

Link Baby's Facial Line Like that of a Human Child.

FULL details of the reported " Missing Link " discovery in South Africa are given by Professor Dart, of the Johannesburg University, in the current issue of "Nature."

"The Daily Chronicle " on Wednesday gave a cable from the Rand which reported briefly the find of what is thought to be a fossilised skull of the much-sought "missing link " between man and the apes, by Professor Dart at Taungs, between Mafeking and Kimberley.

This discovery and others of a similar nature in Africa, writes Professor Dart, "lend promise to the expectation that a tolerably complete story of higher primate evolution in Africa will yet be wrested from our rocks.

"The specimen is of importance because it exhibits an extinct race of apes intermediate between living anthropoids (i.e., gorillas, chimpanzees, and ourangs) and man."

Three of the grounds on which Professor Dart bases the importance of his find are that the cranium (the part of the skull enclosing the brains), the teeth, and the lower jaw-bone all show " humanoid " rather than " anthropoid " characteristics.

CHILD MISSING-LINK.

He states that in this skull, which is that of a juvenile, the ridges above the eyes are entirely absent, and the relative measurement from the

forehead to the back of the skull is due to brain and not to bone. The eye cavities "rise steadily from their margins in a fashion amazingly human."

"The specimen is juvenile, for the first permanent molar tooth only has erupted in both jaws on both sides of the face, i.e., it corresponds anatomically with a human child of six years of age.

HALF-ERECT; NOT HAND-WALKING.

"Owing to the remarkably human characters displayed by the deciduous dentition, when contour tracings of the upper are made, it is found that the jaw and the teeth as a whole take up a parabolic arrangement comparable only with that presented by mankind among the higher primates."

A study of the poise of the skull upon the spine, says the professor, " points to the assumption by this fossil group of an attitude appreciably more erect than that of modern anthropoids.

"The improved poise of the whole body and the better posture of the head and mean that a greater reliance was being placed by this group upon the feet as organs of progression, and that the hands were being freed from their more primitive function of accessory organs of locomotion.

"Their hands were assuming a higher evolutionary role, not only as delicate, tactual, examining organs, but also as instruments of the growing intelligence in carrying out more elaborate, purposeful, and skilled movements, and as organs of offence and defence.

"Whatever the total dimensions of the adult brain may have been, there are not lacking evidences that the brain in this group was distinctive in type, and was an instrument of greater intelligence than that of living anthropoids.

"The brain presents a rounded and well-filled-out contour, which points to a symmetrical and balanced development of the faculties of associative memory and intelligent activity.

SOME COMMON SENSE.

"This group possessed to a degree nearer to those of hu unappreciated by living anthropoids the known apes. the use of their hands and ears, and the "So that, so far a consequent faculty of associating with cerned, the creature the colour, form, and general appear-and not human. ance of objects, their weight, texture, resilience, and flexibility, as well as the significance of sounds emitted by them.

"In other words, their eyes saw, their ears heard, and their hands handled objects with greater meaning and to fuller purpose than the corresponding organ in recent apes.

"They laid down the foundations o that discriminative knowledge of the ap pearance, feeling and sound of thing that was a necessary milestone in the acquisition of articulate speech.

"The 2,000 miles of territory which separate this creature from its nearest living anthropoid cousins is indirec testimony to its increased intelligence and mastery of its environment.

"It is manifest that we are in the presence here of a pre-human stock, which neither chimpanzee nor gorilla possesses a series of differential charac ters not encountered hitherto in any anthropoid stock. It is therefore logically regarded as a man-like ape.

"I propose tentatively, then', adds Professor Dart in his article in "Nature," "that a new family of homo-simidæ be created for the reception of the group of individuals which it represents, and that the first-known species of the group be designated Australopithecus-africanus,

in commemoration, first, of the extreme Southern and unexpected horizon of its discovery; and, secondly, of the continent to which so many new and important discoveries connected with the early history of man have recently been made, thus vindicating the Darwinian claim that Africa would prove to be the cradle of mankind."

VIEW OF PROFESSOR G. ELLIOT SMITH.

Not Enough Data Yet to Show More Than the Anthropoid.

Professor G. Elliot Smith, of the University, of London, told a "Daily Chronicle" reporter last night that there was not sufficient evidence yet to show whether what is popularly called the "Missing Link " had been found.

Asked for a definition of the missing link he replied:—

An ape which shows closer affinity to the human family than any yet known, but which has not got the definite characteristics of man.

Professor Smith, who had an array of apes' skulls and brain models on his desk, said, "This article in ' Nature ' in shows quite definitely, I think, that Professor Dart has found an anthropoid ape.

"It seems to differ in genus and species from the only anthropoid apes, the gorilla and the chimpanzee, at present living in Africa, but whether or not it is appreciably any nearer to the human family than the gorilla still remains to be determined.

"There are not sufficient data in the article.

BRAIN STILL SIMIAN.

"The brain apparently is no bigger than that of the gorilla; and even taking into consideration the fact that it is at of a child and would continuing for a year or so, it still would

not attain propor nearer to those of hu

So that, so far a cerned, the creature and not human.

reaction was 'criticism rather than adoration of their potential ancestry' as he has written,[11] but criticism is part of the process by which interpretative science proceeds; and a scientist with new evidence has some obligation to present it in the fullest possible scientific manner. Dart continued to promote his interpretations of the discovery in the popular press. Meanwhile, expert opinion was steadily hardening towards the conclusion that *Australopithecus* was a form of chimpanzee, its man-like attributes due to the phenomenon of parallel evolution.

It is generally supposed that Dart and the Taung specimen were unfairly attacked by the scientific establishment of the day. In the publication commemorating the fiftieth anniversary of the discovery, it is told how the fossil caused 'sensation and argument' wherever it was mentioned and brought 'an avalanche of scorn' upon Dart. But was the scientific reaction really unfair, given the year and the circumstances?

In the first place, Dart's reputation did not inspire confidence. According to Sir Wilfred le Gros Clark,[12] the memory of an unorthodox theory Dart had once proposed about the evolution of the nervous system still lingered in some minds, suggesting a readiness to draw far-reaching conclusions from limited evidence. Secondly, significant portions of the Taung report depended upon the interpretation of an endocranial cast, while such interpretations in general were still regarded with some scepticism. And then there was 'the extraordinary repetitious coincidence between Dart's discovery and that of Dubois in Java', as le Gros Clark puts it. Both Dart and Dubois were anatomists with an interest in the evolution of mankind. Both went to outlandish places and both found a 'Missing Link' within a few years of arrival. The coincidence of Dubois' discovery was remarkable enough. That Dart should now come along with an almost identical second coincidence 'seemed almost too much of a good thing', writes le Gros Clark. 'At any rate,' he continues, 'combined with the few awkward features of Dart's preliminary article . . , it seems to have alerted the minds of anthropologists generally to the possibility that in his too enthusiastic zeal Dart had claimed far more for his *Australopithecus* skull than was warranted by the evidence.'

Eventually some casts of *Australopithecus* were made, and Dart produced a head and shoulders representation of the creature, but the manner of their subsequent display in London did little to improve his standing. The casts, in fact, were not intended for appraisal by his senior colleagues; on the contrary they were intended to edify the general public – from a showcase in the South African pavilion at the British Empire Exhibition which opened at Wembley in the summer of 1925. When Sir Arthur Keith wished to inspect the cast he had to peer at it

Cutting from Raymond Dart's scrapbook

through a glass case, jostled by other visitors, standing beneath a banner proclaiming 'Africa: The Cradle of Humanity', set before a chart alleging that all mankind had evolved from the ancestor represented by the Taung child.

Once again Dart had flouted convention and Sir Arthur, for one, was not amused. He wrote to *Nature*[13] complaining that students of fossil man had not been given an opportunity of purchasing casts of *Australo-pithecus* but must visit the Wembley exhibition if they wished to make further study of the specimen. But despite the limited facilities for calm scientific appraisal at Wembley, Sir Arthur was able to conclude that the Taung skull had belonged to a young anthropoid ape 'showing so many points of affinity with . . . the gorilla and the chimpanzee that there cannot be a moment's hesitation in placing the fossil in this living group'. Any claim of Missing Link status was preposterous, he said, and as for its being the ancestor of mankind, well, that was like claiming 'a modern Sussex peasant as the ancestor of William the Conqueror'.[14] The last remark referred to Dart's apparent inability to provide data contradicting suggestions that the skull was younger than he claimed, younger even than Piltdown or Heidelberg, to which he said it was ancestral.

Dart attempted to make light of these remarks, but he had nothing substantial to add and fared badly, the more so when his letter appeared in *Nature* together with another cold rejoinder from Sir Arthur on the same page.[15]

Thereafter, Dart and the Taung child were hardly more than a music-hall joke, while in the study of fossil man Dubois' release of the Java material, and the discovery of hominid fossils in China, diverted attention. In South Africa, Dart concentrated on building up the Witwatersrand Medical School. He did not instigate any exploration of cave deposits around the country, or actively seek more remains of *Australopithecus*, but he did complete the monograph on the Taung specimen.

In 1930, he sent the manuscript to Elliot Smith for consideration by the Royal Society, and he himself followed a year later, hoping to convince everyone that *Australopithecus* really was all he claimed for it. He arrived in London with the fossil six years to the day after the initial *Nature* announcement. Finally Dart had bowed to convention, but he was too late to be persuasive.

Elliot Smith, Smith Woodward and Keith welcomed him warmly enough, but they were all much more interested in telling him about the skull recently discovered in China than in hearing the Taung tale all over again. Elliot Smith had just returned from Peking and was to address the Zoological Society on his visit; he invited Dart to accompany him to the meeting, suggesting that he might like to tell the audience of the Taung child. Dart readily agreed, for it seemed a splendid opportunity to present his case properly; but the result was otherwise. 'This was no setting in which to vindicate claims once daring but now trite,' he has written.

> I stood in that austere and chilly room, my heart bounding with the hope that the expressions of polite attention on the four score faces before me might change to vivid interest as I spoke. I realized that my offering was an anti-climax but with undiminished optimism launched into my story. . . . What a pitiful difference between this fumbling account and Elliot Smith's skilful demonstration! I had no plaster casts to pass round, no lantern slides to throw on the screen to emphasize my points. I could only stand there with the tiny skull in my hand, telling the audience what I saw as I looked at it – all of which had been previously published, with illustrations. . . . My address became increasingly diffident as I realized the inadequacy of my material and took in the unchanging expressions of my audience. . .[16]

Dart found little joy in London that year, and just before returning to South Africa he was told that the Royal Society would only publish the section of his monograph concerned with the teeth of *Australopithecus*. Why the rest of it was rejected is not known, although Sir Wilfred le Gros Clark has suggested that it may have been written in an unsuitable style. Sir Wilfred has also wondered 'why some of the senior anatomists in London at the time did not advise and help him redraft his monograph in a form acceptable for publication'.[17]

Meanwhile Sir Arthur Keith had acquired a cast of the specimen and was preparing to publish nearly one hundred pages on the Taung skull in the revised edition of his text book *New Discoveries Relating to The Antiquity of Man* (1930); and the Austrian anatomist Wolfgang Abel published another one hundred pages on the fossil in a European journal.[18] Both these authors opposed Dart's interpretation of the fossil. Keith aligned it with the chimpanzee, while Abel chose the gorilla. A third author, Louis Leakey, similarly cast doubt upon the validity of Dart's claims by omitting all mention of *Australopithecus* from his book *Adam's Ancestors*, published in 1934.

The trouble was that although Dart had drawn the right conclusions from the Taung skull, it was more by inspired speculation than anything else, for there was very little evidence to substantiate his conclusions. The fossil could be ancestral to man, but it had many ape-like characteristics too. Moreover it was a juvenile specimen, which made final diagnosis almost impossible because juveniles and adults differ greatly in all primate species and juveniles of different species resemble each other more than adults do. More than anything else, Dart needed more evidence – fossil evidence – to support his contentions, and it surely existed in the South African cave deposits; but he chose not to look for it.

In 1925 Dart refused the Witwatersrand Education Department's offer of money and time to travel abroad and write his monograph with access to comparative collections and good libraries. He did not want to leave his anatomy department and his home for so long, he has written, and was unwilling to be bound by the condition that he should donate the Taung fossil to the University.[20] But now, over fifty years later, the fossil is part of the University's permanent collection and Raymond Dart regrets that he did not accept the offer and even tour the world in search of support for his *Australopithecus*. 'It's no good being in front if you're going to be lonely,' he says.[21] And equally regrettable is the fact that while Dart was lonely, for ten years and more, untold numbers of *Australopithecus* remains were probably burned in the lime-kilns. But no one bothered about that at the time, of course. They were much more interested in the discovery of Peking Man or, more correctly, a series of discoveries made between 1921 and 1937 representing a number of Peking men and women.

Raymond Dart in 1978, with the original fossil and the issue of Nature *that announced its discovery*

Chapter Five

Peking Man
(1926)

THE STORY OF Peking Man is an intriguing tale with an unhappy ending, but like a good fairy story it begins with dragons. Not the malignant, fire-breathing dragons of Western mythology whose purpose is best fulfilled on the end of Saint George's lance; no, in Chinese mythology dragons are benign creatures – all-powerful perhaps, but kindly disposed towards mankind. They rule the seas, the rivers and the rainfall; when dragons quarrel above the clouds, thunder and rain results; when dragons are thirsty they suck the land dry before retiring to palaces beneath the sea. Thus dragons were believed to control the seasons and, therefrom, dragon worship pervaded the life of the rural Chinese. Emperors were born of dragons who attended their mothers on stormy nights, it was said; beautiful azure dragons descended from the skies to be present at the birth of wise men like Confucius; rubies were petrified drops of dragon's blood; perfume was dragon's saliva; and, more down to earth, dragon bones and teeth, pulverized and mixed in strange potions could cure a multitude of ills. This particular belief still persists: ethnic Chinese drugstores (in London and San Francisco as well as Shanghai and Hong Kong) still dispense Lung Ku – dragon's bones – and Lung Ya – dragon's teeth. But what are these dragon relics, and where do they come from? They are fossil bones and teeth, found in the ancient sedimentary deposits of China and purchased from peasants who 'mine' them during the dry season, when the dragons are in their watery palaces and there is little profit in agriculture.

'Dragon bones' were first brought to the attention of paleontologists and anthropology by K. A. Haberer, a German naturalist who travelled to China in 1899, hoping to explore the hinterland. Unhappily, the disturbances of the Boxer Rebellion restricted his movements severely; he was confined to the ports, so explored the drugstores instead of the hinterland and returned to Europe with a collection of 'dragon' bones representing no less than ninety species, with not a single reptile among them – dragon or otherwise. Haberer's collection was described by Professor Max Schlosser in a monograph entitled *The Fossil Mammals of China* (1903). Schlosser gave details of fossil elephants and camels, bears, hyenas, rhinoceros, giraffe, horses – and a solitary primate, represented by an upper molar tooth that Schlosser felt could be either human or ape. The tooth's affinities were no more certain than that, he said, while adding the tantalizing observation that China might be a good place to search for the early ancestors of mankind. Nowadays that particular tooth is regarded as representing an ape, but in the first decades of the century Schlosser's observations accorded well with a growing conviction that mammalian life had originated in Asia and from there had dispersed to populate the world; and any tooth of the higher primates was enough to suggest the birthplace of man. Schlosser's monograph aroused a good deal of interest among paleontologists and anthropologists.

But, of course, they were not the first westerners to find China interesting. Following the footsteps of Marco Polo, enterprising 'foreign devils' travelled extensively through the country during the late nineteenth and early twentieth century. Some were naturalists, others were adventurers, but none travelled without an eye for some kind of foreign profit and exploitation. By the time of the First World War, however, the Chinese authorities believed they were directing foreign exploration towards the greater benefit of Chinese interests. Thus it was that Johan Gunnar Andersson, a Swedish mining expert appointed as adviser to the Chinese Government, discovered large deposits of iron ore that were exploited by Chinese entrepreneurs most profitably while war raged in Europe. Demand fell with the advent of peace however; so did the incentive to pay Andersson's salary as regularly as he expected, and Andersson therefore sought an income elsewhere.

Andersson's hobby was collecting fossils. Perhaps prodded by Professor Wiman of Uppsala University, who was certainly aware of China's potential as a repository of paleontological treasures, and no doubt using the salary default to full advantage, Andersson negotiated an arrangement with the National Geological Survey of China whereby he would collect Chinese fossils for Swedish institutions. Expenses (including Andersson's salary) would be met by the Swedish China Research Committee, established expressly for that purpose and its chairman, His Royal Highness the Crown Prince of Sweden, personally attended to the diplomatic aspects of the negotiations. In return for the collecting privileges, the Chinese would receive a duplicate set of fossils. As Andersson later wrote,[1] it was an arrangement 'both beneficial to Chinese science

and generous to Swedish museums'. It was also a coup that gave Sweden considerable control over paleontological investigations in China for a decade and restricted American expeditions to the further reaches of the Gobi Desert when they searched for early man in Asia during the 1920s.

One might imagine that after centuries of medicinal exploitation 'dragon bones' would have been scarce in China. But not so: Andersson's endeavours met with immediate and considerable success. Soon he was excavating several sites at once and, when his first collections were lost in a steamer sunk by a typhoon, he was able to replace them all during the following year. It is difficult to assess exactly how much material Andersson collected, but it is hardly an exaggeration to say that Professor Wiman built Uppsala's Paleontological Institute around the fossils he sent to Sweden; even today, the material is still not fully described.

By 1921 Wiman had gathered a select band of scientists and students to assist with the preparation and description of the Chinese material, but he was becoming concerned about the manner in which the fossils were collected. Andersson was not a paleontologist; furthermore, he left the excavating to his Chinese labourers, who were not as careful as was desirable. Wiman felt there should be an expert in charge and persuaded Otto Zdansky, a young Austrian paleontologist, to spend three years in China ensuring that the excavations were handled 'in a more businesslike way'.[2] Zdansky had recently completed his doctoral thesis on fossil turtles and was willing to go to China but, because Wiman offered no remuneration beyond travel and living expenses, only on condition that he was given the right to describe his finds himself. 'After all,' Zdansky explains, 'the publications would be all I got out of my stay in China.' Wiman accepted the condition and so, with Schlosser's monograph prominent among his baggage, Zdansky set off for China in the summer of 1921.

Zdansky quarrelled with Andersson very soon after arrival. He threatened to return to Europe immediately; Andersson placated him, but thereafter the relationship between the two men was decidedly cool. Zdansky went to the regions Andersson suggested, but once he was there, the excavations were entirely Zdansky's affair. To familiarize himself with Chinese conditions before venturing into the more remote regions, Zdansky first investigated a disused lime quarry about fifty kilometres from Peking known to contain large quantities of recent fossils. He established his headquarters in the neighbouring village called Chou K'ou Tien and began work on a column of secondary infill which the limeworkers had left standing in the quarry. The column was packed with fossils; there were some rodents and small predators among them,

'Dragons' teeth' bought from a Chinese drugstore, and a recipe for their preparation as medicine

but most seemed to be of common and possibly still surviving forms.

Not long after Zdansky had begun exploring the deposits, Andersson paid a visit, bringing with him Dr Walter Granger, chief paleontologist on the American Museum of Natural History expedition in search of early man, which was just then getting under way; and that day a local resident advised the three men of another deposit with bigger and better 'dragon bones' in a quarry about 150 metres from the Chou K'ou Tien railway station. In a matter of hours the new site provided fossils of rhinoceros, hyena and bovids, and that evening a 'happy trio' raised their glasses to the prospect of further discoveries. Zdansky agreed to spend two or three weeks exploring the site.

Andersson had noticed fragments of quartz dotted through the deposit; he became convinced they were primitive tools of early man and on a subsequent visit said to Zdansky: 'I have a feeling that there lie here the remains of one of our ancestors and it is only a question of your finding him. Take your time and stick to it until the cave is emptied, if need be.'[3] Zdansky, however, did not agree that the quartz fragments might be tools. He felt they were just splinters fallen from the veins of quartz that traversed the limestone.

Nonetheless, he did find evidence of early man at Chou K'ou Tien during the late summer of 1921 – a single molar tooth that was unmistakeably human. 'I recognized it at once,' Zdansky recalls, 'but I said nothing. You see hominid material is always in the limelight and I was afraid that if it came out there would be such a stir, and I would be forced to hand over material I had a promise to publish. So I said nothing about it.'[4] The fossil tooth Zdansky had found was, in fact, the first evidence of Peking Man.

Andersson's interest in finding early man may have been awakened by Schlosser's monograph, but it was surely encouraged by Dr Walter Granger, and undoubtedly was confirmed by the arrival in Peking of all the experts and equipment that were to explore Mongolia and China under the auspices of the American Museum of Natural History. The expeditions conducted from 1921 to 1928 were inspired by the 'brilliant prediction' of Professor Fairfield Osborn, then President of the Museum, that 'Asia would prove to have been a great dispersal center for northern terrestrial mammalian life'.[5] But whatever the inspiration, the avowed intention of the expeditions was 'to seek and discover the ancestry of man'. Popularly known as 'The Missing Link Expeditions', the scale on which they were organized and the flamboyance with which they were conducted might have seemed to guarantee success, but they were restricted by one important consideration – namely a 'gentleman's agreement' with Andersson, and a formal undertaking with the Chinese National Geological Survey, that 'the expeditions would not enter upon geological, paleontological or archaeological explorations in Northern China.'[6] Which effectively confined the Americans to the wastes of Mongolia, an area of deposits so ancient they could never contain the remains of man. As cynics suggested, they might as well have looked for fossils in the Pacific Ocean.

Nonetheless, the Americans were provided with ample resources; $600,000 to be precise, with undertakings of more to follow. Their leader, Roy Chapman Andrews, a colourful zoologist and explorer, envisaged ten years of exploration in China. The problems he faced were enormous, but Andrews found a solution for many of them in motorized transport. Cars and trucks could travel one hundred miles a day, ten times faster than a camel, and thus should enable the Americans 'to do approximately ten years' work in one season', Andrews reasoned; and he claims to have achieved that ratio. But for all their benefits, motor vehicles brought problems peculiar to themselves. Accidents were frequent, with 'many people killed and injured'; and fuel was a constant headache. The fleet of five cars and two trucks required 4000 gallons each season, which weighed twelve tons and would have left little space for the expedition's personnel, equipment and discoveries if carried in the vehicles themselves. So Andrews resorted to camels, employing several score as a fuel train. Forty-four-gallon drums proved difficult to pack on a camel's back, and they had to be returned after use, so disposable five-gallon cans were used instead. Each camel carried twelve of these, weighing 400 pounds – perhaps an excessive load, but one that quickly lessened as the cans expanded, rubbed and leaked when subjected to a camel's rolling gait under a desert sun. A full fifty per cent of the fuel was lost in this way the first year, but Andrews reported that better packing reduced leakage to twenty-five per cent in 1925.

Logistics notwithstanding the American expeditions achieved remarkable results. They found a fossilized redwood forest, and the graves of a shovel-tusked mastodon with jaws five feet long; they sent over 26,000 specimens back to America and described more than one thousand fossil and living forms new to science. In all they collected enough data for hundreds of scientific articles and for twelve volumes of final reports. But in respect of fossil man, the expeditions were a failure. As Andrews wrote in a paragraph of his report headed 'The Unfinished Task': 'we have not been successful in one object of our search – the "Dawn Man". It is a scientific tragedy that Chinese opposition to foreign investigations should end our work when that goal might be attained.

Still, we have shown the way, broken trail as it were. Later, others will reap a rich harvest. We are more than ever convinced that Central Asia was a paleontological Garden of Eden.'

The expulsion of the American Museum team from their newfound 'Garden of Eden' was due, in no small part, to the manner in which they disposed of some fossilized reptiles' eggs they discovered there. It happened like this:

> On July 13 [1923] George Olsen reported at tiffin that he had found some fossil eggs. Inasmuch as the deposit was obviously Cretaceous and too early for large birds, we did not take his story very seriously. We felt quite certain that his so-called eggs would prove to be sandstone concretions or some other geological phenomenon. Nevertheless, we were all curious enough to go with him to inspect his find. We saw a small sandstone ledge beside which were lying three eggs, partly broken. The brown, striated shell was so egglike that there could be no mistake. Granger finally said "No dinosaur eggs ever have been found but the reptiles probably did lay eggs, these must be dinosaur eggs, they can't be anything else." The prospect was thrilling, but we would not let ourselves think of it too seriously and continued to criticize the supposition from every possible standpoint, but finally we had to admit that eggs are eggs and we could make them out to be nothing else. It was evident that dinosaurs did lay eggs and that we had discovered the first specimens known to science [7]

The expedition found twenty-five dinosaur eggs that year and the news caused excitement everywhere. When Andrews returned to America, newspapers clamoured for exclusive rights to the story, some offering thousands of dollars. But Andrews refused all in favour of *Asia* magazine, to whom he was contracted for popular articles. Eventually the story and pictures were made available to the press free of charge, but Andrews and his colleagues at the American Museum determined to cash in on the enormous interest aroused by auctioning one egg to the highest bidder. Not only would the sale contribute directly towards expedition expenses the following year, they reasoned, it would also publicize the shortage of funds and perhaps encourage private donations. The egg went to Colonel Austin Colgate for $5000 and Andrews raised $284,000 that winter, but he soon had reason to wish the publicity campaign had not been quite so successful. The Chinese, Mongolian and Russian authorities assumed that every egg obtained was worth $5000 and, not surprisingly drew the conclusion that the fossil collection Andrews and his team had removed from Central Asia was of enormous commercial value. They never could be persuaded otherwise, and, with a change of government and internal strife not helping, co-operation gradually turned to direct opposition until the American Museum had to withdraw, pending 'the dawn of a more tolerant era of sympathy and co-operation with foreign scientific endeavour', as Andrews writes in his report, *The New Conquest of China*.

Rather more successful in his relationship with the Chinese during this period, though in respect of only his own individualistic mode of exploration and without any intention of looking for early man, was Sven Hedin. Born in 1865, educated with royalty and the last man in Sweden to be knighted, Hedin was a romantic figure who spent the greater part of his life in the Far East. He wrote several books on his travels and achieved popular fame with one in which he claimed to have re-discovered Marco Polo's Silk Road, which even the Chinese had been unable to find. Hedin was an adventurer more than a scientist or a businessman. He managed to allay Chinese suspicions that he was removing valuable treasures from the country, but his expeditions did have their commercial undertones: in 1925 for instance, his travels through Tibet, Mongolia and China were financed by Lufthansa, who were then anxiously seeking topographical details of their proposed air route to Peking.

The Hedin image was subsequently tarnished by his support for the Nazis. In his defence it is said that he once refused to dine in the company of Quisling, the Norwegian traitor – though his defenders may neglect to mention that the dinner was in Berlin and the host was Hitler. But while Andersson and Andrews sought early man in China such notoriety was still to come.

In the 1920s the Hedin star was in the ascendant, perhaps aided by his belief in the protective properties of the Llama's ring he always wore. Hedin knew how to manipulate the Chinese authorities to his own ends, and he knew how to raise money in Sweden and elsewhere. As such he was a threat to both the American and the Swedish explorers: even though he declared no interest in the search for early man his presence compounded the uncertainties of an already complicated situation.

While Hedin tramped a solitary path and the Americans raced about in cars with the Stars and Stripes boldly fluttering until they were expelled, the Swedish team resorted to the transport of the country – railways, rickshaws, donkeys, and in Shantung, carts pulled by coolies and aided by a sail when the wind was favourable. Andersson's expeditions were not flamboyant, they were much cheaper than the American Museum's, but not less successful. Apart from the fact that Zdansky had actually discovered the remains of Dawn Man within weeks of arriving in China, he and Andersson also uncovered the beginnings of deciduous vegetation among the fossils of Southern Manchuria; in Central China they found a rich field of fossil plants including many new to science. Fossil fish, turtles, cockroaches and dragonflies came from eastern China – from there too came some strange dinosaurs. One of them was fully ten metres long; Zdansky and his men cut out the near complete skeleton in great blocks of sandstone and, in Sweden, four men spent a year preparing and reassembling the bones. From the structure of the bone and the form of the skeleton, Professor Wiman deduced that the creature had lived in the water rather like a very large, long-necked hippopotamus. He called it *Helopus zdanskyi*, which means marsh-footed and acknowledges its discoverer. Wiman regarded *Helopus* as a most important discovery.

But despite the success of the expeditions' paleontological endeavours, it was a recurrent disappointment to Andersson that all the sites they investigated were far too old to contain the remains of man. In fact the only site they had encountered with fauna recent enough to have been contemporary with man was the very first they had visited – Chou K'ou Tien. And there, of course, he had seen the quartz fragments. 'I could never forget the thought of hominid remains in this cave,' he wrote later; and in 1923 he persuaded Zdansky to return to the site. Of course, Zdansky already had in his pocket – so to speak – the very thing Andersson most wanted, the hominid tooth found two years earlier. He was aware of the world-wide interest in the search for early man. But still he said nothing of the tooth to Andersson. The fact that he disliked the man eased any qualms and, in any case: 'I wasn't interested in what Andersson wanted,' Zdansky recounts, 'I wanted only the fauna of the cave.'

Zdansky returned to Sweden in 1923 to study and describe his discoveries and later that year published a preliminary paper on the Chou K'ou Tien deposits, with Andersson as co-author.[8] The hominid tooth was not mentioned, and indeed its existence might have remained a secret until Zdansky published his monograph[9] (1928) if the Crown Prince of Sweden had not made a visit to Peking in 1926. It will be recalled that the Crown Prince was Chairman of the Swedish China Research Committee which had funded Andersson's work. To mark the Prince's visit to Peking in the course of a world tour, Andersson arranged a scientific meeting and wrote to Professor Wiman, asking for details of any important discoveries that could be announced to coincide with the Prince's visit. Wiman responded with a description of the magnificent

Helopus zdanskyi and asked Zdansky if he had anything to contribute that might 'give an additional spice to the meeting'. 'Yes I have,' replied Zdansky and promptly dispatched a description of two hominid teeth from Chou K'ou Tien (he had found a second while sorting the material), together with photographs and lantern slides.

Andersson's first response to this sudden revelation that Zdansky had found the ultimate prize and never disclosed it while in China is not recorded. Later he wrote that Zdansky had thought the first tooth was an ape's when he found it, but in October 1926 he kept his counsel and saved the 'spice' for the very end of the meeting. As Zdansky had expected, the news caused a sensation: his discovery was immediately labelled 'Peking Man' and reported as 'The oldest human type whose remains have been found in the strata of the earth'.[10]

As a paleontologist of uncompromising determination, Zdansky had resolutely avoided the glamour of the search for early man; he sought the broad picture of ancient life, in which man was an insignificant detail. But in the audience at the Peking meeting sat an anatomist with an interest in fossils among which fossil man filled the entire canvas. His name was Davidson Black, a Canadian who was Professor of Anatomy at the Peking Union Medical College – an establishment generously endowed by the Rockefeller Foundation of New York.

Black was inspired by the Chou K'ou Tien teeth. With only the photographs and a written description to hand (reports that Black worked from the originals are erroneous, says Zdansky: the fossils have never left Sweden), Black compiled a report on the discovery which he submitted to *Nature*[11] and *Science*.[12] The teeth are 'two specimens of extraordinary interest', he wrote 'which cannot otherwise be named than *Homo? sp.* . . . the actual presence of early man in Eastern Asia is no longer a matter of conjecture,' he said and, recalling Schlosser's prediction, concluded that 'the Chou K'ou Tien discovery . . . furnishes one more link in the already strong chain of evidence supporting the hypothesis of the central Asiatic origin of the Hominidae.' Thus wrote the anatomist.

A few months later Zdansky published a preliminary paper[13] presenting the more cautious view of the paleontologist. Noting that the discovery was 'decidedly interesting but not of epoch-making importance', he said:

> I am very sceptical towards a great deal of prehistoric-anthropological literature, and convinced that the existing material provides a wholly inadequate foundation for many of the various theories

based upon it. As every fresh discovery of what may be human remains is of such great interest not only to the scientist but also to the layman, it follows only too naturally that it becomes at once the object of the most detailed – and, in my opinion, too detailed – investigation. I decline absolutely to venture any far-reaching conclusions regarding the extremely meagre material described here, and which cannot be more closely identified than as ?*Homo sp.*

With this honest and accurate assessment of the evidence and inclinations then prevailing in the search for early man, Otto Zdansky retired from the story of Peking Man. He completed his monographs in 1928 and thereafter was appointed professor at Cairo University. And with his retirement, the Swedish option on early man in China effectively lapsed. The two teeth Zdansky dug from the Chou K'ou Tien deposit still reside in the Paleontological Institute at Uppsala, but the subsequent discoveries they inspired were destined for a much less satisfactory resting place.

Within days of the sensational announcement of the fossil teeth at the Peking meeting, Black convened a smaller, more select gathering in his office. With the Crown Prince in the chair, representatives of the Geological Survey of China, and of the Rockefeller Foundation in attendance, Black and Andersson gained unanimous approval for a joint Chinese/Swedish/American expedition to Chinese Turkestan two years hence. But while he was negotiating this cooperative endeavour (which never came to fruition owing to the activities of Sven Hedin already alluded to), Black was also applying to the Rockefeller Foundation for money to conduct a systematic two-year research project on the Chou K'ou Tien deposits. The Foundation responded generously. Black arranged that the project would be conducted in conjunction with the Geological Survey and undertook to study any hominid fossils recovered in his laboratory in Peking.

The second round of excavations at Chou K'ou Tien began on Good Friday 1927. Otto Zdansky had been invited to take charge but declined in favour of the Cairo appointment. In his stead Professor Wiman sent another of his graduate students, Birger Bohlin, who had recently completed his doctorate on the fossil giraffes Andersson had sent from China. Like Zdansky, Bohlin was primarily interested in the broadest aspects of paleontology but, unlike Zdansky, his work in China was narrowly circumscribed from the start. 'I went to China chiefly because I wanted to go somewhere.' says Bohlin, 'but I was ordered to find man.

Hominid teeth found by Otto Zdansky among the Chou K'ou Tien deposits, 1921–3, with a third tooth found in the course of further examination of Chou K'ou Tien material held at Uppsala

You could see from a distance that Davidson Black wanted fossil man. The rest was just by-product. He gave me some directions of how to work at Chou K'ou Tien: he said I should remove the whole deposit in six weeks and take it back to Peking. In the first few days I saw that this was impossible.'[14]

With five thousand dollars' worth of explosive, a small army of Chinese labourers and the able assistance of C. Li, a Chinese geologist, Bohlin managed to blast and examine 3000 cubic metres of deposits in six months. He uncovered the plan of the cave, revealing a deposit about 800 metres square and between eleven and seventeen metres thick. But for all that, evidence of early man eluded them until three days before work was to finish for the year. Then, on 16 October, Bohlin found a single hominid tooth poling from a corner of the cave. 'Here you are,' he told Li triumphantly, 'we can go home now.'

'Do you think one is enough?' replied Li.

Not long after Bohlin's return to Peking, Davidson Black identified the single tooth to his satisfaction as a child's, matching the second that

Davidson Black and X-rays of the Sinanthropus pekinensis *type specimen*

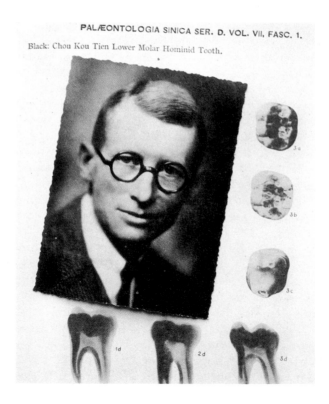

PALÆONTOLOGIA SINICA SER. D. VOL. VII. FASC. 1.

Black: Chou Kou Tien Lower Molar Hominid Tooth.

Zdansky had discovered in Uppsala. On reflection, he decided that both must come from the same jaw, and both must have been related to the adult represented by the third tooth – remarkably fortuitous discoveries among such a vast quantity of excavated deposit. Then, comparing the Bohlin tooth with corresponding teeth from a chimpanzee and a ten-year-old child, Black concluded that 'the newly discovered specimen displays in the details of its morphology a number of interesting and unique characters, sufficient it is believed, to justify the proposal of a new hominid genus.'[15] He called the creature *Sinanthropus pekinensis (Black and Zdansky)*, and so despite his caution Zdansky found his own 'extremely meagre material' used in a manner he could never approve, with his own name appended in honour of the first discovery.

In the light of subsequent finds at Chou K'ou Tien, Davidson Black's creation of a new genus on the basis of one tooth is often viewed as a bold and inspired move. At the beginning, though, many authorities considered the announcement irresponsible. The first announcement produced no correspondence in the journals and little comment in the newspapers – though the indifference which greeted *Sinanthropus* was probably not unrelated to almost simultaneous dethroning of *Hespero-pithecus haroldcooki*, another solitary molar hailed as a human ancestor and, in view of its relation to the story of Peking Man, worthy of a brief digression.

Hesperopithecus had been presented to the world in April 1922 by Henry Fairfield Osborn (the very same who inspired the AMNH expeditions to China). The specimen comprised a small water-worn tooth found in the Snake Creek fossil beds of Nebraska by Harold J. Cook, geologist. Cook sent the tooth to Osborn who, on receipt, replied:[16] 'The instant your package arrived I sat down with the tooth, in my window, and I said to myself: "It looks one hundred per cent anthropoid" ... we may cool down tomorrow, but it looks to me as if the first anthropoid ape of America had been found.' This was an event that American anthropologists had been 'eagerly anticipating' for some time. *Hespero-pithecus* means 'ape of the land where the sun sets', but in the London *Times* on 20 May 1922 Grafton Elliot Smith extended the description somewhat and welcomed the tiny tooth as 'the earliest and most primitive member of the human family yet discovered ... one would regard so momentous a conclusion with suspicion,' he continued, 'if it were not for the fact that the American savants' authority in such matters is un-questionable.' The shape and structure is like a palimpsest to the ana-tomist, he said, revealing the ancestry of the creature that once owned it. The paleontologist Arthur Smith Woodward took a different view of

Hesperopithecus – if the tooth were set differently in its hypothetical jaw, he remarked, its owner could just as well have been an extinct form of bear as an early kind of man.[17]

The arguments surrounding *Hesperopithecus* were as much concerned with detail absent from the tooth as with detail present on it; by 1925 they were still unresolved, inspiring Osborn to write: 'In the whole history of anthropology no tooth has ever been subjected to such severe cross-examination as this now world famous tooth of *Hesperopithecus*. Every suggestion made by scientific sceptics was weighed and found wanting'.[18] Subsequently, however, a Mr Thompson of the AMNH searched for more specimens of *Hesperopithecus* in the Snake Creek deposits. He found several teeth, some quite unworn, among which there was sufficient resemblance to the original tooth to establish their overall affinity beyond doubt, and sufficient detail on the unworn specimens to show quite clearly that all the teeth had come from the jaw of an extinct wild pig.

'An ancient and honourable pig no doubt, a pig with a distinguished Greek name,' commented *The Times* in a leader when the news was released, 'but indubitably porcine'. *The Times* wondered whether the worshippers who had so eagerly proclaimed themselves made in the image of *Hesperopithecus* were now left desolate; and concluded: 'If there is a place where the spirits of forsaken gods congregate . . . to condole with one another on ruined temples and smokeless altars, there also, aloft in the branches of a monkey puzzle tree overlooking the asphodel meadow, . . . conscious of his own distinction as one who has received the offering of unsuperstitious science, should sit the spirit of the Evening Ape.[19] Paleontologists had been badly bitten by the Nebraska tooth, Elliot Smith remarked later.[20]

As this salutary lesson on the dangers of applying bold and inspired interpretations to limited evidence was rumbling to its climax, in Peking Birger Bohlin had painted a charming portrait of Peking Man among the flowers of Chou K'ou Tien (which he photographed and has continually painted and repainted throughout his life), and Davidson Black set off for America and Europe with *Sinathropus pekinensis* in a specially made brass capsule that was variously suspended from his watch chain, or about his neck. Ostensibly he was on holiday, but he also toured the world of anthroplogy to present *Sinanthropus*. The trip was not marked with much success. Some colleagues were critical, some indifferent and others plainly rude. But Black was unmoved; according to Elliot Smith, rejection had no effect on Black 'beyond awakening his sympathies for anthropologists who are unfairly criticized and to make him redouble his

Birger Bohlin in 1978 with some of his paintings of Peking Man (and Woman) – all variations on the original he painted in 1927 and based, he says, upon the evidence of the single tooth he found!

efforts to establish the proof of his claim'.[21]

A little more of that proof awaited Black on his return to Peking in December 1928 – half a lower jaw with three teeth in place. Again, Bohlin had found the fossil, and again it was found a few days before excavations ceased – the only hominid fossil among over 400 cases recovered that year. The teeth matched *Sinanthropus*, and the shape of the jaw seemed to show ape-like characteristics, so Black felt his earlier claims were vindicated, but even so, the evidence of early man recovered from Chou K'ou Tien during his years of expert, expensive and extensive excavations was not impressive: four teeth and a fragment of jaw.

The Rockefeller Foundation grant had been for two years' work; now that the money was spent, could these meagre hominid finds possibly convince the trustees in New York that further investment was justified? On the face of it, probably not, and it is therefore quite likely that but for the collapse of his plans to explore Chinese Turkestan with Andersson for two or three years beginning in 1929, Black would not even have asked. It was at this point that the devious dealings of Sven Hedin worked to the benefit of those seeking the fossil evidence of early man. Naively perhaps, Black and Andersson had sought the advice of Hedin while planning their joint Chinese/Swedish/American expedition two years before. They had confided its destination, objectives and intent; and when Hedin subsequently returned to Sweden, he organized an expedition of his own to fulfil these purposes, thereby absorbing all the Swedish money available for such an undertaking. The Swedes would not support a second expedition; the Americans (that is, the Rockefeller Foundation) would not foot the entire bill to duplicate what was, in effect, Sweden's unilateral action, and the Chinese had no money at all, so the Black and Andersson enterprise was abandoned.

The expedition had long been Black's cherished dream; he had already arranged a three-year release from his duties at the Medical College and was sorely disappointed that his plans could not proceed – but he quickly saw that the collapse of one project could be turned to the advantage of another. He knew that the Rockefeller trustees were sympathetic to his plight; and as money had already been budgeted for the expedition (Black had requested $20,000 per year), perhaps it could be used to extend the search for early man. Black applied to the Foundation accordingly. But the proposal that reached the New York offices in January 1929 was not simply for funds to continue excavations at Chou K'ou Tien; it was much more ambitious. Black proposed the creation of a laboratory to investigate cenozoic geology and paleontology throughout China (cenozoic is the name of the geological era extending from the present to about sixty-five million years ago). The Cenozoic Research Laboratory should be a special department of the Geological Survey of China (then in dire financial straits and kept afloat by private mining interests), Black proposed, though it would be housed in the Anatomy Department of the Rockefeller-funded Medical College. Eventually the laboratory would deal with all aspects of geology and paleontology, nationwide, including prehistoric archaeology, but Chou K'ou Tien would be of particular concern from the start. An important condition was that all fossils and artefacts must remain in China – research material would never again be sent abroad for study and preparation. Black presented an impressively bold and inspired plan, and the Rockefeller Foundation responded with a grant of $80,000 to cover its initial establishment. Black's mood changed from depression to jubilation – 'things have turned out very differently than I . . . supposed possible,' he wrote to Sir Arthur Keith, 'it's better to be born lucky than rich.'[22]

At the conclusion of the first Chou K'ou Tien excavations Birger Bohlin had joined Sven Hedin's expedition (where an early task was to negotiate the purchase of the American Museum of Natural History's equipment on their expulsion), but Black did not look again to Sweden or to America for a replacement. Instead he relied on Chinese geologists and paleontologists to manage the excavations under his own direction, with the further help of occasional visitors like Teilhard de Chardin, the Jesuit priest become expert of fossil man who subsequently contributed extensively to the study of the geology and the fossil fauna of the Chou K'ou Tien deposits.

By 1929, a total of 8800 cubic metres of fossil-bearing deposit had been removed from the site and 1485 cases of fossils packed off to Peking. There were a few more hominid teeth among them, but substantial remains to underpin the shaky foundations of *Sinanthropus pekinensis* still eluded Davidson Black. He may have been confident all along, but not until December 1929 – at the very end of the season once again – did the combination of Rockefeller dollars and Black's conviction finally pay the dividend his critics demanded – a relatively complete skull.

The skull was discovered by one of the Chinese scientists, W. C. Pei, just when work had been halted forty-two metres below the highest point of the deposit by rock that could be breached only by extensive quarrying. Pei was curious to know what lay beyond, and found two caves opening away from the southern extremity of a fissure low in the deposit. He was lowered into one of them on a rope and explored it 'with great difficulty', finding only a few hyena vertebrae.

The other cave was not so deep and since it opened horizontally he was able to enter without much difficulty and explored the interior on 29 November. The weather was bitterly cold. On 1 December he began removing the uppermost part of the accumulation filling the cave. At four o'clock the next afternoon he encountered the almost complete skull embedded partly in loose sands and partly in a hard matrix so that he was able to extricate it with relative ease. On 6 December Pei left Chou K'ou Tien in the early morning and deposited the specimen in the Cenozoic Laboratory by noon the same day.[23]

The skull Pei had found represented the culmination of Davidson Black's work in China, substantiating his claim that fossil evidence of early man would be found in Peking, and presenting scientists with the first hint in many years of something both new and believable. The specimen served to divert attention from the Piltdown riddle and helped to eclipse the significance of Raymond Dart's *Australopithecus*. Once all the matrix had been removed from the skull, however, it became clear that *Sinanthropus pekinensis* was not so unique after all. Despite the slight dental distinctions Black had emphasized when proposing the new genus and species on the basis of teeth alone, the new specimen was very similar to the *Pithecanthropus erectus* fossils that Eugene Dubois had found in Java.[24] Subsequent discoveries at both sites confirmed the association, and the Java and Peking fossils were grouped together as *Homo erectus*. But Davidson Black did not live to see this. He died suddenly aged forty-nine of a heart complaint while working at his bench in the Cenozoic Research Laboratory during the night of 15 March 1934.

After Black's death, Teilhard de Chardin took charge of the Chou K'ou Tien excavations; Black's deputy was appointed Professor of Anatomy and a year later Dr Franz Weidenreich arrived in Peking to take over as head of the Cenozoic Research Laboratory. Within two years, excavations at Chou K'ou Tien were abandoned in the face of guerilla fighting in the surrounding hills and the growing menace of Japanese occupation of the whole of north eastern China. But by that time a large section of the hillside had been removed. In all, fourteen skulls in varying degrees of completeness were found, together with eleven mandibles, 147 teeth, portions of seven thighbones, two upper armbones, one collarbone (of doubtful attribution) and one wristbone.[25] During a total of 1873 days worked on the site, the excavators had blasted and sifted through the equivalent of a solid rock 'haystack' about twenty-three metres long, fifteen metres broad and forty-six metres high. Of course, such effort pales into insignificance against the tons of rock that are mined from holes kilometres deep to produce every ounce of gold, but the

Casts of Weidenreich's reconstructions of the Peking fossils are all that now remain.

remains of Peking Man were no less a treasure for all that.

When the military menace finally halted the excavations in 1937 Weidenreich retired to the laboratory, where he devoted himself to the detailed study of the fossils' anatomical structure. Careful casts and drawings were made, photographs were taken and Weidenreich issued a stream of authoritative monographs on the mandibles, the teeth, the brain casts, the long bones, and finally, a truly monumental work on the skull. No fossils had ever been so assiduously documented.

Because of its American connections, the Cenozoic Research Laboratory was regarded as a pocket of foreign interest during the early stages of the Japanese incursion, and was not molested. But with the beginning of the Second World War in September 1939, the growing danger of conflict between Japan and America posed a serious threat to the laboratory and the fossils it housed. The official understanding, of course, was precisely as Davidson Black had defined it: the Chou K'ou Tien fossils must remain in China. But the Chinese seem to have overlooked their responsibilities in this respect when the government moved from Peking. In January 1941, the director of the Geological Survey, Dr Wong, suggested from his refuge in South West China that Weidenreich should take the fossils with him on his return to America. Weidenreich declined. He feared the fossils would be confiscated if customs officials found them among his personal baggage and, in any case, considered them much too valuable to expose to an unprotected voyage in so dangerous a time. The diplomatic pouch was the obvious alternative and apparently Weidenreich suggested to the American Ambassador that the fossils should be sent to the United States in official baggage not subject to customs examination. But his suggestion was rejected and so, while Weidenreich travelled safely to America in April 1941 with a complete set of casts, photographs, drawings and data, the original fossils remained in the safe at the Cenozoic Research Laboratory.[26]

At this late stage, the wisest course probably would have been to hide the fossils somewhere in China, but in July they were packed in two large boxes, taken to the United States Embassy for safe keeping and, in August, Dr Wong himself asked the U.S. ambassador to arrange their shipment to America. The ambassador could hardly refuse such a direct request but, for some unexplained reason, three months passed before his instructions reached the appropriate authorities. By then it was mid-November 1941; the Japanese attack on the American naval base at Pearl Harbour was barely three weeks away.

Now the story becomes confused, but it seems certain that the fossils left Peking early in December in the care of a U.S. Marine contingent who were to sail for America in the *S.S. President Harrison*. War was declared between Japan and America while the marines were on their way to the port. The *President Harrison* ran aground trying to evade a Japanese warship and never docked. The marines were held by Japanese troops, and the fossils in their care have never been seen again. The casts, and Weidenreich's work on the originals, are all that remain.

Since the war, Chinese researchers have resumed excavations at Chou K'ou Tien. In 1966 two skull fragments were found that make a whole skull when joined with the casts of two other fragments found in 1934.[27] More teeth have also been recovered, and at another site, Lantien, a *Homo erectus* skull and mandible have been found.

In America, scientists are still studying the Chinese fossils that Roy Chapman Andrews collected in such vast numbers. In Sweden, Professor Bohlin continues his work on the fossils Andersson sent back, and on those he collected himself on the Hedin expedition. And at the behest of NASA his colleague on that journey, the geographer Professor Norin, is correlating the ground data he collected with modern satellite pictures. The teeth Zdansky found are still there too, the only original remains of Peking Man. It is ironic to reflect that had Otto Zdansky been a less determined scientist, and more concerned with the romance of early man, if he had told Andersson of that first tooth and spent the next two years in the Chou K'ou Tien cave, he might have found the fossils that Black's endeavours subsequently discovered. Then, too, Peking Man would be safe in Sweden instead of wherever he now resides.

Chapter Six

Australopithecus substantiated
(1936)

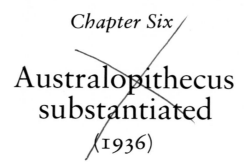

WHILE THE scientific establishment continued to argue over the merits of Piltdown Man and was diverted by the discoveries from Peking, the significance of the South African fossil that Raymond Dart had named *Australopithecus africanus* in 1925 was neglected. After his skirmish with fame and controversy Dart applied his talents to the creation of a creditable anatomy department at the Witwatersrand Medical School. Meanwhile, lime-quarrying kept pace with the country's development and the cave deposits, together with the fossils they undoubtedly contained, were shovelled into the kilns with hardly a thought for anthropological significance. That the potential Dart had identified was left unexploited, even wasted, was the result of circumstance and temperament unhappily combined, as we have seen. That it was exploited twelve years later, and Dart's claims subsequently vindicated, was entirely due to the initiative and effort of one man – Robert Broom.

The distinguished biologist J. B. S. Haldane once described Broom as a man of genius, fit to stand beside Shaw, Beethoven and Titian;[1] and a biographer offers the observation that Broom was about as honest as a good poker player.[2] On reflection, these compliments may not seem wholly appropriate to a dedicated scientist, but the evidence of Broom's life and work suggests that both are true and neither is a discredit to the man or science.

Robert Broom was born in Scotland on St Andrew's Day 1866. Poor health and his family's pecuniary problems permitted him only four years of unbroken schooling. Nonetheless, he entered Glasgow University at the age of sixteen and emerged a Bachelor of Medicine and Master of Surgery at twenty-three. Thus he was introduced to the natural sciences while they were still freshly inspired by the work of Darwin, Lyell, Huxley and Haeckel. He was a great believer in 'Missing Links' and

Robert Broom, some of his writings, drawings, a fossil and newspaper comment

TRANSVAAL, TUESDAY, APRIL 19, 1938.

NEW LIGHT ON EVOLUTION OF MAN

DR. BROOM'S DISCOVERIES AT STERKFONTEIN

HUMAN CHARACTERISTICS OF ANTHROPOID APE

Dr. Robert Broom, F.R.S. the celebrated scientist, to-day described two discoveries, in connection with Australopithecus, to the Pretoria representative of The Star.

"Professor Dart's discovery of the skull of a very young ape from Taungs, which he described as Australopithecus Africanus, was made in 1924," said Dr. Broom. "The specimen gave rise to considerable controversy. Dart considered that it represented a form of anthropoid ape much more nearly allied to the human stock than to the chimpanzee or gorilla, and probably near to the human line. Elliot-Smith, Gregory and others considered that it was, in the main, right. Others considered that Australopithecus was not far removed from the anthropoid apes.

"As the only specimen was of a young being developed, a human child of five years might be inferred that the case was not fully settled and preferred to wait until a better skull was discovered.

FIND NEAR KRUGERSDORP

In 1936 Dr. Broom began the Transvaal limestone caves in range of finding more evidence of Australopithecus. In August, during for fossils at Sterkfontein, near Krugersdorp, the greater part of a skull of an adult, but without the lower teeth. This specimen, which evidently of a much later geological age than the Taungs ape, Dr. Broom described as Australopithecus Transvaalensis. An account of this find was published in The Star about the end of August, 1936.

"At that time," said Dr. Broom, "I had the greater part of the top of the skull, the base of the skull, with ridges and other bones, and the complete upper jaw of the right side with the second pre-molar, the first and second molars and also the detached third wisdom tooth. Some weeks later there was discovered in the matrix much of the upper left protube with the beautifully preserved pre-molars and the first and second molars, and with the sockets of the incisors and canine."

FURTHER FINDS

When Dr Broom was in America during the first half of 1937 nothing further was discovered, but on his return he again began hunting at Sterkfontein and succeeded in finding the lower wisdom tooth, the upper wisdom tooth, much of the upper first incisor and the badly worn wisdom tooth of an old individual.

"The hunt has been continuing week after week," continued Dr. Broom. "Ten days ago I was fortunate in discovering the lower canine tooth, but it was so nearly human that I hesitated to say much about it in case it might prove to be human. This week, near the same spot, I have been lucky in finding a good right upper jaw with the incisor, canine, a pre-molar and a molar."

This new find was only second in importance to that of the type. That it was the same species of the type could not be doubted. The pre-molar and first molar are closely similar to those of the type in size and structure.

ENLARGED CANINE

"We have the rather startling fact revealed that the canine tooth is enlarged as in the chimpanzee or gorilla, and is typically human. It is even smaller than in the male Australian skull, which has the second incisor is also smaller than in most human skulls.

"Further, there is no gap between the incisor and the canine, so that the teeth form a continuous series as in

man. The grinding of the teeth is exactly as in man, as will be seen from the photographs. The top of the second incisor and the top of the canine and of the pre-molar are ground down to practically the same level.

"If the cast of these teeth had been sent to all the anatomists of the world," said Dr. Broom, "probably 95 per cent would have been satisfied that they were human. The size, the arrangement and the wearing all have human

like those of modern man than is the canine of Eoanthropus (the Piltdown man), which is undoubtedly the primitive human type.

"The gap between the anthropoid ape, like Australopithecus, with a brain of 500 to 600 c.c., and the most primitive true man, the Pithecanthropus of Java, with a brain of 950 c.c., is still a large one. Perhaps the transformation of the pre-human type like Australopithecus into the primitive man came about fairly rapidly from the development of a large brain, but how this change came about is still mysterious," concluded Dr. Broom.

searched for them assiduously in later life, but in effect he became a link himself – between the eccentric, idiosyncratic enquiries of Victorian science, among which he was reared, and the calculating, statistical investigations of the mid-twentieth century among which he died in 1951.

Broom held firm beliefs that were often provocatively displayed. He was inclined, for example, to remove all his clothes while hunting fossils in remote hot places (he once misplaced them altogether), in order to enjoy more fully the sunshine he considered so beneficial in health; and to demonstrate the benefits of sunshine in sickness, he once left an African 'flu victim inside a hut to die while another sat outside in the sun and was cured.[3] To further his anthropological researches he boiled skulls clean on the kitchen stove and buried dead Bushmen in the garden, to be exhumed when decomposition was complete. In another field of scientific endeavour, Robert Broom found and described important fossil evidence of the evolutionary link between the reptiles and the mammals but, although he accepted the theory of evolution, he rejected Darwin's proposal of Natural Selection as the driving force.[4] In Broom's view the process was too complicated and the results much too wonderful to be the product of mere chance. He believed that life on earth was the work and concern of a divine creative force.[5]

To a casual eye, a predilection for the odd and quirkish is immediately evident in the bibliography of 456 papers, books and monographs that Broom published during his lifetime. But a closer look suggests that the explanation of the odd and the quirkish was in itself a theme central to the purpose and intent of his scientific enquiries. Robert Broom's first paper, published when he was nineteen, was 'On the volume of mixed liquids'[6] and showed that two and two do not add up to four in the case of some chemical solutions – when mixed together the whole becomes less than its parts. His second paper (1888) was an 'a monstrosity of the common earthworm' and described a worm with two tails, each 'furnished with a perfect anus'. In 1895 he described the anatomy of a four-winged chick, and the Organ of Jacobson in the duck-billed platypus.

The Organ of Jacobson, a tiny accessory sense organ in the nose of many mammals, was one of Broom's lifelong interests. As a student he collected a specimen from a kitten and the comparative anatomy of the organ later became the subject of his doctoral thesis. Subsequently he described its anatomy in anteaters, squirrels, moles, horses, bats, shrews and marsupials and, during the First World War, his collection was enhanced by the addition of a rare and fully developed specimen plucked from the nose of an unsuspecting woman on whom he was operating for a quite different purpose.

Broom's interest in the Organ of Jacobson developed into a reasoned belief that since the organ was not affected by habit, its varying structure and form should provide clues to the zoological distinction between mammals whose appearance was otherwise very similar. Indeed, he did split a group of the Insectivores into three different orders on the basis of such evidence.[7] And in Australia, where he practised general medicine from 1892 to 1896, Broom found that the Organ of Jacobson in the duck-billed platypus is supported by a structure remarkably similar to that found in the snakes and lizards. The platypus is a mammal that lays eggs, as do the reptiles, and Broom's work on the Organ of Jacobson in its snout provided further detail of the manner by which the mammals had evolved from the reptiles.

Broom moved to South Africa in 1897 and, turning from living creatures to the evidence of fossil remains, sought clues to the origin of the mammals among the fossil reptiles preserved in the ancient sediments of that country. He identified several important mammalian features in their skeletons and ultimately assembled a series of fossil forms that showed how a group of reptiles had gradually evolved into mammals.

In 1920 Broom was elected a Fellow of the Royal Society; in 1928 he received the Society's Royal Medal for his work on the origin of the mammals. The citation read:

> At the time he went to South Africa thirty-five genera and sixty-five species (of fossil reptiles) had been identified. Little was known of their structure and the classification was hopelessly confused. He trebled the number of genera, quadrupled the number of species and worked out the details of the anatomy of most groups and established a classification that is universally accepted.[8]

In South Africa, however, Broom's work on the fossil reptiles was not quite so well received. Throughout his life Broom earned a living from medical practice; but for many years he also ran what amounted to a wholesale fossil business from his consulting rooms, paying collectors to bring him fossils, and selling them to museums abroad. In this manner a substantial number of important specimens went to the American Museum of Natural History, who paid rather better than other establishments. Of course, this flow of fossils aided Broom's research as well as his pocket – as the Royal Society Medal amply demonstrated – but the South African museum authorities did not recognize such subtle distinctions. The fossils belonged to South Africa, they said, and Broom had no right to sell them abroad for his personal gain. His behaviour was held to be reprehensible and dishonest. In the early 1920s Broom was forbidden all access to the collections of the South African Museum and his esteem in South Africa thereafter sank very low indeed, despite accumulating acclaim from abroad. The position eased a little with the death of the Museum Director, and was further improved by the interventions of General Smuts, Raymond Dart and the affairs of *Australopithecus africanus*.

When the first reports of *Australopithecus* were published in February 1925, Broom immediately wrote to Dart, congratulating him on an important discovery and noting that although he (Broom) had achieved so much, still he had not been 'so blessed by fortune' as Dart. 'The missing link is really glorious,' he wrote, 'what a new chapter you will be able to add (to the story of human evolution). Possibly an adult skull or perhaps a whole skeleton will yet turn up.'[9]

Two weeks later Broom visited Dart's laboratory. Unannounced, and ignoring both professor and staff, he strode over to the bench on which the skull reposed and dropped to his knees 'in adoration of our ancestor', as Dart recalls his actions and words.[10] Broom spent a weekend examining the fossil and found nothing to confound Dart's contentions. Although probably no older than the Pleistocene, the specimen was undoubtedly a 'missing link', he reported in April 1925,[11] connecting the higher apes with the lowest human types. *Australopithecus* was surprisingly similar to Java Man, he wrote, and probably the forerunner of Piltdown Man. Broom demonstrated these affinities with a drawing of the adult *Australopithecus* skull he envisaged (and in which jaw and dentition almost precisely duplicated those parts in Piltdown Man), and concluded his report with a reference to the 'considerable probability' that adult specimens would be found.

In common with other authorities, Broom was fully aware that adult specimens were essential if the significance of Dart's interpretation of the juvenile *Australopithecus* from Taung was to be properly examined. But adult specimens were not found, nor hardly sought, in the years immediately following the 1925 announcements; and they were still undiscovered in 1934, when Robert Broom finally gave up medical practice and, at the instigation of General Smuts, accepted the post of paleontologist at the Transvaal Museum in Pretoria. For nearly two years he worked on the collection of fossil reptiles, writing sixteen papers on twenty-three new genera and forty-four new species until, in May 1936, he decided to look for 'an adult Taung ape', as he put it.[12] By then the cave deposits had been neglected for nearly twelve years and Dr Robert Broom was sixty-nine years old. He already considered himself the greatest paleontologist that ever lived, Broom later remarked, and saw no reason why he should not become the greatest anthropologist as well.[13]

It is never unreasonable to suppose that where one of a kind has been found there may be more, but in the case of *Australopithecus* the problem confronting Robert Broom in 1936 was not so much whether the fossils existed as whether there were any left. The original Taung fossil owed its initial discovery to the activities of limeworkers, as we have seen; twelve years later, in a country short of lime, there were likely to be more scenes of devastation than discovery. Broom deplored the fact that the deposits had been ignored for so long ('Dart was not much of a fighter,' he said, and had been too easily discouraged by opposition to his pronouncements).[14] But Broom found some consolation in the thought that even if he did not find the remains of *Australopithecus* he was certain to find some interesting Pleistocene mammals. He could not afford to travel to Taung, so he began his investigations on some old limeworkings around Pretoria. Within a few weeks he had discovered half a dozen new species of rats and moles, a small sabre-toothed tiger and a giant baboon.

Cave deposits and limeworkings similar to those on which Broom was first engaged are common features of the dolomitic region to the north and west of Pretoria and Johannesburg. There are some near Krugersdorp, and if circumstances had ever taken Robert Broom to that small market town about sixty kilometres west of Pretoria, he probably would have noted Mr Cooper's general store on the main street where a sign beside a small display of fossils invited one and all to 'Buy Bat Guano from Sterkfontein and find the Missing Link'. Prodigious quantities of bat guano are frequently deposited in caves; it is a very good fertilizer and, as such, was a profitable adjunct to Mr Cooper's sale of agricultural and building lime from limeworks at Sterkfontein, ten kilometres away.

The man in charge of the Sterkfontein quarry was Mr Barlow, who had been manager at Taung when the first *Australopithecus* was found. No doubt Barlow's interest in fossils had inspired Mr Cooper's window display, but it was one of Professor Dart's graduate students, Trevor Jones, who eventually brought Sterkfontein and its fossils to the attention of Dr Broom.[15] Some of Jones's colleagues regretted the intervention of Broom,[16] feeling perhaps that the subsequent discoveries ought to have been reserved for Professor Dart, but there can be no doubt that Broom had more time and enthusiasm for the quest than Dart had shown. Broom pursued the investigation most energetically and found an adult *Australopithecus* skull at Sterkfontein on 17 August 1936, nine days after his first visit to the site and just three months after he had decided to look for one.

The discovery was almost an exact repetition of events at Taung twelve years before (if Dr Young's account of those events is accepted). An endocranial cast was found after blasting in the morning, and rocks containing associated pieces of skull and face recovered from the rubble during the afternoon and the next day. The cast was undistorted and lacked only its rear portion, but the face and side of the head were badly crushed and, furthermore, the fossil bone was extremely friable and therefore very difficult to remove from the much harder rock in which it was embedded. Four upper teeth were also preserved however, and one of these, together with the braincast, were in fact the only diagnostic features available in the new specimen. Broom acknowledged the inherent difficulty of comparing such fragmentary evidence of an adult with more complete juvenile remains, but reported to *Nature*[17] that the 'newly-found primate probably agrees fairly closely with the Taung ape', despite 'certain distinctive details' in its teeth. Broom was no less confident of the fossil's human affinities and, in the *Illustrated London News*, described his find as 'A New Ancestral Link between Ape and Man'.[18]

The skull was first called *Australopithecus transvaalensis*, Broom proposing specific distinction from the Taung specimen on the grounds of his belief that the Sterkfontein deposit was appreciably younger. Subsequently, however, he decided that the differences he had noted in the teeth merited generic distinction and re-named the creature *Plesian-thropus transvaalensis* – which means 'near-man' of the Transvaal and defines Robert Broom's opinion of its position in human evolution rather more closely than *Australopithecus* – 'southern ape'.

In November 1936 Robert Broom celebrated his seventieth birthday; in February 1937 he showed casts of the new discovery at a Congress of Early Man held in Philadelphia; in June he received an honorary doctorate from Columbia University; and during six months abroad he was enthusiastically applauded wherever he lectured. But the acclaim was for Robert Broom more than for the fossil of which he spoke. The Sterkfontein discovery was notable, but hardly conclusive enough to persuade everyone that Raymond Dart had been right after all. Interest in the South African claims had dwindled considerably by 1937; the works of Keith and Abel (see page 93) were widely regarded as the definitive appraisals of *Australopithecus*, and, although disagreement may have persisted on the question of whether the creature was related to the gorilla or the chimpanzee, there was general agreement with the contention that *Australopithecus* was not an ancestor of mankind. Polite scepticism characterized the majority view that Broom encountered abroad, but his belief in the ancestral status of *Australopithecus* was undiminished and, on returning to South Africa in August 1937, he immediately resumed the search for more substantial evidence.

In fact, Broom's investigations were significantly dependent upon the financial arrangements he made with Mr Barlow, who was encouraged to look out for interesting specimens exposed by the quarrying operations but expected to be paid for fossils of merit. Between August 1937 and May 1938 Broom bought from Mr Barlow a wrist bone, a facial fragment, the lower end of a thigh bone and a nice piece of upper jaw with four teeth in place. All undoubtedly were remains of *Australopithecus* but none matched the significance of the first skull. And then on 8 June, Barlow produced a palate with one molar still in place that Broom knew to be worth more than the £2 he gave for it. Perhaps Barlow knew too, for he would not reveal precisely where the fossil had come from, and nor would the workmen when Broom returned to question them in Barlow's absence a day or two later.

Broom then tried a more straightforward approach: the specimen was very important, he told Barlow, it had belonged to a large ape-man quite different from those previously found at Sterkfontein. But some teeth had been freshly broken off, he said, and in the interests of science Barlow should assist the search for the missing teeth and more remains of the creature. Where had the fossil come from?

Relenting, Barlow directed Broom to Gert Terblanche, a young boy whom Broom found at school some five or six kilometres away. In the presence of his headmaster Gert 'drew from the pocket of his trousers four of the most wonderful teeth ever seen in the world's history', Broom recounts.[19] They were the teeth missing from the palate; Broom promptly purchased them, transferred them to his own pocket and, after enthralling pupils and staff with an impromptu lecture on cave formations and fossils, walked with Gert to the hillside where the palate had been found in an outcrop of eroded cave deposit. The place was called Kromdraai; it was but three kilometres from the Sterkfontein site and, as Broom had suspected, the deposit contained more remains belonging with the palate. Within a few days Broom assembled a specimen comprising practically the entire left side of the skull, the palate and a large portion of the right lower jaw.

The face of the Kromdraai skull was flatter, the jaw more powerful and the teeth larger than in the Sterkfontein specimen. The whole aspect of the specimen was larger, more robust and, Broom believed, more man-like than either the Taung or the Sterkfontein skulls, so he afforded the new specimen generic distinction from both of them and called it

OVERLEAF, LEFT *Fossil endocranial cast and facial remains of adult* Australopithecus *(right) found at Sterkfontein by Robert Broom in 1936, with three other endocranial casts from Transvaal cave deposits.*
RIGHT *Broom's Kromdraai fossils: type specimen of* Paranthropus robustus; *elbow, hand and ankle bones.*

Paranthropus robustus, which means 'robust equal of man'. In *Nature* he described the anatomical features of the new fossil[20] and in the *Illustrated London News* it was described as 'The Missing Link No Longer Missing'.[21] The scientific establishment responded predictably – chiding Broom for creating new genera on 'extremely slender grounds', advising greater caution and remaining unmoved by the new evidence.[22] Broom was equally unmoved by the criticism and continued the search for more remains.

Lime quarrying at Sterkfontein ceased in 1939 and the advent of the Second World War similarly curtailed explorations at Kromdraai, so Broom conducted his investigations in the laboratory at the Transvaal Museum, where he worked on the blocks of fossil-bearing rock he had previously removed from the deposit. From the block in which the *Paranthropus* skull had been embedded he recovered much of an elbow joint, an ankle bone and some hand and finger bones. Their close proximity to the skull implied the bones must have belonged to the same individual and, although they hardly comprised the adult skull and skeleton Broom had hoped Dart would seek and discover, the scant collection did substantially vindicate Dart's claim that a small-brained, bipedal man-like ape with manipulative skills had once inhabited Southern Africa. The ankle bone Broom had found was quite unlike that of either the gorilla or the chimpanzee, for instance, and more closely resembled the human condition, strongly suggesting a habitual upright bipedal gait. The hand bones were slender and more suited to manipulative dexterity than to walking on all fours, and the elbow joint was similarly man-like. If the bones had been found separately no anatomist would have doubted their human affinities, but at Kromdraai they were associated with a small-brained ape-like skull which many scientists believed to be more closely related to the gorilla or the chimpanzee than to man. Was Broom's new evidence substantial enough to overcome the negative predispositions this association might arouse?

Proper presentation of the evidence was important; preliminary reports appeared in *Nature*,[23] and Broom distributed casts of the Kromdraai remains, but the War undoubtedly diverted attention and judgement was effectively suspended while Broom gathered together all the evidence of the South African fossil ape-men for publication in a comprehensive and convincing monograph.[24] He worked on the volume during much of 1944 and 1945, describing the Taung, Sterkfontein and Kromdraai fossils in turn; attributing them all to one sub-family – the australopithecinae – while defining the basis of the generic distinctions he made between them. Broom's text filled 133 pages and was illustrated with well over one hundred anatomical drawings, all his own work. A further hundred pages of the monograph, reviewing the evidence of the endocranial casts, was the work of the Johannesburg anatomist G. W. H. Schepers. In discussing the affinities of the australopithecinae Broom concluded that 'these primates agreed closely with man in many characters. They were almost certainly bipedal and they probably used their hands for the manipulation of implements. . . . The dentition . . . agrees remarkably closely with the dentition of man,' he said, and the brain, though smaller, was of the human type. 'What appears certain,' wrote Broom, 'is that the group, if not quite worthy of being called men, were nearly men, and were certainly closely allied to mankind, and not at all nearly related to the living anthropoids. And we may regard it as almost certain,' he wrote, 'that man arose from a Pliocene member of the australopithecinae probably very near to *Australopithecus* itself'.[25]

The monograph was published in Pretoria on 31 January 1946, a little over two months after Robert Broom's seventy-ninth birthday, and its authoritative and comprehensive presentation was afforded careful appraisal everywhere. The work won a large measure of support for *Australopithecus* and for the first time the scientific establishment began to suspect that Raymond Dart might have been right after all. Sir Arthur Keith acknowledged the man-like attributes of *Australopithecus* but continued to doubt its ancestral status. Wilfred le Gros Clark, the eminent Oxford anatomist, was more wholly impressed by Broom's work. He wrote a favourable review for *Nature*[26] and subsequently visited South Africa to examine the original fossils. He found good anatomical reasons to support the contention that *Australopithecus* represented the stock from which mankind had evolved.

Though over eighty Robert Broom continued to search for more *Australopithecus* remains in 1947; but, while his work and the South African cave deposits were finally achieving recognition, some authorities were becoming concerned about Broom's apparent lack of regard for geological evidence and the recording of stratigraphic detail. There was some justification for this concern. It was well known that the South African cave deposits do not lie in simple chronological order (an upper layer may be older than those beneath, because it may have been deposited in a tunnel that opened to the surface before those lower down). Now that Broom had found some important fossils, clearly some stratigraphic record was essential if the relative ages of his discoveries were to be incontrovertibly established – especially at Sterkfontein, where the cave entrances had eroded away and limeworkers had removed most of the interior.

Perhaps over hastily, the Historical Monuments Commission issued a ruling which expressly forbade Robert Broom to excavate without the assistence of a 'competent field geologist'. The ruling presumably was intended to do no more than correct a deficiency, but its effect was three-fold. First it insulted Broom excessively – after all, he had been a medallist in geology at Glasgow University, and had held the Chair of Geology at Stellenbosch University for seven years. Second, the ruling inspired Broom to begin excavations at Sterkfontein on 1 April in direct contravention of the Commission, believing, as he wrote later,[27] 'that a bad law ought to be deliberately broken'; and third, the ruling thus led to the discovery of a superb *Australopithecus* skull on 18 April. The specimen was undistorted and complete but for the teeth and the lower jaw. Broom described it as 'the most important fossil skull ever found in the world's history'; and indeed, its significance was readily acknowledged by scientists in Europe and America. In South Africa, however, Broom was unanimously condemned at a meeting of the Commission and once more banned from the Sterkfontein site.

The irony of a world-renowned scientist being banned from the site of his investigations immediately following an important discovery did not escape the press and their cartoonists. Public and private pressure mounted and the ban was lifted a few weeks later. Broom triumphantly resumed work at Sterkfontein – with increased good fortune. At the end of June 1947 he discovered a fine lower jaw, which fully confirmed the man-like, rather than ape-like, attributes of the *Australopithecus* dentition; and in August he unearthed the ultimate prize – a nearly complete pelvis and vertebral column with associated leg bone fragments, part of a shoulderblade and upper arm. At last, twenty-two years after Raymond Dart announced the new species, Robert Broom had assembled teeth, skulls and skeleton of the adult *Australopithecus* – and the assemblage presented irresistible evidence of the creature's man-like affinities. 'Congratulations on brilliant discoveries. Proof now complete and incontestible,' cabled Wilfred le Gros Clark. 'All my landmarks have gone,' said Sir Arthur Keith, 'you have found what I never thought could be found': a man-like jaw associated with an ape-like skull – the exact reverse of the Piltdown evidence.

Keith's conversion to the belief in the ancestral status of *Australopithecus* was absolute. 'Professor Dart was right and I was wrong,' he conceded in a letter to *Nature*. And in *A New Theory of Human Evolution*, written in his eighty-second year and published in 1948, Keith agreed that 'of all the fossil forms known to us, the australopithecinae are the nearest akin to man and the most likely to stand in the direct line of man's

Partial skeleton from Sterkfontein: the first conclusive evidence that Australopithecus *walked upright.*

ascent'.[28] They represented the pre-human stock from which the various divisions of mankind had evolved in the late Pliocene, he said;[29] adding the suggestion that for the sake of brevity – if not contrition – they should be re-named 'Dartians'.[30]

With *Australopithecus* presenting such convincing evidence that the enlargement of the brain was the final stage of mankind's evolution from an ancestor shared with the apes, Keith now attempted to define the point at which the man-like ape could be said to have become man. In *A New Theory of Human Evolution* he proposed brain size as the measure, suggesting that just as the eruption of the first permanent molar provides a convenient mark for determining the end of infancy and the beginning of childhood in the individual, so the acquisition of a certain brain size could mark the species' evolutionary transition from apehood to manhood. Taking the largest known brain size in the gorilla (650 cubic centimetres), and the smallest known in man (855 cubic centimetres) as the most valid determinants, Keith proposed a cranial volume of 750 cubic centimetres as the 'cerebral Rubicon' to be crossed before the ancestors of mankind may be called truly human. By this measure, Java Man (with an estimated mean cranial capacity of 850 cubic centimetres) and Peking (ranging from 915 to 1225 cubic centimetres) were justifiably assigned to the genus Homo, while *Australopithecus* had not yet crossed the Rubicon.[31]

Of course, Keith's *New Theory of Human Evolution* in part also re-affirmed views he had expressed thirty-six years before when he described the erect posture as mankind's most ancient attribute and the large brain as a relatively recent acquisition (see page 56). But the evidence of the large-brained, early Pleistocene Piltdown Man he had championed for so long was not so easily accommodated in the new theory. 'If we could get rid of the Piltdown fossil fragments, then we should greatly simplify the problem of human evolution,' wrote Keith,[32] but 'getting rid of facts which do not fit into a preconceived theory' is not the manner usually pursued by men of science, he continued, and proposed instead that in terms of his new theory, Piltdown Man should be regarded as an 'aberrant' type who first found lonely refuge in England, and then extinction there sometime after the late Pliocene.

Meanwhile Broom continued the search for more remains of *Australo-pithecus*. In September 1948 a site was opened under his direction at Swartkrans, another disused lime quarry across the valley from Sterk-fontein. *Australopithecus* fossils were found within days, and many more have since been found there. In 1950 Broom published another mono-graph[33] on the Sterkfontein hominids (with J. T. Robinson and G. W. H.

Fossil jaw and teeth from Swartkrans.

Schepers as co-authors) and by then he felt that the impact of his discoveries and publications was such that only two eminent scientists remained unconvinced that the Australopithecines represented the ancestors of mankind. The dissidents were Professors W. L. Straus and S. Zuckerman, both of whom still maintained that the fossils were related to the apes, not to man. Zuckerman, a zoologist, bothered Broom most; he had once made a pioneering behaviour study of the residents of Monkey Hill in the London Zoo and was a scientist of standing and repute. Zuckerman believed in figures and statistical method and would not accept findings that did not demonstrate some metrical consistency. So, as Broom produced the fossils and his collaborator, le Gros Clark, published reports defining their man-like affinities, Zuckerman (aided by E. H. Ashton) checked their assertions by comparing the dental dimensions of the fossils with the corresponding dimensions of assorted apes. In all, he checked a total of forty-eight overall dimensions in the fossils with those of eighty chimpanzees, ninety gorillas and sixty orang utans.[34] The results, said Zuckerman, showed that the fossils were more like the apes than like man.

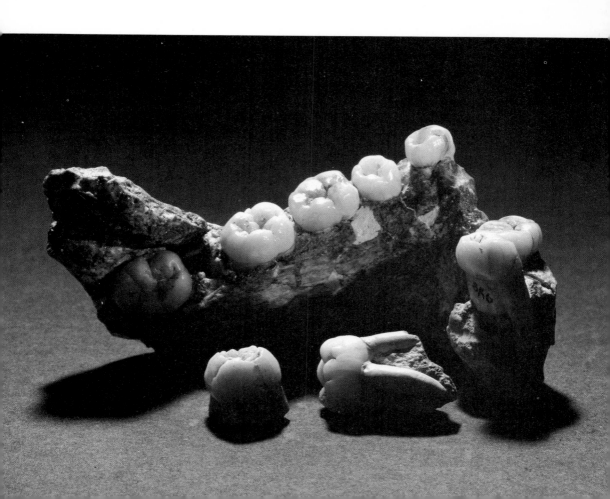

Broom had little respect for mathematical method and scoffed at the findings. 'I suppose that because the molar teeth of horse and cow are often identical, Zuckerman would conclude that a horse is a cow,' he said. Le Gros Clark was similarly sceptical, once remarking that measurements of length, breadth and height would proclaim a cube, a sphere and a pointed star identical.[35] Nonetheless he felt obliged to respond in kind and, using even more diagnostic measurements than Zuckerman, compared the fossils with the adult dentition of 238 gorillas, 276 chimpanzees and thirty-nine orang utans, as well as with the juvenile dentitions of eighty-nine gorillas, 105 chimpanzees and twenty-nine orang utans.[36] The new results directly contradicted Zuckerman's findings. Some lively correspondence ensued, in the course of which a statistician revealed that the Zuckerman team had neglected to divide by the square root of two in some vital computation.[37] But 'the mistake was due to a misunderstanding in the interpretation of the analysis of variance', replied Zuckerman,[38] and made no difference whatsoever to the overall result. Clark disagreed, but contrary to popular myth[39] the factor $\sqrt{2}$ did not settle the argument either way. Indeed it stands best as a symbol of the gulf separating the idiosyncratic, qualitative approach of an earlier age that Broom employed, from the statistical quantitative methods of the mid-twentieth century.

Robert Broom died on 6 April 1951; he was eighty-four. More than any scientist or discovery before or since, Broom's work on *Australopithecus* fundamentally and irrevocably revised the study of fossil man. At first glance he may seem to have confused the story of mankind's evolution with a profusion of complicated names, new genera and new species, not all of them justified and several introduced as 'Missing Links'. But the significant point is that Broom assigned all except one of these 'species' to a single zoological subfamily – the australopithecinae – and made it quite clear that the habitually erect and bipedal autralopithecinae with their man-like dentition and relatively small brains were good candidates for the ancestry of mankind. After Broom, scientists were obliged to fit *Australopithecus* somewhere in their schemes of human evolution. The australopithecinae that Broom knew are now said to comprise one genus and two species – the lightly-built *Australopithecus africanus*, which is often referred to as the 'gracile' *Australopithecus* and includes both the Taung specimen and Broom's *Plesianthropus*; and the heavier *Australopithecus robustus*, known as the 'robust' *Australopithecus* and including Broom's *Paranthropus*.

Indisputably, Broom's work confirmed the potential and importance of South Africa's cave deposits. Since his death other researchers have

Excavations at Swartkrans continue under Dr C. K. Brain: two holes in the Australopithecus *skull he has discovered (foreground left) precisely fit the canines of the fossil leopard jaw beneath.*

contributed significant data to the studies that Dart initiated and Broom made scientifically respectable, but their work has always been circumscribed by the difficulty of assessing the age of the South African fossils with any certainty. Since 1961 this difficulty has acquired another dimension.

In that year the attention of paleontologists all over the world switched from South Africa to East Africa, when a hominid fossil found in Olduvai Gorge was given an absolute age of 1.75 million years by the newly developed potassium argon dating method. This method can only be used on minerals of volcanic origin and therefore is not applicable in the South African cave deposits. The East African fossil beds, however, are eminently suitable and the advent of potassium argon dating contributed significantly to the value of discoveries made in Tanzania, Kenya and Ethiopia during the 1960s and 1970s.

Chapter Seven

Zinjanthropus boisei
(1959)

LOUIS LEAKEY often expressed affection and admiration for Raymond Dart and Robert Broom, but he never accepted their contention that *Australopithecus* was a direct ancestor of mankind. Leakey believed that human evolution has been a long slow affair, and that man – in common with the rhinoceros and the flamingo, for instance – was shaped millions of years ago and has remained relatively unchanged ever since. The fossil record shows, he said, that most, if not all, vertebrate lineages have their dead branches along which related forms have evolved to extinction, and he saw no reason why the *Homo* lineage should be any different.

In Leakey's view, the hominid line leading to man, and the pongid line leading to the apes, branched away from their common ancestral stock about twenty million years ago,[1] and he believed there have been many more branches since then. *Australopithecus*, for instance, left the *Homo* line about six or seven million years ago, he said, and virtually every fossil mentioned in the preceding chapters similarly was no more than an 'aberrant offshoot' from the human stem. Neanderthal, Java, Peking and *Australopithecus* were all, in Leakey's view, evolutionary experiments that ended in extinction. They were 'rather brutish creatures', he said, who may have existed at the same time as the true human ancestor, but played no direct part in the story of human evolution.

These views echo the early pronouncements of Arthur Keith, Leakey's mentor; but whether they were wholly the product of his learning, or whether an upbringing as a missionary's son had already predisposed Louis Leakey towards a belief in the antiquity of man's lineage, it is only certain that the views were formed early in his career and never changed. Throughout his professional life Leakey expressed the belief that man's ancestry is a long direct line on which the enlargement of the brain was a decisive feature, thin skull bones a distinctive characteristic and the ability to make stone tools a crucial development.

Stone tools are the key to the story of Louis Leakey, his wife Mary and their discoveries at Olduvai Gorge. They are also perhaps the most evocative relics of our ancestors. Fossil bones may reveal the physical characteristics of the creatures whose flesh once clothed them – their height, their weight, the relative proportions of their bodies – but the tools they have left behind add an unexpected dimension of understanding. A stone tool may have lain undisturbed for more than a million years, but we can be certain that the hand that made it differs hardly at all from the hand that picks it up today. We heft it, consider using it, perhaps even imagine our lives depending upon it. That we are here to wonder is in itself proof of the evolutionary success of the lifestyle adopted by the early toolmakers. The cutting edge was the beginning of culture and technology. The crude stone tool is a tangible link with those origins.

Louis Leakey perceived the magic of this connection as a boy and undoubtedly it heightened his sensitivity to the subject, predicating his important discoveries and underscoring his success in print and the lecture hall. Uniquely, Louis Leakey was able to envisage and communicate the predicament of early man; and on that plane it is irrelevant that the bold and inspiring story he told was as much the product of his intellectual and emotional preconceptions as it was a reflection of the evidence and the facts.

Young Louis' earliest ambition was to become a missionary like his father.[2] He was born on 7 August 1903 in a mud and wattle house that his parents occupied on the mission station established by the Church Missionary Society among the Kikuyu people at Kabete, fifteen kilometres from Nairobi. When he was twelve years old, Louis received a book on the Stone Age as a Christmas gift from a cousin in England and was immediately inspired to search for flint arrowheads and axeheads in the vicinity of Kabete. He had no clear idea of what he was looking for, or even of what flint was, but this deficiency was probably an advantage, for there is no flint in East Africa and if the young enthusiast had searched assiduously for what was not there he might have overlooked the obsidian flakes that were quite common in the road cuttings and exposed ground of the region. Assuming the shiny black material to be flint (actually it is volcanic glass), Louis collected every scrap he encountered. Subsequently he learned from Arthur Loveridge, his hero and curator of the Nairobi Museum, that his collection was obsidian, not flint, but included some pieces that were undoubtedly Stone Age implements. The boy's delight can be imagined. Loveridge encouraged him to make a record of his finds and at the age of thirteen, Louis Leakey embarked upon a study of the Stone Age in East Africa, determined to continue until he knew all about it.[3]

Many years later Leakey learned that in 1912 two American archaeologists had visited Kenya in search of early man, intending to initiate extensive investigations if they found any worthwhile evidence. But, trained in the European tradition, they were looking for flint tools and of course found none. Leakey was convinced that had they not searched under this misconception they would have recognized the obsidian implements, discovered the archaeological potential of East Africa and preempted his entire career.

An upbringing among the Kikuyu hardly prepared the sixteen-year-old Leakey for life in the English public school he entered in 1920 in pursuit of formal education and his ultimate ambition of a degree in anthropology from Cambridge. He had gained a fair knowledge of French, Latin and mathematics from his father and the tutors brought to Kabete, but he had no knowledge of the English academic system. He did not know the meaning of the word 'essay', understood nothing of Greek or cricket, made few friends and by his own account was very unhappy. But it appears he was an extremely bright pupil in whom pride produced a fierce determination.

He caught up in most things (including cricket) and at Cambridge his upbringing proved to be a distinct advantage, enabling him to gain acceptance for the anthropology course by offering Kikuyu for the Modern Languages Tripos. In his autobiography Leakey says that although the University authorities were perplexed by the proposition, there was no regulation by which Kikuyu could be disallowed – it was spoken by a large living population, the Bible (translated by Leakey's father) was evidence of its written form, and Leakey could produce two certificates of competent knowledge – one from a missionary and the other bearing the thumb-print signature of a tribal chief. The only problem was to find an instructor. In the event, Leakey found himself obliged to teach Kikuyu to his supervisor, who subsequently became his examiner as well.[4]

At the beginning of his second year Leakey suffered concussion on the rugby field. Severe headaches ensued whenever he attempted any reading and his doctor recommended a year's absence from all academic work. This was a serious setback to his ambitions, but Leakey solved the pressing problem of financing a year's enforced holiday by joining a British Museum of Natural History expedition to Tanganyika, where its leader, W. E. Cutler, hoped to recover the fossil remains of dinosaurs from some excavations at Tendaguru begun by German archaeologists before the war.

Cutler had collected fossil reptiles in America most successfully, but he had never been to Africa. Leakey's knowledge of the continent and its people were undoubtedly useful to Cutler, but Leakey himself appears to have been the major beneficiary of the expedition. He gained invaluable practical experience in excavating and preserving fossils, although the fossils they found were of minor significance. Leakey celebrated his twenty-first birthday at Tendaguru and returned to Cambridge with over one hundred ebony walking sticks, carved by the workmen in their spare time, which he sold on commission through some Cambridge tailors and thus financed a portion of his college bills. W. E. Cutler died of black-water fever at Tendaguru some months after Leakey had left.

With first class examination results and sheer enthusiasm to encourage grants, stipends and other financial support, Leakey managed to organize a series of four archaeological expeditions of his own to East Africa between 1926 and 1935. The first two of these explored caves and burial sites in Kenya. An abundance of stone tools and recent skeletal remains was recovered. The later expeditions continued the investigations in Kenya, but also explored Olduvai Gorge in Tanzania and here set the scene for the culmination of Louis Leakey's career.

Olduvai Gorge is an unavoidable feature of the south-eastern Serengeti Plains. The popular story of its accidental discovery by Professor Kattwinkel in 1911 is hard to credit, though Louis Leakey particularly enjoyed recounting how the German lepidopterist had apparently nearly plunged to his death over the cliffs of the gorge while in absent-minded pursuit of some exotic butterfly. Recoiling from the brink, Kattwinkel descended into the gorge in a more orthodox manner and discovered large quantities of fossil bone lying about the erosion slopes. He made a small collection that aroused excitement in Berlin when it was found to include some bones from a three-toed horse. This extinct creature was well known in Europe from deposits of the early Pliocene period, but the Olduvai deposits seemed much younger than that, implying that the three-toed horse had survived longer in Africa than it had in Europe. This was a startling idea that called for further investigations and so – with the Kaiser's personal blessing – an expedition set off in 1913 to make a thorough study of Olduvai Gorge.

Its leader was Professor Dr Hans Reck from the University of Berlin. In three months his team completed a geological survey, collected more than 1700 fossils and confirmed the geological antiquity of the Olduvai deposits, but the significance of this work was quite overwhelmed by the controversy that arose when Reck claimed that a human skull and skeleton found in the lower deposits of the gorge was as old as the extinct animals from the same level. Reck returned to Berlin with the skull wrapped in his personal linen, while the skeleton followed with the other fossils. He announced the discovery in March 1914, and the London Times[5] reported him as saying that the ribs and breast were akin to those of the ape, while the skull was unmistakeably human; an observation which he subsequently claimed as proof 'that the human race more or less as it is now is of considerably greater antiquity than has been imagined.'[6]

The skeleton had lain on its side, knees drawn up in the foetal position. Sceptics suggested that it had belonged to a tribesman of the recent past, whose fellows had buried him in the more ancient deposit. But Reck remained firm in his belief that the skeleton was contemporary with the extinct animals among which it was found, even though they were definitely of Lower Pleistocene age, a time when the human ancestor might be expected to look a little less modern than the large-brained Olduvai Man.

To resolve the problem, Reck planned another expedition to Olduvai. Quite independently, but presumably attracted by the controversy, three other German expeditions to the gorge were planned as well; all four were actually on their way when war was declared in August 1914. None reached their destination. Reck stayed in Tanganyika as a government geologist and became a prisoner of war when the British took the Territory in 1916. After the war, Tanganyika became a British Mandated Territory, no longer so readily available to German science, with the result that the problem of Olduvai Man was still unresolved when Leakey's first East African Archaeological Expedition returned to England in 1927.

Some fossilized human remains that the expedition had recovered from a burial site near Lake Elmenteita in Kenya resembled Olduvai Man, Leakey thought, but the fossil fauna seemed very different; so he went to Germany to examine the Olduvai collections and discuss the matter with Reck, now returned to the University of Berlin. Reck still believed in the great antiquity of Olduvai Man, but Leakey could not agree; he found the state of preservation very different from that of the extinct animal fossils and this, combined with the faunal disparity between Olduvai and Elmenteita, convinced him that the skeleton was younger than Reck believed, though not as young as the critics had suggested.

In this conclusion Leakey was essentially correct, but he was to change his mind before the problem of Reck's Olduvai Man was finally resolved, and meanwhile his second East African Archaeological Expedition (1928–9) added another twist to the mystery. Skulls were discovered in a

OVERLEAF *Olduvai Gorge photographed by Emory Kristof,*
© *National Geographic Society*

cave near Elmenteita which were even more like the Olduvai skull than the specimens found in 1927, yet the associated fauna was very much younger. And then there was the question of tools – why had none been found at Olduvai? At Kariandusi in Kenya, Leakey and his colleagues had collected impressive numbers of handaxes from deposits that Leakey was certain were the same age as Olduvai, yet Reck insisted that despite a most diligent search he had found no stone implements of any kind, anywhere in the gorge. But could he have overlooked them? Leakey suspected there was a good chance that he had. Quite apart from the circumstantial evidence, he recalled noticing a rock among Reck's geological specimens in Berlin which strongly resembled the handaxes from Kariandusi.[7]

With further investigations patently necessary, Leakey included Olduvai Gorge in the itinerary of his Third East African Archaeological Expedition and Professor Hans Reck among its participants. Leakey became so confident that there must be some evidence of Stone Age culture in the Gorge that he bet Reck £10 he would find a stone tool within twenty-four hours of arriving there. Reck was equally confident he would not. The party arrived at Olduvai Gorge just before 10 am on 26 September 1931 and spent the rest of the day establishing their camp and water supply. In the latter endeavour Reck spent most of the night as well. He had difficulty locating the spring he had used eighteen years before and, having awaited the rise of the full moon to light his way back to camp, was frustrated by the occasion of a total lunar eclipse that night. No doubt he had intended to sleep late the next morning, but that plan was frustrated too – by the excited Louis Leakey who had left camp at dawn and found a perfect handaxe very soon thereafter. 'I was nearly mad with delight,' he writes, 'I rushed back with it into camp and rudely awakened the sleepers so that they should share in my joy.'[8] One of the principal objects of the expedition was achieved within twenty-four hours of arrival and Reck lost £10 as well as his night's rest.

Subsequently, thousands of stone tools have been found at Olduvai, and doubtless thousands remain. Why had Reck not seen them on his first visit? It transpired that like the young Leakey at Kabete, Reck had been looking for flint tools but, unlike Leakey, he knew flint very well. Of course there is no more flint at Olduvai than there is at Kabete; the tools that litter the gorge are made from a variety of volcanic lavas, chert and quartz, and Reck simply did not notice them (though apparently he took at least one back to Berlin as a rock sample). It is a classic example of how training can create preconception.

It was at this point, at the age of twenty-eight, with virtually the whole of East African prehistory laid before him, that Leakey's own preconceptions began to colour his interpretations – particularly those concerning the antiquity of large-brained *Homo sapiens*. This tendency was clearly revealed when Leakey and Reck reassessed the contention that Olduvai Man was as old as the Pleistocene fossil fauna found at the same level. Within four days of their arrival at the Gorge Leakey abandoned the evidence of the physical and faunal inconsistencies he had found so persuasive while examining the fossils in Berlin, and accepted instead his senior colleague's interpretation of the geology, concluding that the large-brained skeleton was as old as Reck had claimed.

Within a week of arrival, the expedition leaders sent a note to *Nature*[9] proclaiming that the problem of Olduvai Man was solved. Stone tools reinforced Leakey's conviction. In marked contrast to Reck's previous visit, the 1931 expedition found tools in each of the five geological beds; and among them Leakey claimed to see an evolutionary sequence of manufacturing skills, from the simplest pebble tools of Bed I to the advanced handaxes of Bed IV. Later he claimed these discoveries were important enough 'to startle the scientific world and lead paleontologists to revise their concepts of the age of *Homo sapiens*.' Reck's Olduvai Man was probably the maker of an intermediate pebble tool culture, he wrote in *The Times*,[10] suggesting that 'Homo *sapiens* goes back to East Africa to an age in the evolution of modern man far more remote than the evidence found anywhere else in the world suggests'. A few weeks later tools and traces of fire attributable to Peking Man were found in the Chou K'ou Tien cave and, in a revealing comment, Leakey told readers of *The Times* that although Peking Man was probably the same age as Olduvai Man he represented a cousin, not an ancestor, of *Homo sapiens*. Further excavations at Chou K'ou Tien probably would show that *Homo sapiens* had lived there, Leakey suggested, and was responsible for the tools, the fire *and* the remains of Peking Man – the latter representing 'the relics of his meat feasts', Leakey said.[11]

After the Olduvai interlude Reck returned to Europe while Leakey and the rest of the party set off to explore some deposits near a village called Kanjera in the vicinity of Lake Victoria. Fossils had been found there in 1913 and Leakey was anxious to see if the deposits matched the age of those at Olduvai. In a matter of weeks the contemporaneity was confirmed to Leakey's satisfaction – not least by the discovery of two fragmentary skulls as sapient as modern man and his alleged ancestor from Olduvai Gorge, and then by a scrap of hominid mandible from another site (Kanam West) which Leakey claimed also represented *Homo sapiens* and was even older than Olduvai Man. 'The world's earliest *Homo*

sapiens,' he called it, 'one step further back than even Olduvai'.[12]

Neither the Kanjera skulls nor the Kanam mandible were particularly impressive fossils, nor was the evidence for the antiquity of Olduvai Man very convincing; but such was the status of Louis Leakey in the early 1930s that he persuaded a number of important people to agreement on all counts. Sir Arthur Keith for instance, who had rejected Reck's claim in 1914, wrote: 'In the light of the discoveries made by Mr Leakey in the Rift Valley, there can no longer be any doubt as to the antiquity of Oldoway (sic) man ... I have had to reconsider my opinion and acknowledge that Dr Reck was in the right when he claimed Oldoway man as a representative of the Pleistocene inhabitants of East Africa.'[13]

At Cambridge in March 1933 a conference organized by the Royal Anthropological Institute expressly to examine all aspects of the Kanjera and Kanam finds unanimously agreed with Leakey's interpretations and congratulated him 'on the exceptional significance of his discoveries'.[14] Leakey had achieved considerable success at a relatively young age, but how much of it was due to the fact that his views so closely echoed those of his mentors? Is it simply ironic that Sir Arthur Keith, Professor Elliot Smith, Sir Arthur Smith Woodward and Dr W. L. H. Duckworth (the triumvirate of British anthropology plus one), who all congratulated the thirty-year-old Louis Leakey in 1933, were the very same gentlemen who had cast doubt upon the announcement of *Australopithecus* by the thirty-two-year-old Raymond Dart seven years before? Or does the irony reveal the predispositions of those involved? *Australopithecus* was an ape, the eminent gentlemen had said; but Leakey's fossils differed hardly at all from *Homo sapiens*, despite their apparent antiquity. 'A most startling discovery,' commented Sir Arthur Smith Woodward.[15] However, while Dart's pronouncements were corroborated by later discoveries, Leakey's were soon discounted.

Leakey's moment of unalloyed success was brief. It was first tainted by the findings of independent geologists reconsidering the antiquity of Olduvai Man. They showed that the body had been buried comparatively recently in an ancient Bed II surface exposed by faulting that was subsequently covered again during the deposition of Bed V. Reck and Leakey had to agree.[16] Olduvai Man was not the oldest *Homo sapiens*. Reck had been wrong all along and Leakey had only the dubious comfort of learning that his first interpretation of the evidence had been correct. But even that comfort was lacking when a voice of dissension was raised soon thereafter concerning the provenance of the Kanam and Kanjera fossils. It came from the Professor of Geology at Imperial College, Percy Boswell, who suggested that more evidence of the geology and paleon-

Louis Leakey on an early expedition; original fragments of the two skulls found at Kanjera; and, in the foreground, the Kanam jaw fragment

tology ought to be collected.

Boswell was a senior Fellow of the Royal Society, a most important figure, and it is a measure of Leakey's conviction and straightforwardness that his response to the implied criticism was an invitation for Boswell to join the Fourth East African Archaeological Expedition then being planned. If the Royal Society would finance Boswell's trip, Leakey would be happy to accompany the gentlemen to Kanam and Kanjera so that he might assess the evidence for himself and science. However, commendable though this action was, it did nothing to strengthen Leakey's case; in fact, Boswell's assessment virtually destroyed it.

The first essential was that Leakey should prove to Boswell that the remains had been found in the deposits precisely as claimed, and not washed or carried there from somewhere else. For some reason Leakey had neglected to make a map recording the position of each discovery in 1932, an omission which became doubly unfortunate when, on returning with Boswell nearly three years later, he found that local tribesmen had removed all the iron pegs he had hammered into the ground to mark the spots. Furthermore, a camera fault had rendered all Leakey's photographs of the sites useless, and those of another expedition member proved to have been incorrectly labelled when he attempted to locate the sites from them. In short, it was impossible to show Boswell the precise location of the finds. This did not entirely disprove Leakey's claims, but Boswell would not accept them on trust. 'It is regrettable that the records are not more precise,' he commented in *Nature*, and 'disappointing, after the failure to establish any considerable geological age for Olduvai Man . . . that uncertain conditions of discovery should also force me to place Kanam and Kanjera man in a "suspense account".'[17]

Louis Leakey's attempts to explain the debacle[18] were not persuasive and, although his own belief in the conclusions remained unshaken, Boswell's attack dealt a serious blow to Leakey's reputation. Thereafter controversy (spiced with a measure of good luck), rather than academic approval, distinguished his career.

After the Kanam confrontation Boswell returned to England and the Fourth East African Archaeological Expedition spent several months at Olduvai Gorge, where Leakey's research team comprised himself, a geologist, a zoologist, a surveyor and a young archaeologist named Mary Nicol. The expedition concentrated its attention on sections of the Gorge not thoroughly explored on previous visits, noting geology and collecting paleontological specimens. Large numbers of Stone Age implements were recovered too, from horizons throughout the sequence, which enabled Leakey to substantiate (to his satisfaction at any rate) the evolution of the stone tool culture at Olduvai that he had proposed in 1931. He described the simple pebble tools of Bed I as the Oldowan Culture, and traced the growth of manufacturing skill from the Oldowan, through eleven stages, to the relatively sophisticated tools of Bed IV, which he compared to the Acheulean flint handaxes of Europe.[19]

In all, the vast potential for prehistoric research at Olduvai was fully confirmed. In 1931 and 1935 Leakey's expeditions explored about 300 kilometres of fossiliferous exposures up and down the Gorge, ranging in depth from seventeen to one hundred metres of cliff and slope face. They discovered more than thirty promising sites, identifying them with the initials of expedition members followed by the letter 'k' for 'korongo', which is the Swahili word for 'gully'.

At FLK Louis Leakey had found the first stone tool in 1931, signifying the beginning of his work at Olduvai; he named the site for his wife, Frida Leakey. At MNK, towards the close of the 1935 season, Mary Nicol found two fragments of a fossilized human skull among remains of antelopes and pigs and a scattering of stone tools. They searched for more but found none. The pieces were small and isolated but undeniably hominid. In effect they marked the end of the first stage of Leakey's Olduvai investigations with a hint that Olduvai possibly held the sort of evidence that no critic could dispute – the campsites of early man, on which his fossilized bones might be preserved, along with his stone tools and the remains of his meals. And if the gorge held the fossils of man in each of its geological levels, then Leakey would be able to show the process of human evolution from the Lower Pleistocene to recent times . . . a prehistorian's dream.

In 1936 Louis Leakey was divorced by his wife and married Mary Nicol, bringing upon himself and her the opprobrium such behaviour attracted at that time. Leakey's biographer implies that the divorce precipitated their move to Kenya – once he realized that, combined with the Kanam affair, the divorce rendered him unsuitable in some eyes for the academic posts he sought at Cambridge.[20] But in any event, it was not until 1951 that stage two of his Olduvai investigations seriously commenced.

For many years academic and government institutions were Leakey's main source of funds, significantly supplemented from his own pocket and by the proceeds of his popular writings. In 1948 however his financial problems were eased by the generosity of an American-born London businessman with an interest in prehistory, Charles Boise. Early in 1948 *The Times* published a letter from Louis Leakey, describing the problems of conducting such research in Kenya, which caught the attention of

Boise and inspired him to contribute £1000 towards the undertaking. Subsequently Boise visited the Leakeys in Kenya, travelled with them to Olduvai Gorge and became the major contributor towards the cost of the excavations that began there in 1951 – first in the form of direct financial aid, and later through the Boise Fund which he established at Oxford University expressly for the purpose.

Leakey's early Olduvai investigations had been limited to surface explorations, with very little excavation – mainly because of the expense of the petrol that would have been needed to maintain an adequate water supply for a large workforce. Boise solved the money problem, but now time was the limiting factor. Olduvai Gorge was in Tanganyika, Leakey was a Kenya government employee and could hardly explore the prehistoric site of another country on official time – so work there was restricted to his holidays and unpaid leave.

Accordingly, the Leakeys concentrated attention on the most promising of the sites that the surveys had revealed; in particular BK (Bell's Korongo) and SHK (Sam Howard's Korongo). Both were in Upper Bed II, both were living floors and both provided large accumulations of stone implements, waste flakes and the fossilized remains of the animals upon which early man had lived. At SHK there were over two thousand stone implements and evidence of a unique and extensive mammalian fauna. BK proved to be a veritable 'slaughter house', with more than three thousand stone tools littered among numerous animal bones. The remains of *Pelorovis* were especially prevalent: Louis Leakey suggested that a group of hominids had driven a herd of the massive herbivores (now extinct) into a bog there, dragging out the smaller individuals for the slaughter while the largest became inextricably stuck in the mud, where they died. One skeleton was found standing upright.[21]

A remarkable feature of the Upper Bed II fauna was the presence of several giant herbivore species. Louis Leakey suggested that optimum feeding conditions were responsible for their development.[22] The giants included a pig the size of a hippo (whose tusk was at first mistaken for that of a primitive elephant); *Pelorovis*, with a horn span in excess of two metres (first classified as a sheep but later shown to be a relation of the buffalo) and a baboon the size of a gorilla. The size aspect was seized upon in 1954 when the *Illustrated London News* published a review of the latest discoveries from Olduvai Gorge, in which an artist's impression showed the prehistoric creatures looming above their modern counterparts. Olduvai had been the hunting ground of prehistoric man, the headline implied and, at the conclusion of his accompanying article, Louis Leakey wrote: 'the remains of the men themselves still elude us, and it is interesting to wonder whether, when found, they will be giants like the animals they hunted, or of normal stature.'[23]

An answer of sorts was provided four years later when Leakey described two hominid teeth found at the BK site in 1955. One was a canine and the other a molar. The canine attracted little attention, but the molar was unusual enough to fall into the category of uncertainty that inevitably attracts controversy, particularly when Louis Leakey suggested that it had come from the lower jaw of three- to five-year-old human – for the tooth was huge and the child would have been a giant. Leakey's judgement was based upon the cusp pattern of the tooth. In *Nature* he remarked that although the pattern was the most unusual he had ever seen in a deciduous molar, the tooth nonetheless had more affinities with fossil and modern man than with the australopithecines. 'We are, therefore, possibly dealing with a very large true hominid which is not of australopithecine type. The teeth, in fact, suggest we are dealing with a human.'[24] The *Illustrated London News* reported the announcement more colourfully: 'A giant child among the giant animals of Olduvai? . . . a really gigantic human milk tooth has been found at Olduvai Gorge . . . which suggests that [prehistoric] Man in Tanganyika may have been gigantic'.[25]

The tooth was certainly a puzzle, but many found the proposals of Dr John Robinson a more satisfactory explanation of its size. It was not a milk tooth from the lower jaw of a human child, he said, but a permanent tooth from the upper jaw of an australopithecine adult.[26] Dr Robinson had excavated australopithecines with Robert Broom and written a monograph on their dentition; his word carried weight, but before Louis Leakey's reply pleading uncertainty appeared in print,[27] events were overwhelmed by an even more contentious discovery.

By the end of the 1958 season, the Leakeys began to feel they had exhausted the immediate potential of Bed II and decided that in 1959 they would first of all look for living sites among the Laetoli deposits south of Olduvai. Three weeks at Laetoli proved totally unrewarding, but soon after their return to Olduvai a hominid tooth was found at MK I, a Bed I site that had yielded many Oldowan tools since its discovery in 1931. The tooth obviously rendered MK I worthy of immediate excavation, but research funds for the year were exhausted.

Leakey returned to Nairobi and managed to arrange an overdraft on his research account sufficient to cover three weeks' excavations at MK I. He also arranged for the operation to be filmed by Des Bartlett for Armand and Michaela Denis' *On Safari* television series. Bartlett was to arrive on 17 July, bringing with him the Leakey's fourteen-year-old son

Richard. Louis and Mary travelled down a few days in advance. On the morning of the 17th Louis remained in camp, recovering from a slight bout of influenza. Mary took the dogs and walked across to the FLK site where the first stone tools had been found in 1931 and where she and Louis suspected there might be an Oldowan living floor.

At about 11 am she noticed a skull eroding from the slope about seven metres from the top of the bed. At first glance it was not at all like a hominid, for the exposed bone was not solid as in human skulls, but permeated with air cells like the skulls of very large animals where compensation must be made for excessive weight. She brushed away some of the covering soil and two teeth were revealed – unquestionably hominid, but suspiciously australopithecine. 'I was tremendously excited by my discovery and quickly went back to camp to fetch Louis,' writes Mary Leakey.[28] But Louis did not share her excitement. 'When he saw the teeth he was disappointed,' she continues, 'since he had hoped the skull would be *Homo* and not *Australopithecus*.'

Nonetheless, FLK proved to be a site of unique significance. It was a living floor, but an older, less disturbed and more revealing living floor than any that had been found until then. Many thousands of years before the Leakeys began to uncover its secrets, a group of hominids had camped at FLK. The site was beside a lake whose waters rose and fell periodically; it became littered with the debris of their habitation, the hominids moved away and shortly thereafter the rising lake waters combined with a fortuitous shower of volcanic ash to preserve some clues of their presence and lifestyle. Organic matter such as skins, wood and the like soon rotted away, but the bones of the animals they had consumed – many of them broken to extract the marrow – were covered over before the weathering effects of sun and rain could fragment them further. Among the bones, the hominids left many stone tools of the Oldowan culture; and on the same living floor, in direct association with the animal remains and the tools, lay the impressively complete skull that Mary Leakey discovered that July morning.

If the skull had been *Homo* it would have been a splendid vindication of Leakey's claims for the Kanam and Kanjera fossils. The dispute with Boswell doubtless still rankled, even after twenty-five years, but the new skull had obvious australopithecine affinities and its implications struck rather deeper than the disappointment of its failure to settle an old argument. They presented Leakey with an awkward dilemma.

At FLK the Leakeys had discovered – for the first time ever – hominid remains of great antiquity and indisputably associated with stone tools. By definition a toolmaker *was* man,[29] but the skull that lay among the tools was clearly a representative of the australopithecines – the hominids Louis Leakey would not countenance in his story of human evolution and whom most scientists believed incapable of making tools.

By 1959 Louis Leakey may have been the only scientist actively seeking man's origins who still refused to accept Dart's and Broom's assertion that *Australopithecus* was an ancestor of man, but he was one of many still unwilling to accept the contention that the creatures had been capable of making tools. Simple tools of the Oldowan type were known to have been made during australopithecine times, but who made them was another question. The evidence against *Australopithecus* was entirely negative: the brain was not large enough, there was no proof that he had made tools. A few chipped pebbles had been found together with australopithecine fossils in one of the gravel levels of the Makapan caves in South Africa, it was true, and Dart claimed they were tools made by *Australopithecus*,[30] but other authorities were sceptical. The chipping could have been natural, they said, and the specimens were too heavily weathered to be conclusive.

Then too, a sizeable collection of more acceptable tools had been recovered from the Sterkfontein caves between 1956 and 1958, though not associated with any fossils. Who had made these? The site had produced large numbers of australopithecine fossils, as we have seen, but John Robinson thought it more likely that the tools had been made by a more advanced hominid from the Swartkrans site, a mile or so away. In this conclusion Robinson was congratulated by Louis Leakey for proving 'that these "near-men" (australopithecines) were contemporary with a type of early man who made these stone tools and that the australopithecines were probably the victims which he killed and ate'.[31]

This remark echoed Leakey's comment on the occurrence of tools with the *Sinanthropus* fossils at Peking, made twenty-seven years before (see page 145); and indeed, it accurately reflected his long standing and vigorously expounded opinion that the pedigree of Man the Toolmaker was a line of great length and exceptional purity, from which most of the hominid fossils found theretofore were but 'aberrant offshoots'. How extraordinary then, that it should fall to Leakey to discover the most 'aberrant' of those 'offshoots' lying among some of the earliest known examples of stone tools on the world's oldest and best preserved living floor of early man.

Research does occasionally unearth evidence that directly contradicts preconception, but rarely is the confrontation so obvious and unavoidable as that which Louis Leakey found at FLK. The evidence of skull and tools in direct association strongly suggested that a group of australo-

pithecines had made the tools at FLK, where one of their number had died. But if the australopithecines had made the tools then by definition they qualified as human ancestors, a corrollary which seriously conflicted with the Leakey notion of human evolution. So he might have been expected to cling to his preconceptions and suggest that – as at Peking and Sterkfontein – FLK had been the campsite of another hominid – true man, who made tools, ate australopithecines along with all the other animals whose bones littered the living floor, but was still unknown in the fossil record. In the long term, (as we shall see), his preconceptions have proved closer to the truth than the inference of the evidence; but in the short term Leakey took the pragmatic view and resolved the dilemma with a blend of interpretation and preconception that revealed the extent of his faith in both and brought extensive publicity.

Because the skull was virtually intact he concluded that it represented the occupants of the campsite rather than their victims; because of direct association he concluded that the occupants of the site had made the tools with which it was strewn; because the occupants had made the tools he concluded that the skull represented a human ancestor; but because he did not believe the australopithecines had played any part in the evolution of man he concluded that the Olduvai specimen was not an australopithecine, and created a new genus to accommodate the pheno-menon – *Zinjanthropus boisei*. *Zinj* is the ancient name for East Africa, *anthropus* means man, and *boisei* of course honours Leakey's benefactor – *Zinjanthropus boisei*: Boise's East African Man.

Though the recovery of the skull fragments and the subsequent reconstruction of the specimen took some time, Leakey's announcement of the new genus appeared in *Nature*[32] less than a month after the discovery. The skull showed no sign of having been broken before fossilization, he said, so there was no good reason to suppose that its owner had been 'the victim of a cannibalistic feast by some hypothetical more advanced type of man'. It was much more likely that the fellow and his kind had themselves made the tools among which he was found. But, whereas for some this might have proved that *Australopithecus* was a toolmaker after all, for Leakey it meant that the Olduvai toolmaker was not an australopithecine. He conceded general affinities but claimed the new skull differed from both *Australopithecus* and *Paranthropus* much more than the two genera differed from each other; he listed twenty points that he felt supported the call for generic distinction and concluded: '. . . the new find represents one of the earliest Hominidae, with the Olduvai skull as the oldest yet discovered maker of stone tools'.

In the *Illustrated London News* he was bolder: '. . . Zinj was a close

Zinjanthropus boisei: *the original specimen set against the Castle, a distinctive feature of the Olduvai landscape* relative of the "near-men" of South Africa and yet he was a man in the sense that he was a maker of stone tools "to a set and regular pattern" . . . Zinj, moreover, shows a number of morphological characters which are definitely man-like, far more so than any of the South African "near-men" and so he can be regarded almost certainly as being in the direct line of our ancestry.'[33] And in the *National Geographic* he described 'Finding the World's Earliest Man . . . who lived in East Africa more than 600,000 years ago'.[34]

It is unlikely that Leakey persuaded anyone but the innocent man in the street with his cry that Zinj was an ancestor of man and the australopithecines were not. John Robinson called the new genus 'unwarranted and biologically unmeaningful', and claimed that the characteristics Leakey saw as distinctive of *Zinjanthropus* were, in his view, either related to the greater size of the specimen, or were not real differences at all.[35]

But a questionable new genus could not detract from the significance of the specimen itself. The skull was more complete and less distorted than any of the South African forms and its discovery at such an ancient level, along with pebble tools marking the beginnings of human technology, was a major event in the progress of the science. It could hardly have been more appropriate to the centenary of *The Origin of Species'* publication.

In the one hundred years since Darwin had provided a theoretical basis, zoologists had been striving to establish the path of man's evolution from primal origins. At the same time, archaeologists and prehistorians – encouraged by Joseph Prestwich's confirmation of the geological antiquity of stone tools, also published in 1859 – were delving ever deeper for the origins of culture. The two lines of enquiry, both seeking the roots of humanity, appeared to have met when skull and tools were found together on the FLK living floor in Bed I at Olduvai Gorge. The only pity was that the skull at FLK seemed to suggest that Adam's ancestors were not the large-brained man-like creatures Leakey and others had believed in. 'It is now clear that tools ante-date man,' wrote Sherwood Washburn.[36]

The skull's evolutionary significance, and the tools' relationship to the origin of man, were matters of interpretation, quite distinct from the fact of their indisputable antiquity. Whatever the interpretation of their evidence may be, FLK and Olduvai remained a milestone of the science – a reference point against which earlier and subsequent discoveries could be assessed. The certainty of antiquity stemmed from the geological circumstances of the Gorge which, though not uncomplicated, could be followed more easily than most. The Gorge slices through a 'layer cake' of deposits, revealing a sequence of remarkable clarity. Furthermore, it is packed with fossils, and the advent of new species, combined with the extinction of others through the ascending strata, enables paleontologists to determine the relative age of Olduvai fossils with unusual accuracy.

Zinj had died among the tools on the FLK living floor during Lower Pleistocene times. That much was certain, and no one was inclined to dispute Leakey's claim in *The Times* that 'the Olduvai skull represents the *oldest* well-established stone toolmaker ever found anywhere'.[37] But relative age determinations – even when accurate – are of limited value, particularly in attempts to discern the detail of hominid evolution, all of which is packed within the relatively recent geological past. Something more precise was called for – an absolute timescale that would give ages in years rather than in geological eras.

Estimates of fossils' actual ages frequently appeared in books and articles, it is true, but these were very rough estimates based on guesses of how fast evolution proceeds, or how long sedimentary deposits take to accumulate. These estimates were always known to have little scientific value and they were produced primarily for popular publications (where their inconstancy must surely have confused as many as were enlightened). So the suggestion that Zinj was over 600,000 years old would not have disturbed Leakey's colleagues, even if they were unaware that the suggestion had originally come from G. Mortelmans, a science writer.[38] However, not many months later Leakey himself claimed that Zinj was 1.75 million years old; and this claim did startle his colleagues, not only because of the great age, but also because Leakey and his co-authors claimed that this was the *absolute* age of the fossils.[39] This announcement introduced the potassium-argon dating method to paleoanthropology, a development that matched the importance of the fossils themselves.

During the 1950s, as the enquiries of paleontologists and archaeologists approached their rendezvous with Zinj on the FLK living floor, a select group of geologists and physicists in the laboratories of the University of California at Berkeley were discovering how the age of sedimentary deposits could be determined with far greater precision than the geological timescale allowed. The principle upon which the Berkeley group's work was based is simple enough: certain chemical elements are unstable in that spontaneous disintegration occurs within their atoms; as this disintegration proceeds radio-activity is emitted and different chemical elements are formed successively until a stable state is reached. Uranium, for instance, eventually becomes lead. The rate of disintegration is discernible, and if the relative amounts of unstable and stable elements in a given quantity of material are measured then it is possible to calculate how much time has passed since all the material was in its pristine unstable state, and that of course tells how long ago the element was formed and gives the age of the rocks in which it was found.

The uranium/lead decay was actually used to date rocks as long ago as 1913, but since uranium decays very slowly indeed (a given quantity loses half its radio-activity in 4,500,000,000 years) the amount of decay material in a sample accumulates very slowly too; in fact it is infinitesimally small and impossible to measure in all but the very oldest rocks. For more recent rocks a radioactive material with a faster decay rate was called for – and the Berkeley group turned to potassium. But even here they faced problems of daunting proportions. Many rocks contain potassium, but only about one per cent of natural potassium comes in the radio-active form called K.40. K.40 decays into an inert gas called argon (Ar.40), losing half its radio-activity in 1,310,000,000 years – which is considerably faster than uranium but still means that in two or three million years only some 0.1 per cent of the K.40 will have turned into Ar.40.

The quantities were still extremely small, but once the Berkeley group had perfected their extraction methods, and succeeded in developing a mass spectrometer capable of measuring billionths of a gram with consistent accuracy, then potassium/argon dating was available to science. Since Zinj it has become an integral part of early man research. Of course, it is not the fossil itself that is dated, but the deposits with which the fossil is associated – which is both a problem and a limitation. A limitation because the required potassium-bearing rocks do not occur at every fossil site; and a problem because collecting undisturbed, uncontaminated rock samples of known and indisputable association with the fossils has proved – in some cases – to be hardly less complicated than the laboratory procedures themselves.

The skull that had lain undisturbed beneath the Olduvai sediments for 1.75 million years travelled extensively in the months following its re-birth as *Zinjanthropus boisei*. First to Kinshasa, where he was introduced to science by Louis Leakey at the Pan African Congress on Prehistory which opened there on 22 August, and earned the sobriquet 'Nutcracker Man' in respectful acknowledgement of his enormous teeth. Then to London in October, where he was presented at the British Academy and achieved popular fame as the oldest of man's ancestors, though several scientists contested the claim. And in November, Leakey and his charge joined Sir Charles Darwin and Sir Julian Huxley (grandsons) as guests at the University of Chicago's Darwin Centennial (*The*

Professor Garniss Curtis, a pioneer of potassium/argon dating, checks with his associate Dr Bob Drake as a rock sample is heated to extract gases.

Origin of Species was published on 24 November 1859). Zinj was an unexpected guest; not surprisingly he was welcomed as the archetypal Missing Link – found at last.

While in America, Leakey made an extensive lecture tour. He also told the tale of Olduvai Gorge to the research committee of the National Geographic Society where, like a magician saving his best trick for the end of the show, he casually drew Zinj from cotton wool wrappings in his briefcase as he concluded a plea for funds to extend the excavations in the Gorge.[40] The NGS responded with a grant of over $20,000 and has funded the Leakeys' work with annual grants ever since.

After America Zinj travelled to Johannesburg, where he resided for several years in the anatomy department of Professor Phillip Tobias, who subjected him to exhaustive examination, measurement and comparison. The results were published as volume II of the Olduvai Gorge series of monographs and in it *Zinjanthropus* was accorded only sub-generic rank, with his australopithecine affinities firmly asserted: Tobias called him *Australopithecus (Zinjanthropus) boisei*.[31] In January 1965, Zinj made another journey, this time to Dar es Salaam. He has not moved since, but resides permanently and very securely in a sealed glass case, within a small locked box, inside a locked steel cupboard in the air conditioned strong room of the Tanzania National Museum.

Zinj – with Neanderthal arguably the world's most famous fossil – made Leakey a household name, especially in America where Louis's lecture tour became an annual event. The popular attention he received – which frequently bordered on adulation – surely helped Leakey assimilate Zinj into his scheme of human evolution, and the funds he gathered from a variety of sources certainly helped the investigations at Olduvai. In fact they could not have proceeded without it. After Zinj, however, Louis became less and less directly involved with the work at the Gorge. His time was filled with new projects, fund-raising and the promulgation of his theories. The investigations at Olduvai proceeded at the direction of his wife, Mary.

Chapter Eight

Tools

WHEN MARY NICOL joined Louis Leakey's Fourth East African Archaeological Expedition to Olduvai Gorge in 1935 she was just twenty-two years old and her two most important interests in life were archaeology and Louis Leakey. Convention might have suggested that it was not quite proper for a young lady to join four young gentlemen on an extended visit to the wilds of Africa – unchaperoned – especially as her heart was deeply taken by the leader of the expedition, who was married and had two small children. But Mary Nicol was an unconventional young lady who smoked cigarettes, wore trousers and could pilot a glider. Her background and upbringing were unconventional too, and from them she had emerged determined and ambitious as Louis Leakey himself, with an independence of spirit that uniquely complemented his.

Mary was an only child, born when her father was forty-five and her mother ten years younger. Her mother's maiden name was Frere; and in 1797 her great-great-great-grandfather, John Frere, had been the first man ever to recognize that the curiously shaped flints found in gravel pits and the like were actually implements 'fabricated and used by a people who had not the use of metals', who lived at a time 'even beyond that of the present world'.[1] Her father, Erskine Nicol, was a landscape painter, successful enough in the post-war years to maintain an enviable way of life. In the autumn, winter and spring, he travelled about Italy and southern France with his wife and daughter, painting stylish pellucid watercolours that sold well at the exhibitions he held in London during the summer and financed the next trip to Europe. There was never any regular schooling for Mary. The family was always on the move in Europe, and the schools in England were closed whenever they were there. Nonetheless, she picked up French as they travelled, her father taught her the elements of arithmetic, and the excitement of *Robinson Crusoe* read aloud by her parents encouraged her to read the book herself at the age of seven.

Erskine Nicol painted during the mornings only – strictly alone – and devoted the afternoons to his family. Mary remembers a series of afternoons when they were at Les Eyzies in France, near the famous caves where Cro-Magnon Man and the La Ferrassie remains had been discovered not many years before. Excavations were still going on and Mary visited the sites with her father. They talked to the archaeologists, she recalls, and rummaged through the debris from the caves – looking for stone tools. Not as a kind of child's treasure hunt, Mary insists, but because of her father's interest. He was intrigued by the tools' aesthetic qualities, she says, and by the images they evoked of the men who had made and used them. Mary was eleven then, and doubtless the magic of those tangible links touched her too.

Erskine Nicol died unexpectedly of cancer in 1926. With the end of her father's life, Mary's idyllic childhood came to an abrupt end too. Her mother settled them in London, where Mary became an unhappy and rebellious teenager, quite unwilling to follow the path of formal education her mother planned. She persistently ran away from the convents she was supposed to attend, never completed a school course, never sat for an examination and never gained the slightest of academic qualifications. But this did not deter Mary Nicol from pursuing the only subject that really interested her – archaeology and Stone Age man.

At an auspicious moment – she does not recall how, where or when – Mary learned that she could attend lectures at University College, London without entrance qualifications and without having to endure the time-consuming tedium of a full undergraduate course. This discovery she says, marked her 'return to sanity'. She could never get a degree of course, but Mary was more interested in information than accolades and followed lectures in geology and archaeology as assiduously as any enrolled student.

In the summer of 1930 she was invited to join the excavations of an Iron Age fort at Hembury, Devon, under Dorothy Liddell, whose brother-in-law, Alexander Keiller, excavated the Avebury site (1924–39) and pioneered modern archaeological methods. In 1931 she worked under Dorothy Liddell again, at Stockbridge in Wiltshire, whither she returned in 1932 and 1933. The following year she ventured forth on her own and, with Kenneth Oakley handling the geological aspects, excavated a Stone Age site at Jaywick Sands near Clacton-on-Sea in Essex. Jaywick proved to be an important site which resolved some puzzling anomalies concerning the development of stone tool technology.[2] Mary was only twenty-one, but already she was an accomplished archaeologist with significant discoveries behind her.

Not surprisingly, Mary Nicol inherited a degree of artistic sensitivity and talent from her father. It lay dormant throughout her childhood and

In the first stage of making a handaxe, flakes fly from a block of quartzite

adolescence, but blossomed in 1932 at the instigation of a family friend who, possibly sympathetic to both the daughter's ambition and the mother's pecuniary plight, introduced Mary to the archaeologist Gertrude Caton-Thompson just when that lady needed some drawings of implements for her book on *The Desert Fayoum*. Mary was given the task and thus earned some money of her own for the first time. The drawings turned out splendidly. Then – whether by accident or design is not clear – Caton-Thompson introduced Mary to Louis Leakey just when that gentleman needed some drawings of stone tools for his book *Adam's Ancestors*. The occasion was an informal dinner in London, and Caton-Thompson arranged that Louis should sit beside Mary. The attraction was immediate and mutual, Mary says, and supposes that their shared interests rendered the result predictable.

Mary drew the tools for *Adam's Ancestors*; Louis visited the excavations at Jaywick. There was always a plausible professional reason for their meetings, but Mary's mother never approved of Louis. Perhaps in an attempt to forestall the inevitable she took her daughter to South Africa during the winter of 1934–35, but if her intention was that the study of prehistoric sites there should erase thoughts of Louis from Mary's mind, she was disappointed. Mary left her mother at Victoria Falls, flew to Tanganyika to join Louis on his Fourth East African Expedition, and together they spent three months searching for stone tools and the remains of prehistoric man in the fossil beds of Olduvai Gorge.

Forty-five years later it can be said that their investigations have made Olduvai Gorge unquestionably the longest, fullest, most revealing record of early man and his 'predicament' yet found. Evidence is recorded from no fewer than 127 sites ranged along the length and breadth of the Gorge and throughout its geological sequence. From the base of Bed I up to the most recent deposits, the sites span nearly two million years. Artefacts, and the fossilized remains of hominid meals, have been collected in tens of thousands. Among them are stone anvils that have lain undisturbed since they were last used, and tiny fish scales so perfectly fossilized that even their transparency is preserved. The sheer quantity is impressive enough, but the quality of the Olduvai evidence – which distinguishes the Gorge from every other site mentioned in this book – lies in the glimpse it affords of man's earliest cultural activity and development at a single location during a known period of time. The stone tools littering the floor of Bed I are close to the beginnings of humanity, and the increasingly sophisticated tools in the higher beds are a clue to the evolution of skills ultimately responsible for the technological culture that surrounds and supports modern man.

Mary Leakey began the post-Zinj investigations at Olduvai in February 1960, with a full-time work force of sixteen Kenyan labourers and the part-time assistance of visiting scientists, students and family. The first phase of the work, dealing primarily with the oldest deposits, was brought to a close at the beginning of 1964. In forty-six months only thirteen sites were excavated, but together they spanned 700,000 years from the base of Bed I (1.9 million years) to the top of Bed II (1.2 million years). The excavations revealed forty-three distinct levels strewn with the evidence of hominid occupation. The total area of the occupation levels amounted to over 55,000 square feet and every square inch of it was mapped. The position, size and shape of every artefact, every stone, every fossil was plotted before its removal for study and analysis. In all, 37,127 artefacts and 32,378 fossils were recorded; and the latter figure does not include all the remains of birds, rodents, frogs and the like which occurred in prodigious quantities but generally were very small and fragmentary – 14,000 rodent fossils from one site, for instance, weighed less than fifteen pounds.

Mary Leakey's work at Olduvai[3] was roughly equivalent to recording the precise position and physical form of each stone and everything else encountered while digging a trench ten feet wide, ten feet deep and one mile long. Excavating procedures were simple enough. After the over-burden had been removed with pick and shovel the fossil-bearing levels were marked in a grid of one-metre squares, each of which was excavated in ten-centimetre spits with a home-made chisel-like instrument. The matrix surrounding the fossils was removed more judiciously with a dental probe and paint brush before the specimen was coated with a preservative – many fossils were extremely friable. All the debris removed from the grid was sieved through a mesh one-sixteenth of an inch wide – which is how most of the very small fossils came to light. And every artefact, fossil and stone was plotted on a map of the grid, numbered and recorded. But, though the procedures were simple, circumstances were not always favourable. At some sites the deposits were rock-hard when dry and slushy mud when wet; at others the sides threatened to crumble and had to be bolstered with sandbags; at yet others the overlying deposit tore away the fossil level beneath unless it was first thoroughly moistened to separate the two.

The work was tedious for the labourers, and tensive for Mary Leakey. It fell upon her to manage the investigations in general and oversee the work at every site – ensuring, for instance, that the excavations proceeded vertically, that measurements in every plane, the relationship of different levels, and any stratigraphic change were all recorded as well as every find plotted on the map of the site. These things were all crucial and if they were not recorded at the time of excavation, there would be no chance of recording them later on. Supervision, in fact, determined the speed of the investigations. Many more men could have been employed, but Mary Leakey had learned from previous experience that excavations are difficult to control when more than about half a dozen people are working on the site at one time: detail tends to become blurred as speed increases, and detail is everything.

But to interpret the fine detail Mary Leakey's excavations were resolving at every site, the picture of their general context had to be properly focussed too. This task was performed by Richard Hay from the University of California at Berkeley, who produced a masterly geological survey of the entire Olduvai basin.[4] Hay also collected substantial amounts of detailed data during the months he spent in the field, but no less effort was expended in the laboratory, where he analysed the rock samples and the data he had collected.

Hay's conclusions are revealing indeed – a fascinating insight into both the process of geological enquiry and the evolution of a natural landscape, quite apart from the importance of the supportive evidence they lent to Mary Leakey's investigations. In this latter respect Hay's prime objective was to correlate the deposits throughout the Gorge and determine the exact temporal sequence in which the sites occurred. This would be simple if each lay directly above the other in a neat geological sequence, but such is rarely the case. At Olduvai the sites are widely distributed in the horizontal plane, and the geological strata in which they occur are not always at the same height in the vertical plane; this may be because the thickness of the beds varies from point to point, or because they have been disturbed by erosion or by geological faulting. Five major faults associated with the formation of the Rift Valley are known at Olduvai, and there are many smaller ones that further complicate the picture.

Physical exploration and examination of the gorge was essential but complete understanding of its geology was finally achieved in the laboratory, where chemical and microscopic examination of the samples he had collected enabled Hay to determine the characteristics of each deposit and thus relate them to one another at all points along the gorge. This in turn made it possible to state with certainty the sequence in which the archaeological sites had been occupied by early man.

A direct corollary of this research was Hay's interpretative reconstruction of the physical environments pertaining at Olduvai during the times that early man was living there. From the same basic data he showed that numerous small rivers and streams from the south-eastern highlands had maintained a sizable lake in the Olduvai basin during Bed I and lower Bed II times. It had measured roughly ten by five kilometres and persisted perennially for several hundred thousand years, despite periodic inundation by showers of ash from the erupting Kerimasi and Olmoti volcanoes (Ngorongoro and Lemagrut, which dominate the scene today, were extinct before Bed I was laid down). The ash, of course, created the Olduvai deposits and preserved all the artefacts and fossil remains that are found within them.

Helped by the accumulative effect of rapid evaporation in a lake with no regular outflow, the ash was also responsible for the high alkalinity of the Olduvai lake, rendering the water suitable for both the microscopic algae which flourish in such conditions and for fish and birds specialized to feed on them – tilapia and flamingoes for instance. That such creatures lived around the Olduvai lake in large numbers is confirmed by their fossil remains, as indeed is the presence of their predators – crocodiles and man among them. Thus the volcanic ash not only preserved the remains of the early Olduvai inhabitants – that was simply fortuitous; but more fundamentally, because shallow alkaline lakes can support a far larger biomass than other bodies of water, the volcanic ash created the ecological circumstances that encouraged them to congregate there in large numbers.

At about 1.6 million years ago the lake shrank to a third of its earlier size. By 1.2 million years ago it was reduced to a series of seasonal pans dotted about an alluvial plain. One might imagine that volcanic ashes had filled the basin and were responsible for the demise of the lake they had previously made so productive, but there were other factors at work too. Foremost among them, perhaps, was geological faulting which could have reduced the lake very rapidly and certainly was responsible for the eastward movement of the drainage sump until about 400,000 years ago, when it reached the Olbalbal depression, where it rests today.

But at the same time as the faulting, there were also dramatic changes in climate. In Lower Bed I times Olduvai was very wet, with perhaps even a groundwater forest standing around parts of the lake shore. By Upper Bed I times, however, a much drier climate prevailed, reverting to wetter conditions again in Lower Bed II. These climatic changes are revealed by the evidence of fossil pollens that identify the vegetation, by the presence of animals that live exclusively in wet or dry habitats, and by the evidence of windblown and waterborne materials that Hay found in the sediments.

The distribution of the ancient stream channels in the deposits of that time told Hay the drainage pattern had changed too. He found that the streams and rivers from the highlands had merged into a large main stream flowing westward. With time, as the volcanoes continued to puff ash into the basin, laying down Bed III, drainage from the west joined this main stream. Ultimately it turned, and flowed eastward – as it does today. The stream began cutting the gorge about half a million years ago; the deposition of volcanic ashes and lake sediments ceased only about 15,000 years ago, so that some of the younger deposits overlie earlier excisions, which makes the geology difficult to interpret in some places. The spot where Reck's Olduvai Man was found is a case in point.

Relating the positions of the occupation sites to the geology, Hay arrived at conclusions which, combined with Mary Leakey's findings, conjure up a picture of our ancestors at the beginning of humanity. Hay found very little evidence of hominid activity on the savannah and barren floodplains; it occurred principally along with evidence of perennial freshwater, relatively abundant game and vegetation. All twenty camp sites known from Bed I are situated around the lake margin, eighteen of them on the eastern side where most of the streams flowed into the lake in those times. During the depositions of Bed II, when the lake dwindled away to nothing, hominid activity became much more widespread – of the sixty-three known campsites, fifty were to the east of the lake basin and many were situated on the banks of watercourses. In Beds III and IV, the campsite pattern followed the change in drainage, forty out of forty-three sites were to the west of the basin.

Apart from establishing the geological and environmental circumstances of the campsites, Hay's work also tells something of the tools that were found there – and the toolmakers. He identified the sources of nearly all the principal rocks used for making the stone tools. This is yet another point that makes Olduvai unique, for nowhere else are the sources of raw material so thoroughly known. This knowledge is particularly illuminating in that it offers clues to early man's growing awareness that some materials make better tools than others, and suggests his willingness to travel ever greater distances in search of the best. In Bed I and II, Hay found that most tools were made of lava obtainable within two kilometres of the campsite; other materials were used too, but rarely was the source more than four kilometres away. Higher in the sequence however, the variety of material increases and more and more of it comes from further afield. Bed III assemblages include many tools made from rock found eight and ten kilometres away and by Bed IV times the basin is criss-crossed with a veritable network of supply routes. Trachyte from Olmoti is found at sites fifteen kilometres distant; green phonolite from Engelosen occurs twenty kilometres from its source; Kelogi gneiss is found thirteen kilometres to the east. These are distances as-the-crow-flies – on foot it was certainly greater.

Mary Leakey believes it unlikely that large blocks of raw material were carried over the entire distance by members of a single group. The various rocks have quite distinct properties, and perhaps the early hominids had equally distinct uses and preferences for them. Mary Leakey has suggested that the apparently random distribution throughout the basin could indicate some form of barter or exchange among the groups camped closest to the sources of the various rocks – a kind of 'trade' in raw materials, known to have been well-established during the later phases of the Stone Age, possibly just beginning at Olduvai one and a half million years ago.[5]

Mary Leakey's 1960 excavations began at FLK, where Zinj had been found. Given that the skull was relatively intact, there was some hope that the jaw might also be recovered, but it was not. This was regrettable, for the jaw would certainly have helped resolve the nagging question of Zinj's australopithecine affinities (Louis thought the jaw might also reveal whether or not Zinj could talk), but in the event, the absence of a single fossil was of small consequence amid the wealth of detail that the site provided concerning the activities of the earliest known toolmakers – whether or not Zinj was one of them.

The Zinj living floor occupied an area of 3384 square feet. In the forty feet of deposits excavated from the hillside directly above it there were another twenty-one levels at which some evidence of hominid activity was found. The Zinj floor itself was remarkably well preserved and the material on it showed little or no sign of disturbance or weathering – probably because the site had been covered by a shower of ash soon after it was abandoned. It seems likely that the site had been in use for some time, for on it were found 2470 artefacts, 3510 fairly large fossils and literally thousands of bone fragments too small to be numbered.

But the major significance of the excavations at FLK lay not in their extent, nor in the quantity of material, nor its fine preservation, nor even in the skull of Zinj himself – it lay in the site's startling revelation that nearly two million years ago the social structure of our ancestors already included the concept of a 'home'. Until then experts had doubted that man had reached this stage of social development so long ago, but Olduvai proved conclusively that he had been hunting, gathering in groups at a homebase, and occasionally making shelters for at least 1.75 million years.[6]

The first evidence of this remarkable fact lay in the detail Mary Leakey had recorded so meticulously at FLK; it was confirmed at the other sites

and is clearly shown in her site plans.

The site plan of the Zinj living floor shows a scattering of artefacts and faunal remains over the entire area, with a densely concentrated patch on one side surrounded by a narrow, barren zone. The concentration measures about twenty-one by fifteen feet and the assemblage within it is marked by a preponderance of light-weight artefacts and smashed animal bones; the surrounding areas – by contrast – contain mainly large artefacts and many large unbroken fossils. The two assemblages are so different that if they were found separately they would almost certainly be considered as two distinct cultures.[7] Yet at FLK they were together on the same living floor; what is the explanation?

The site plan shows that the faunal remains within the concentrated area are almost exclusively the meat and marrow bearing bones of the carcass, while those outside are mostly jawbones, shoulder blades, hipbones, vertebrae, ribs and the like – all devoid of marrow. To Mary Leakey it seems probable that the concentrated remains marked a place where hominids had gathered to consume the animals they had caught. They would have sliced the meat from the carcass with small flake tools, she suggests, and then smashed the bones to extract the marrow. The large unbroken fossils scattered about the surrounding area would represent the rejects from their meals, and the barren zone in between the two assemblages is precisely where a brushwood shelter might have been erected to break a prevailing south east wind. The skull of *Zinjanthropus*, incidentally, had lain about fifteen feet from the patch of concentrated remains, on the lee side.

Excavations at two other sites revealed living floors on which the distribution of cultural and faunal material was similar to that encountered at FLK, though at each of these there were not one, but two, patches of concentrated material; they were roughly circular and lay quite close together – reminiscent of the way nomadic Bushmen still arrange their camps in the Kalahari. At all three excavations the evidence of structures made by early man was entirely circumstantial, but then it could hardly have been anything else. There was little chance of the brushwood windbreak itself being preserved, so only the bare ground in which it had stood could suggest its existence. At a fourth site however, a group of hominids had camped where there was little or no soil into which branches could be thrust. Here they were supported with rocks instead and today a circle of small rock piles remains as direct evidence of man's earliest known building efforts.

The site is known as DK (Donald McInnes Korongo), and it lies immediately above a lava flow dated at 1.9 million years. A profusion of

Handaxes and cleavers in a variety of materials, all collected at site WK in Bed IV, Olduvai Gorge

flamingo bones and some fish remains indicate its proximity to the lake, and fossilized rhizomes suggest that a bed of reeds or papyrus once grew there. The circle stands on a small hummock. It seems likely that the spot was chosen as one conveniently close to the lake and the creatures that congregated there, but drier than the surrounding areas – perhaps it was a small promontory.

The circle averages thirteen feet in diameter. It is little more than a ring of loosely piled lava blocks, with six small heaps spaced along the northern rim where it is best preserved. Maximum height is about twelve inches. At first sight the circle is far from impressive, little more than a jumble of rocks one might expect to find at the bottom of a gorge, but advance knowledge contributes deeper understanding. With a site plan to hand and time for contemplation, the circle evokes poignant images of our ancestors and their predicament one million nine hundred thousand years ago.

DK is the earliest hominid living site at Olduvai or anywhere else, and the tools found there are the simplest known, both in style and variety. Nonetheless they are tools, fashioned with some purpose in mind. The observation that removing a flake from a stone produces a useful sharp edge was almost certainly the result of natural accident. Rocks tumbling in a river or landslide occasionally break, and hurling stones about in a river bed can produce the same result. But such accidents are more infrequent than might be supposed: tumbling rocks are rounded more often than broken, and hurled stones usually bounce. And besides, the edge formed by accident is entirely unpredictable. So a useful cutting edge must have remained rare until someone perceived the advantage of dependable supply, and set about learning how the results of natural accident could be artificially reproduced.

Choppers are the simplest tools recognizable as manufactured artefacts. They are generally made from oblong, rounded water-worn cobbles that fit comfortably in the hand, and the edge is formed by removing flakes alternatively from either face along one side, or round one end. Deliberately turning a stone into a usable tool requires a surprising amount of skill. Even with our high level of general knowledge concerning technical and mechanical matters, very few people today could decide by themselves which stone is best and precisely where it should be struck to achieve the desired result. We know it can be done – there are many examples of beautiful and sophisticated stone tools to remind us that the effort is worthwhile. But the first toolmakers lacked this incentive. They acquired their skills in pursuit of an end, driven by a need – which means they had reached the conceptual threshold enabling them to identify a problem

Plan of the stone circle at site DK, Olduvai Gorge. The circle lies close to the 1.9 million year level and is the earliest known evidence of a man-made structure.

Stones

Fossils

A

A

B

B

and appreciate the benefits of solving it. Crossing that threshold put our ancestors firmly on the path to *Homo sapiens*.

The simple tools at DK and elsewhere belong to the Oldowan Culture. The term was coined by Louis Leakey, who described its most common variety as 'a crude chopper varying in size from about the dimensions of a ping-pong ball to that of a croquet ball'.[8] He believed that the evolution of toolmaking skills at Olduvai could be traced in a direct line from the simple choppers at the base of Bed I to the fine handaxes at the top of Bed IV. Given the length of time spanned by the deposits it was almost certain that some progress must have occurred, but Mary Leakey's excavations and analysis have revealed that it was by no means as straightforward as her husband had imagined. Which is not to cast aspersions upon Louis' perspicacity: his pronouncements on the Olduvai tools merely reflected the views of European experts. And these were based on the experience of flint – where it was well known that the fine feather-flaking of an Acheulean handaxe (named after St Acheul in France, where they were first found) required far more skill than the deeply flaked Chellean pebble tools (from St Chelles). In the latter, flakes were removed with a hammerstone; in the former a soft, broader hammer was used, wood or perhaps horn.

By experimentally reproducing known tools, the experts assessed the degree of skill needed to make each and established a stone tool chronology based entirely on the number and form of the flake scars. This was used to place sites in chronological order, but could never be confirmed because no European deposits spanned enough time to reveal the development of manufacturing skills from one type of tool to another through ascending levels. But Olduvai spanned many ages. There were no flint tools in the gorge, but perhaps it was natural that Louis Leakey should approach those made of other materials with the same ideas that were held in Europe. And natural too that as he collected and studied specimens from levels throughout the deposits he should seek what Europe's experts had said ought to be there. And he found it – or at least he believed he had found it. On the evidence of flake scars and presumptions of technique Leakey carefully documented eleven stages by which, in his opinion, the technical skills used in the manufacture of Oldowan tools had evolved into those required for making Acheulean tools. The findings were well received in their day, but his wife's work has since rendered them out of date.

Louis Leakey's readiness to impose old ideas upon new evidence typifies the simplifying approach that science initially adopts towards discovery. It is generally the second round of investigation that takes the

Six of the twenty artefact categories Mary Leakey has described from Olduvai Gorge: a) chopper; b) handaxe; c) spheroid; d) cleaver; e) burin; f) proto-biface

a

b

c

d

e

f

more circumspect view, that attempts to gather all available data, and then subjects them to thorough analysis to see if any significant facts or trends emerge. So it was at Olduvai where, with the acknowledged additional benefits of finance, time and patience not available to Louis, Mary Leakey has recorded the physical characteristics of all the 37,127 artefacts collected from Beds I and II at Olduvai. She noted the material of which the artefact was made, the number of flake scars it bore and, where visible, the angle of the striking platform – which is what determines the depth of the flake that is detached.

It was obvious from the start that the collection could be divided into a variety of tool categories, which may or may not provide clues to evolving skills. Mary Leakey eventually identified twenty quite distinct categories. Some of the terms she used to describe them relate to the form of the tool: spheroids, discoids, bifacial points, proto-bifaces, laterally trimmed flakes, polyhedrons, *outils écaillés* ('scaled tools') and débitage (flakes produced during manufacture of other tools but showing some sign of use themselves). Other terms suggest the function of the tool: awls, anvils, choppers, chisels, hammerstones, cleavers, picks, scrapers and punches. In addition she describes manuports (rocks foreign to the site but lacking any sign of modification), and utilized material (artefacts which defy closer description).

In the analysis of all these data, the relative proportions of the various raw materials and categories of tool occurring at each site have been calculated. This is only one of several lines of enquiry but, relating the results to the position of the sites in the geological sequence, significant trends do emerge. We have already noted that raw materials seem to be more specifically selected at sites through the ascending levels. This could reflect an increasingly complicated lifestyle; and the variety of materials, together with developing manufacturing skills, could indicate a growing ability to perceive and solve the problems of that lifestyle.

So what does the evidence show? The toolkit on relevant Bed I living floors contains an average of only six different tools, but in Bed II the average has risen to just over ten different types. During the same period, the ratio of artefacts to faunal remains has changed too: there are fewer bones on the younger sites, and more tools. Why? Because the people in those times had developed the skill to catch larger animals than their predecessors. At each of two butchery sites, for instance, the skeleton of an elephant was found strewn among a profusion of tools. Throughout the upper levels of Bed II the remains of giraffe, hippopotamus and rhinoceros are far more common than lower down. Obviously, one elephant would feed as many people as a whole herd of antelope. These developments occurred over about 150,000 years; at the same time the simple chopper was supplanted by the proto-biface, which is the first known attempt to produce a tool with a joint as well as a sharp edge; and the multi-faceted polyhedron with its several cutting edges probably evolved by progressive stages into the perfect spheroid – a stone ball which the Leakeys believe may represent a transition from passive tool to aggressive missile. They suggest that the spheroids were bolas, like those used in Argentina where two or more are strung together on lengths of hide and flung at the legs of animals to entangle and halt them.

So among the wealth of detail there is a good deal of accumulative evidence suggesting that early man's technical skills developed considerably during the period of time spanned by the Olduvai deposits. The simple Oldowan Culture evolved into what Mary Leakey termed the Developed Oldowan Culture. Tools became more refined, and the toolkit was enlarged by the addition of different types of tools and different raw materials.

But, while her work traced our ancestors' increasingly complicated lifestyle and heightened conceptual perception, Mary Leakey uncovered an intriguing puzzle too: from the base of Bed I the Oldowan Culture evolves into the Developed Oldowan A and thence into the Developed Oldowan B – but it does not evolve into the Acheulean handaxe culture as Louis Leakey had surmised. The Developed Oldowan persists virtually unchanged through Beds II, III and IV, while the Acheulean arrives suddenly and fully fledged in the middle of Bed II. Thereafter the two cultures are contemporary, Mary Leakey says, in one part of the gorge they are found within a few hundred metres of each other, on the same geological horizon. But there is no mingling. In Leakey's view they remain culturally distinct despite such close proximity.

Since there is no sign of the Acheulean having evolved at Olduvai, it is presumed to have been intrusive. But where did it come from? No one knows; its arrival coincides with the disappearance of the lake, when there was an abrupt change in climate, fauna and hominid activity in the basin. Perhaps another group migrated into the region at this time, bringing with them the superior skill of handaxe manufacture. But then why did not the Oldowan toolmakers already there also acquire that skill and incorporate it in their own toolkit?

The primary factor that distinguishes the two cultures is the ability to remove from a boulder the large flakes essential to handaxe manufacture. This is not difficult once the idea is there, and one might expect that during the course of a few thousand generations the Oldowan people would have learned the trick – by example if not by instruction, for abandoned Acheulean handaxes were there to be picked up in their time just as in ours. With the skills they already possessed they surely could have copied them. But no, the Acheulean and the Developed Oldowan remain culturally distinct.

Another puzzle was encountered among the Acheulean handaxes themselves – though this one proved more susceptible to solution. There are two sites in Bed IV whose stratigraphic relationship is indisputable but appears to be contradicted by the evidence of the handaxes they contain. Site HEB is lower in the sequence and therefore must be older than WK, but its handaxes seem finer, more sophisticated and therefore more recent than those at WK. How is it possible that younger handaxes can occur on the older site? This apparent anomaly puzzled the experts, Mary Leakey included, and the fact that it was seen as an anomaly at all indicates the strength and persistence of the traditional views on stone tool manufacture.

The WK handaxes were considered to be primitive because very little flaking had been done on them while the HEB handaxes were flaked over most of their surface – and fine flat flaking at that, which everyone believed was a difficult and sophisticated technique that must have developed after the 'cruder' work at WK. The most plausible explanation of this apparent regression in manufacturing skill has come from the work of Peter Jones, a young man who assisted Mary Leakey at Olduvai for several years while pursuing his own researches into stone tool cultures.

Jones suggests that, far from denoting a regression in skills, the 'crude' WK handaxes actually represent a more sophisticated approach.[9] Like Louis Leakey sixty years before, Peter Jones was caught by the fascination of stone tools at an early age. But unlike Leakey he lived in England, became familiar with flint and developed more of an interest in making tools than in looking for them. By trial and error, reading, and the examination of extant examples he learned to make a respectable hand-axe and a passable arrowhead. He spent a summer working with François Bordes in the Dordogne and was pleased to discover that he actually had tips to offer the master, as well as some to learn.

In 1976 Jones joined Mary Leakey at Olduvai and began duplicating the tools that had been found there. He soon discovered that, with the exception of chert, none of the materials used by the early toolmakers behaved much like flint. Though the principle, of course, was essentially the same, different rocks required subtly different techniques. With hindsight this might not seem an especially surprising observation, but at the time it was noteworthy for, although Louis for example had made tools at Olduvai and even skinned goats with them, no one had set about

Handaxes from site WK (TOP A, profile and side views) appear more primitive and therefore older than those from HEB (TOP B, profile and side views) although they come from a more recent site. Modern copies (BOTTOM, with removed flakes) resolve the anomaly. The amount of flaking required indicates that the WK tools (LEFT) represent a more sophisticated approach – they were made more quickly in a more effective material than the tools from HEB.

A B

A B

duplicating the Olduvai toolkit in all the various materials, recording the best techniques and how much time each required.

In his experiments Jones found that some rocks were suitable for one class of tool and not for another, techniques were not always inter-changeable, some tools could be made quickly, others took more time. Mary Leakey and Richard Hay had noted that the increasing variety of raw materials used at Olduvai was a significant development, but Jones has shown that the development was more complex than they realized. The WK/HEB anomaly is a case in point. The WK handaxes can be made in less than a minute because the material used produces a good clean sharp edge on the first flake struck from the boulder and requires a minimum of retouching. The material at HEB, however, is not suitable for this treatment; the edge has to be prepared by flaking all round, which may take five or seven minutes. The WK handaxes, then, represent a considerable advance in manufacturing efficiency over those at HEB – their only drawback is that their fine edge cannot be retouched. Once a WK handaxe has been blunted in use, it is necessary to make a new one.

Jones began by simply copying the Olduvai tools – as he had copied the European specimens – but he discovered that actually using his results added an important new dimension to his perception of their purpose, and of how they ought to be made. He quickly appreciated the advantages of a really heavy tool, for example, when he tried to skin a zebra with a light specimen; and he soon realized that the process of resharpening the right sort of large skinning tool produces numerous flakes perfectly suited for the subsequent task of disjointing the carcass, cutting the sinews and scraping the skin. It thus became obvious to Jones that the early toolmakers need only have carried a hammerstone and a few large tools to a butchery site in order to be fully equipped for every task that the job presented – a conclusion which explains the apparent superfluity of small tools at some sites that had previously puzzled many investigators.

Like many contemporary researchers, Jones is more concerned with function than with form. His work lends strength to the belief that traditional views on stone tools have been unduly and unfortunately biassed by aesthetic considerations. Flint tools can be beautiful and museum collections contain many outstanding examples, but do the aesthetic qualities we perceive today necessarily reflect the functional value of tools made one million years ago?

Peter Jones's work is a valuable extension of Mary Leakey's investiga-tions into the predicament of early man at Olduvai Gorge. But what of early man himself? Who was he, the fellow who first took one stone to make a tool of another? We shall never know the colour of his skin, how he talked or whether he smiled, but what *do* we know of him? One thing is certain: he was not very numerous. Amid a total of well over 100,000 artefacts and faunal remains collected at Olduvai there are fifty-eight hominid fossils to date, including several skulls, a quantity of isolated teeth and a number of skeletal parts. Some of the fossils are fragmentary, some are non-diagnostic and some are controversial . . . .

Chapter Nine

Homo habilis
(1964)

WE HAVE SEEN that to accommodate *Zinjanthropus boisei* within his scheme of human evolution, Louis Leakey subjected both the interpretation of the evidence and his own preconceptions to some distortion. He claimed the specimen resembled modern man more closely than it resembled the South African australopithecines, which even the most casual observer might have disputed; and he accepted the unseemly creature as a direct ancestor of man – which must have offended his notion of the antiquity of the pure *Homo sapiens* line. How ironic then that not many months after Zinj was proclaimed man's earliest ancestor, the excavations funded by Leakey's energetic publicity campaign should have produced a more worthy candidate: a series of fossils that could be accommodated much more readily than Zinj within the Leakey scheme of human evolution. The fossils in question were found together with tools, some of them on living floors even older than that on which Zinj was found. They were more lightly built in tooth and bones, and estimates of cranial capacity suggested that the fossils represented a hominid whose brain was large relative to body size.

Without embarrassment Louis Leakey embraced the new evidence and returned to the comfort of his former beliefs. He promptly demoted *Zinjanthropus boisei* to the status of non-toolmaking aberrant offshoot from the human line and hailed the new discovery as the true maker of the Oldowan tools – an entirely new species of human being from which *Homo sapiens* had evolved in Africa (by way of Kanjera man) before migrating to Europe. The discovery pushed man's origins back another 1.25 million years, he said, and would require many experts to rewrite their textbooks because it proved that *Australopithecus* was not an ancestor of man but simply another hominid lineage that had existed at the same time, just as he had said all along. The new species was called *Homo habilis* – handy man. Scientists of the day were quite willing to accept Leakey's latest discoveries as further proof that Olduvai Gorge

National Geographic *tribute, Louis Leakey's personal copy of* Zinjanthropus *paper, and the type specimen of* Homo habilis *with the original* Nature *publication*

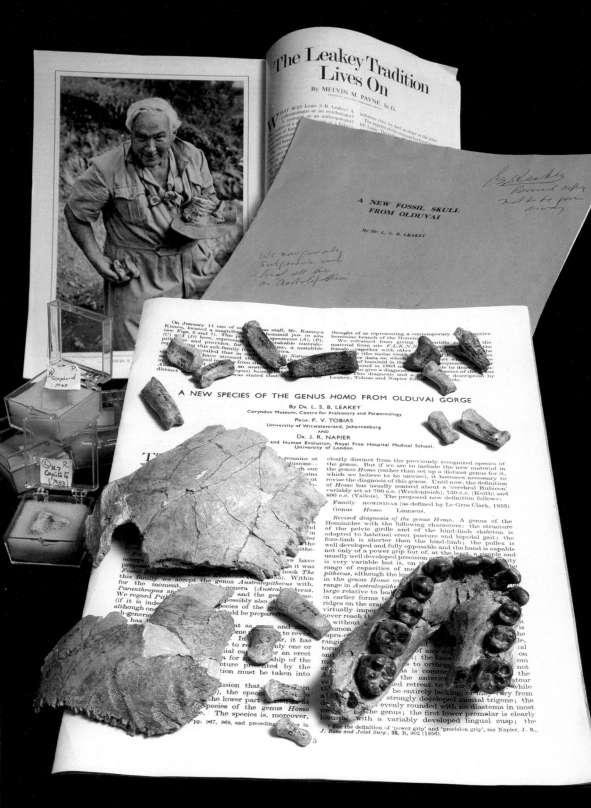

was 'the finest prehistoric site on earth . . . geologically and archaeologic-
ally sensational', and they did not dispute the 'immense value of his
discoveries', but they found his interpretations open to question.[1]
Controversy ensued.

Of the fossils now attributed to *Homo habilis*, the first to be discovered were a tibia and a fibula (the bones of the lower leg) found on the
Zinj living floor at FLK. Like Zinj, they lay outside the area of concentrated remains and were unbroken. They were found some distance from
the skull, several yards apart. At first it was presumed they had belonged
to Zinj himself, even though they seemed too lightly constructed for a
creature with a skull of such large proportions. And indeed, the presump-
tion had to be revised when remains of similarly light construction were
found at other sites.

The first came from FLK NN, a few hundred metres north of FLK
(another site – FLK N – lay in between). The site was discovered quite
fortuitously by Leakey's eldest son, Jonathan, then nineteen, who had
just finished school and was helping at Olduvai. Wandering away from
the main excavations at FLK on a fossil hunt of his own one day in
May 1960, Jonathan found an unusual lower jaw eroding from a nearby
slope. Though not immediately recognized as belonging to a sabre-
toothed cat (a rare find), the specimen was deemed interesting enough to
warrant a brief search for more remains of the creature. The surface
soil of the slope was sieved. Nothing more of the cat turned up, but a
solitary hominid tooth and a single fingerbone were compensation with
far greater promise. To locate the level from which the tooth and fingerbone had eroded, a step trench 1.53 metres wide and six metres long (in
total) was cut into the slope. On 13 June Jonathan found a hominid
collarbone, followed a few days later by several fragments of a very thin
hominid skull, all lying on what was clearly an occupation floor.

As the excavations were extended to left and right (eventually an area
17 by 12.3 metres was uncovered), an interesting collection of hominid
remains, artefacts and debris was revealed. Most of the floor appeared to
have eroded away some time before Jonathan chanced upon the cat's
jaw; only the outer limits were left and, as with the area surrounding the
'windbreak' at FLK, the remains found upon it were mainly of the
non-marrow-bearing variety. Among a total of 2158 fossils, there were
the ribs, vertebrae, shoulder blades and jawbones of pig and bovid; six
catfish skulls and seventeen tortoise shells. Artefacts were not plentiful
(only forty-eight are recorded), but hominid remains were scattered
about the entire floor.

They comprise a curious assortment of bones, and they were curiously distributed. Twelve associated foot bones, for example, were found among a variety of ribs, vertebrae and the sundry remains of horse and bird. Six metres away, twenty-one hand bones lay beside a pig's skull; and nine metres from the hand bones, a piece of lower arm bone lay beside a pig's jaw. Towards the south western edge of the site, one toe bone and one finger bone lay in splendid isolation more than six metres from both the hand and the foot to which they may – or may not – have belonged. In the vicinity of the trial trench that had produced the collarbone and skull fragments already mentioned, Jonathan found more skull fragments scattered over a wide area: 4.3 metres separated the most widespread, and a left and right parietal, which together formed the central arch of a skull, lay three metres apart. A solitary mandible completed the hominid collection: this important specimen was found about two and a half metres from the left parietal, where it lay with an unidentified rib between two tortoise shells.

The FLK NN living floor posed several intriguing questions concerning the content and distribution of the fossil collection Jonathan Leakey found there. Why such a strange assortment of bones? Why were they spread across the floor in such a curiously random fashion? The answers so far available are neither complete nor absolutely conclusive, but they demonstrate that modern paleoanthropology is a multi-disciplinary affair, with a variety of independent scientific investigations adding their findings to the growing knowledge of our ancestors' predicament.

Geologists identified the stratigraphic level of the FLK NN living floor, and geochronologists determined that it had been occupied at least 1.7 million years ago. Archaeologists found the distribution of fossils similar to that pertaining at FLK, and felt it likely that, before erosion, the FLK NN floor had also borne evidence of a crude shelter. Paleontologists identified animals the occupants must have killed and eaten. Anatomists determined that three individuals were represented among the hominid remains; they found evidence of two adult left feet, while the parietals, hand bones and mandible all had belonged to a juvenile.

The individuals had died of natural causes, anthropologists believed, suggesting the bodies had been left outside the FLK NN encampment when the rest of the group moved on – a procedure that has been recorded among modern nomadic people. Taphonomists, who study the processes affecting the nature of fossil assemblages, believe the corpses were almost entirely devoured by scavengers. Some skull fragments and some foot bones bear characteristic teeth marks, and the widespread scattering of the few remains is typical of hyena activity, for instance.

At first glance the hominid fossils from FLK NN seem ill-assorted and

not especially revealing of early man's physical form. But in fact, together
with the leg bones from FLK, they constitute an extraordinarily comprehensive collection which has supplied a good deal of new information –
just about all of which lent strength to Louis Leakey's belief that the
remains represented the earliest ancestor of true man. Among the hand
bones, anatomist John Napier found evidence of at least two hands (one
juvenile and one adult), an opposable thumb and the physical capacity to
manufacture the Oldowan tools found on the living floor.[2] From the foot
bones another anatomist, Michael Day, reconstructed an almost
complete adult left foot; it was entirely human, with no sign of the ape's
divergent big toe and every indication that its owner had stood erect
and walked with a bipedal and free-striding gait[3] – a view which a third
anatomist, Peter Davis, confirmed in an independent study of the tibia
and fibula from FLK.[4] In the mandible, Leakey found the front teeth
relatively large and the cheek teeth relatively small – quite different
from the australopithecines, he said, and quite appropriate for a new and
distinct type of early hominid.[5] From the parietals and other fragments
yet another anatomist, Phillip Tobias, reconstructed a skull and estimated
its cranial capacity as 680 cubic centimetres; nicely beyond the australopithecine average and approaching the *Homo* range.[6]

So the scanty remains from FLK NN appeared to represent a hominid
with a relatively large brain, thin human-like skull bones, *Homo*-like
dentition, manipulative hands and the ability to make stone tools –
evidence which, together with the age of the FLK NN living floor, most
persuasively suggested that the new fossils must represent man's earliest
ancestor. It seemed likely that Zinj had been an intruder – or a victim – at
the FLK campsite after all. The evidence was surely more compelling
than much around which Louis Leakey had constructed theories in the
past, but this time he did not rush to publish his conclusions.

Brief descriptive announcements appeared, but they did not assign the
fossils to any particular genus or species. The new species was finally
announced in April 1964,[7] by which time several more specimens had
been found at Olduvai. Among them, the end joint of a big toe hardly
affected the contentions, but two skulls, an upper and a lower jaw held
considerable corroborative value. The skulls were broken, but the bone
was indisputably as thin as the FLK NN specimen and their cranial
capacity appeared equally large. The dentition of the new and earlier
finds was very similar. Perhaps even more important, the finds were
seen to range from the base of Bed I to the middle of Bed II, a span of about
three quarters of a million years during which there appeared to have
been very little change in physical form – implying that *Homo habilis*

The type specimen of Homo habilis: *note the scavenger
teeth marks on skull fragment, top left*

had been a successful and durable species.

Furthermore, to add to the significance of the *habilis* fossils, classic *Homo erectus* remains were found in Upper Bed II – about 1.2 million years old. The first of these was a skull found by Louis Leakey himself, the only hominid fossil he ever found.

For many paleoanthropologists, Leakey's discovery of a *Homo erectus* skull represented the last link in the Olduvai story of human evolution: the sequence *Homo habilis – Homo erectus – Homo sapiens* made a perfectly acceptable evolutionary continuum. Some have also suggested that the presence of *Homo erectus* in Upper Bed II could explain the puzzle of the Acheulean culture that appears so suddenly in slightly earlier deposits (see page 177). Were the handaxes brought in by *Homo erectus*? The fact that only tools of the Oldowan culture have been found with *Homo habilis*, and the discovery in 1970 of *Homo erectus* skeletal remains alongside Acheulean handaxes[8] are two points that Mary Leakey interprets as suggesting that *Homo erectus* may have been responsible for the Acheulean culture of Bed II. But while the suggestion solves one puzzle it raises another, one in which the evidence of fossils and culture appear to contradict one another. The point is this: if it is accepted that man evolved from the primal stock via a lightly built toolmaker, then the *Homo habilis – Homo erectus – Homo sapiens* continuum is eminently reasonable. But if *Homo habilis* with Oldowan tools evolved into *Homo erectus* with Acheulean tools, why do the two cultures not show a similar connection? Why should the Oldowan and Acheulean cultures be contemporary and quite separate in the Olduvai deposits if they are the products of an evolving hominid lineage?

The puzzle is still unsolved, but for Louis Leakey it never even arose. He had described *Homo erectus* as an aberrant offshoot from the human line long before the discovery of *Homo habilis*. In his view, the apparently conflicting evidence of the new skull (which was especially thick-boned) simply confirmed his earlier beliefs and proved that three hominid lineages had existed at Olduvai – that is: the robust australopithecines as represented by Zinj; *Homo erectus*; and the true ancestor of man – *Homo habilis*.

The advent of *Homo habilis* marked the first time that an assortment of fossil bones was used to define a new hominid species. Most, if not all, species until then were founded on the evidence of skulls or teeth demonstrably belonging to just one individual. The mandible from FLK NN held a full set of teeth, but Leakey and his co-authors Napier and Tobias decided that its evidence ought to be augmented by including the skull and hand bones in their definition, even though this implied that the remains had all belonged to one individual – an implication that could never be verified and must, therefore, remain open to doubt. So the remains 'of a single juvenile individual from site FLK NN Olduvai, Bed I' were given as the type specimen of *Homo habilis*.[9] The foot bones and other fossils were listed as paratypes.

Leakey and his co-authors believed that *Homo habilis* represented a hitherto unknown stage in the course of human evolution, so they felt obliged and entitled to revise the standing definition of the genus *Homo* in accordance with their new evidence. This may seem an audacious step, but in fact the genus was never more than provisionally defined,[10] and Leakey's proposals were more an extension than a revision of those already existing.

Most authorities believed that absolute brain size was the distinguishing feature of the evolving *Homo* genus, and variously had proposed cranial capacities from 700 to 800 cubic centimetres as the limit beyond which a hominid brain could be termed human. Leakey and his co-authors scrapped this notion; the *Homo* brain was highly variable in size, they said, and proposed relative brain size as a more accurate indication of generic status. The most important factor, in their view, was that the evolving *Homo* brain was large in relation to body size. In respect of the other evidence, the new generic definition accepted skull shape, facial form and bipedal gait as previously given, while extending the list of dental characteristics and adding the opposable thumb as distinguishing features of the genus.

Since publication, *Homo habilis* has been subjected to frequent reassessment. It has been suggested that one of the hand bones is a vertebral fragment, two may have belonged to an arboreal monkey, and six came from some unspecified non-hominid.[11] But despite these enquiries, the evidence remains valid. Its significance, in fact, was never doubted – it was Leakey's interpretation that caused offence, mainly because he chose to stress differences rather than similarities and created a new species rather than squeeze the specimens into one that already existed. And then, most provocative of all, he reinforced his own conception of human evolution by calling the new specimen *Homo* instead of *Australopithecus*, which most others believed had stood on the path of human evolution at that point. His critics responded with complaints that the conventions of classification had been flouted;[12] they said that the distinctiveness of the new species had been inadequately demonstrated,[13] and claimed there was insufficient 'morphological space' for another species between *Australopithecus* and *Homo erectus*.[14] But at the same time, critics and supporters alike accepted the association of

OVERLEAF LEFT *The earliest* Homo habilis *specimen (not less than 1.8 million years old) from Olduvai Gorge; in the foreground is a cast of the skull before reconstruction*
RIGHT Homo erectus *skull found by Louis Leakey; above: fragments of another* erectus *skull from Olduvai*

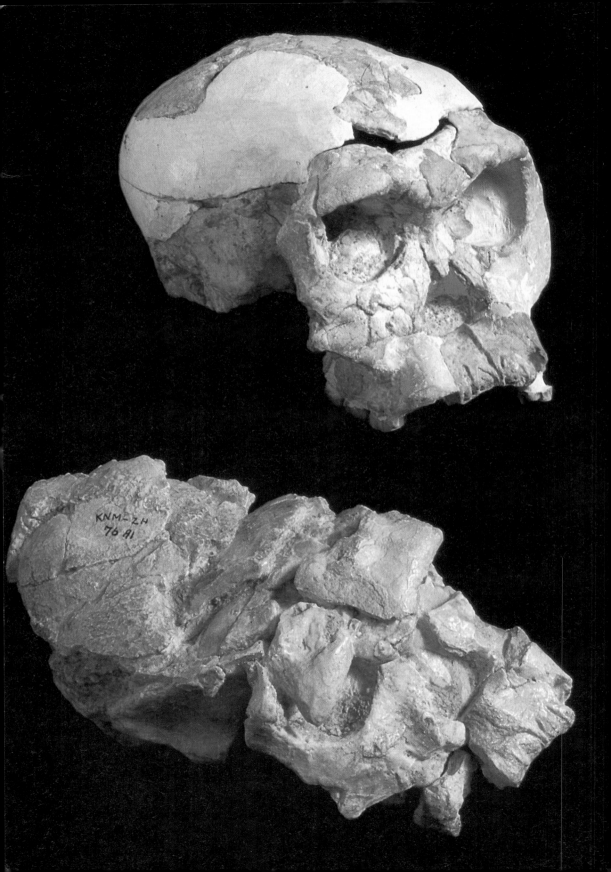

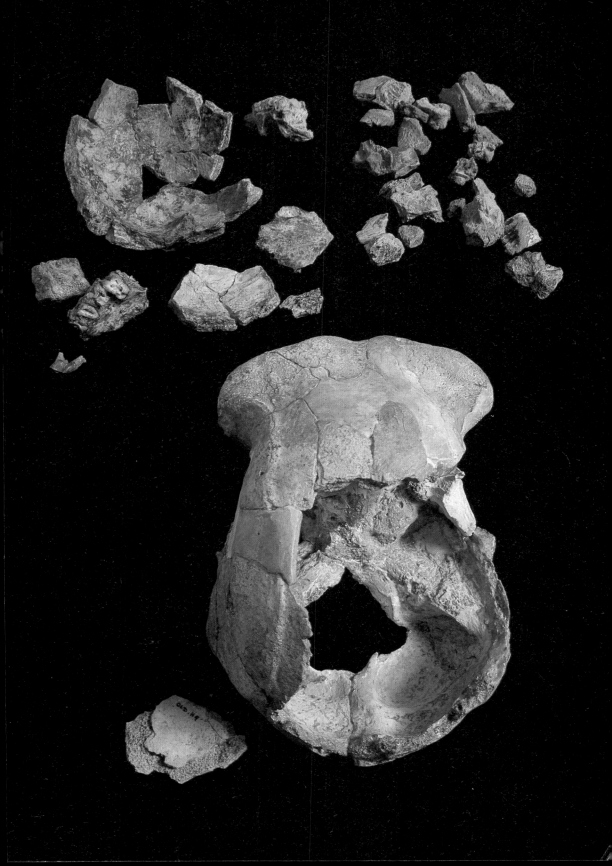

stone tools as evidence that the hominid Leakey had discovered was responsible for the Oldowan culture and therefore qualified as a human ancestor; and all agreed that the enlarged brain was a significant step in the direction of *Homo sapiens*.

In essence, then, it was agreed that *Homo habilis* was an ancestor of man and, for those who believed *Australopithecus* had stood on the human line, the controversy had more to do with name than status. Was *habilis* the most advanced *Australopithecus* or the lowliest *Homo*, they asked? Given the difficulty of determining when one species becomes another on a lineage where evolution is presumed to be gradual, this purely academic question could never be answered. As the debate reached the correspondence columns of *The Times* even the anatomists Tobias and Napier confessed that the association of stone tools was the most convincing evidence of *habilis's* affinities with the genus *Homo*.[15] But such an assertion was hardly adequate. Classification is determined by morphology, not by inferred behaviour.[16] And besides, Leakey had offered exactly the same argument as evidence that *Zinjanthropus* was an ancestor of mankind, and that claim had proved to be incorrect.

Acknowledging that the fossils needed a label, most authorities would probably have accepted *Australopithecus habilis*. Indeed, that label has been applied.[17] But for Louis Leakey, of course, such a name was a contradiction in terms: he had never believed that *Australopithecus* was a human ancestor, while he had known since a boy that stone tools were made by the ancestor of man – who would be called *Homo*. Therefore in his view *Homo habilis* was the only name that could be applied. But where did that leave *Australopithecus* in the story of human evolution?

The practice of drawing ancestral trees has been introduced to the study of fossil man at an early stage, and became a legitimate means of expounding hypothesis. The arrangement of stems, branches and dead twigs varied enormously as fossils were discovered and concepts changed, but even so, by 1964 most authorities shared the view that *Australopithecus* had played an important role in the evolution of mankind. Louis Leakey had never agreed, and the announcement of *Homo habilis* in 1964 in effect contended that he was right and the others wrong. *Homo habilis* firmly dismissed *Australopithecus* to the rank of aberrant offshoot from the *Homo* lineage, he said, and would require many scientists to revise their concept of human evolution. Thus *Homo habilis* quickly polarized opinion to one side or the other of a most divisive question: what was *Australopithecus*? Ancestor of mankind, or distant cousin?

Chapter Ten

1470

(1972)

IN THE LAST decade paleoanthropology has become less the pursuit of individuals, calling more and more for the collaboration of expert specialists. But at the same time, ironically, the public and the media continue to demand their scientific heroes. Richard Leakey has been called 'the organizing genius of modern paleoanthropology'.[1] The research he initiated at East Turkana in northern Kenya has been carried out by a large number of invited specialists. As scientist, Leakey has played only a minor role, but undoubtedly he has directed the investigations with extraordinary success. His background (some say his birthright) may have contributed to the East Turkana project's initial impetus, but its subsequent success is entirely due to Richard Leakey's ambition, determination and impressive administrative skill.

Following his father's death in October 1972 Richard Leakey devoted much time and effort to the establishment of The International Louis Leakey Memorial Institute for African Prehistory (TILLMIAP). He raised the money, negotiated the covenant and saw the Institute's impressive new building opened in Nairobi: a son's monument to his father.

But now Richard Leakey's ambitions extend beyond the search for early man,[2] and he wants the East Turkana Research Project to become less his personal enterprise and more a function of the Institute. In this he is hoping to pioneer a more impersonal trend in the science, whereby the predispositions of a discoverer (or expedition leader) may be lost, or at least diffused, while the fossils are studied by groups or appropriate experts.

But meanwhile Richard Leakey has become a public figure, and his public statements tend to overshadow the scientific utterances. He expounds his views fluently and frequently in magazines, newspapers, books and on television, so that despite his avowed conviction that less public and more impersonal scientific procedures should prevail, Richard Leakey, personally, has become today's most celebrated champion of the theory of man's distant ancestry.

Like his father, Richard Leakey believes that the ancestry of mankind is very long indeed, and that *Australopithecus* has played no direct part in it since the two lines split from the common ancestor about six or seven million years ago.[3] Others, equally vehement, champion the opposite view, that *Australopithecus* was the ancestor of mankind, and that the *Homo* and *Australopithecus* lineages split from a common ancestor little more than two million years ago. The new evidence used to support the two theories is the same – fossils found at East Turkana and in Ethiopia. Each side interprets the evidence differently, but the arguments are united by familiar undertones – each reflects preconception as much as interpretation, and each reveals as much of the scientist as of science.

The field base camp of Richard Leakey's East Turkana Research Project is situated on the shores of Lake Turkana, near a sandy spit called Koobi Fora. It is an oasis of comfort in a hot and windy wilderness. Water is the most important attraction. Only a hundred metres or so separate the camp buildings from the lake, and from the shore water extends to the horizon. The water is unpalatable and slimy to the touch because of its extremely high alkalinity, and it has to be shared with hippos and crocodiles. The cool sandy shore stretches away in the distance; flamingoes, pelicans and plovers congregate in large numbers. Zebra, antelope and gazelle gather on the flats, the sun sets across the lake, the wind drops – it is a place of exceptional beauty.

The camp buildings are constructed with flagstones from the lakeshore and kept cool by the draught that circulates beneath the low thatched roofs. In the dining area there is always squash available, large pint glasses, ice in the fridge and a canvas watercooler hanging in the breeze. Essential supplies are brought by a lorry which constantly plies the rough five-day, eight-hundred-kilometre 'road' to and from Nairobi. Richard Leakey flies in for a few days whenever he can, bringing with him fresh meat, fruit and lettuce. Visitors are always impressed by the fresh salads he serves, and by the very good French dressing he makes to accompany them.

Leakey has made Koobi Fora a most desirable place, but it is only a base-camp. Scientists are likely to spend only the weekends here – a well earned respite in which to soak up water, wash clothes and hair – after a week of work conducted from satellite camps where conditions are less congenial and where meals consist monotonously of corned beef.

Working conditions on the distant landscapes where the East Turkana fossils are found are probably among the most testing on earth. For an hour or so each morning and evening, when the shadows are long and the sky is a saturated blue, the temperature is comfortable. For the rest of the

Richard Leakey in 1978 with the Australopithecus
skull he found at East Turkana in 1968

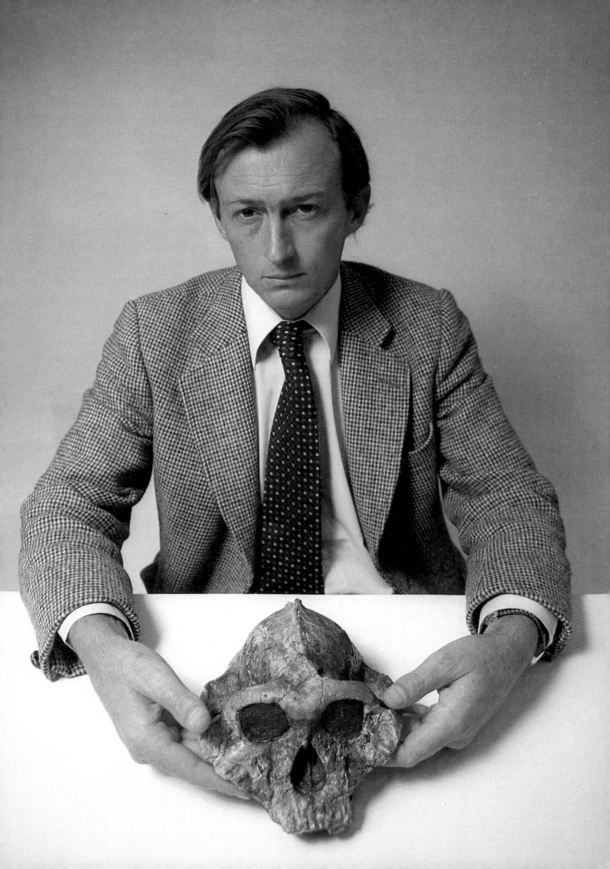

day, however, the heat is overwhelming: bleached sky, burned vegetation, glaring reflections from burnished lava cobbles. And then there is the wind. An easterly gale blows most of the day, most days, and the best to be said of it is that conditions are far more uncomfortable when it drops. Everything radiates heat, and without the wind tiny sweat bees and midges cluster on the exposed damp skin. They whine about the ears and irritate body and mind.

In these circumstances it might be imagined that stress would arise between individuals. In fact the sun and wind do not so much shorten tempers as they exhaust everyone, creating silences around the tea table and in the casual moments when people usually chatter and gossip after a day's work. Scientists working from the satellite camps often feel unusually vulnerable: one told me that he needed a long thick book to preserve his serenity.

Most of the East Turkana hominid fossils have been found by a group of Kenyans known colloquially as the Hominid Gang. Generally there are six of them and they scour the exposures six hours a day, six days a week, six months a year. They cover virtually every square metre of 800 square kilometres every year. In eleven years (aided by the scientists who have occasionally accompanied them) they have brought back more than 5000 fossils. Of these, some 200 are hominid, of which less than twenty are whole bones, nine are reasonably complete skulls, thirty or so are mandibles in varying states of preservation and the rest are isolated teeth, skeletal and mandibular fragments. Hominid hunting is hard work.

Finding fossils at places like East Turkana is an expensive business. In ten years Richard Leakey had channelled more than $800,000 into his East Turkana Research Project. Government institutions and the more august bodies that fund scientific research do not rate the search for fossil evidence of human evolution very highly among their priorities, and initially Leakey found all his money elsewhere. The National Geographic Society gave him $25,000 in 1968; in succeeding years other foundations have contributed too and, all along, participating scientists have been required to find some independent funding for their travel and research. The East Turkana Research Project has shown that money is available for a wide range of investigations associated with the search for the origins of mankind. In some seasons a total of up to fifty specialists have worked at East Turkana, for most of whom the research was part of a personal academic programme. Their results have contributed significantly to the overall investigations at East Turkana, but dependence upon such individual research and piecemeal funding has hindered the development of the long term programme.

If annual grants totalling the $800,000 Richard Leakey has spent had been guaranteed when the project began, there can be no doubt that both research and results would have benefited. But such long term planning was impossible. Grants were made irregularly and ran for just a few years; the National Geographic Society, for example, decided upon its contribution annually. Thus funding was most readily encouraged by short term results and the prospect of more to come. In this respect hominid fossils were the most valuable result of the research at East Turkana, even though their scientific value depended heavily upon other, less colourful, investigations. So the search for more hominids became fundamental to each year's research programme at East Turkana, and Richard Leakey was obliged to find something interesting to say about each new discovery.

All scientists are obliged to report upon their investigations and most would like to reach the widest audience possible, but few are so fortunate in their subject as those studying the evolution of man. For one thing, the very nature of their investigations – *human* evolution – is bound to arouse popular interest; and paleoanthropologists have not hesitated to take advantage of this.

The 'Missing Link' was a flag waved for many years. There are enough Missing Links in the popular record to merit their classification as a distinct species, but during the sixties and seventies they were superseded by the 'Oldest Man' as the image of paleoanthropology that best caught the public attention. The advent of potassium/argon dating was the primary cause of the demise of the Missing Link. It enabled scientists to determine the absolute age of fossils from suitable deposits and, since they turned out to be much older than anyone had thought likely, it is not surprising that the press releases stressed their age before the significance of any discernible evolutionary context.

Richard Leakey's 1968 season at Lake Turkana produced fossil remnants of extinct pigs and elephants 'about four million years old', and a few fragments of australopithecine jaw – poorly preserved but enough to strengthen Leakey's application for more funds with the suggestion that 'near-man had lived along the eastern shore of Rudolf [the name was changed to Turkana in 1974] between two and three million years ago'.[4] Further investigations 'would turn up further evidence of man's ancestry', he said, and the Society responded with funds for another year.

The ages Leakey had attributed to these fossil fauna were educated guesses based on the evidence of other sites. The pigs, for instance, seemed older than those from Olduvai. In 1969, he determined that the age of his

OVERLEAF *The fossil beds at East Turkana*

finds should be more accurately assessed as part of a geological and stratigraphical survey of the 800 square kilometre deposits that would be undertaken by Kay Behrensmeyer, a graduate student of geology at Harvard University. Early in her endeavours, Behrensmeyer found some stone tools. She selected samples of the volcanic ashfall in which they appeared to have been embedded and dispatched them to Cambridge University for potassium/argon dating by Drs Fitch and Miller. The first tests included an age of 2.4 million years, which was enthusiastically celebrated at Koobi Fora.[5] Subsequently, further tests of additional samples caused Fitch and Miller to revise their first estimate to a 'more accurate date of very close to 2.6 million years, plus or minus 260,000 years'.[6]

Meanwhile Leakey had found a complete hominid skull about fifty kilometres north of the tool site, and one of his Kenyan assistants found fragments of another – but different – skull nearby. According to Behrensmeyer's stratigraphic work, the hominid site lay below the geological horizon on which the tools had been found. In Leakey's estimation, the fossil fauna confirmed her correlation and so, he deduced, the tools and the hominids must all be at least 2.6 million years old. The oldest evidence of toolmaking known theretofore had come from Olduvai, as we have seen, from beds dated at close to 1.9 million years. So after his second season at East Turkana Richard Leakey could claim to have pushed the toolmaking phase of mankind back nearly three quarters of a million years. Furthermore, his expedition had discovered two skulls as well – one magnificent, the other mysterious. The first was an undistorted version of Zinj, a wonderful specimen that was found, incidentally, ten years almost to the day after Richard's mother had found the original at Olduvai. There could be no doubt about its affinities: robust australopithecine. The second was incomplete, puzzling and, in the short term, more useful for that very reason.

Leakey referred to the mystery skull in *Nature*[7] and *National Geographic*.[8] Although the skull was too fragmentary to permit conclusive interpretation, certain things, wrote Leakey, were clear. There was not much of *Australopithecus* to be seen in it, and not much of *Homo* either; but he believed the slight morphological evidence of the latter was strengthened by the associative evidence of stone tools. It was generally agreed, he pointed out, that australopithecines had not made tools. Therefore a second hominid species must have existed at East Turkana. Was this it? If so, then the remarkable repetition of events at Olduvai might have seemed sufficient precedent, and *Homo habilis* might have seemed the obvious candidate for the East Turkana toolmaker as well.

But Leakey could see little of *habilis* in the mystery skull either.

If not *habilis*, what was it? Could it be a prototype of *Homo erectus*, he wondered, making tools at East Turkana over two million years before appearing in Java and Peking? Richard Leakey believed it was quite possible. 'We will find the answer, I am sure,' he told *National Geographic* readers, 'for among the strata of the East Turkana desert lies a fascinating volume of prehistory, holding untold chapters of the origin of mankind . . . we have scarcely turned the first page, and I am eager to get on with the reading.'

Funds flowed, fossils too. In 1970 sixteen hominids were found, followed by another twenty-six in 1971. Among these were some important mandibles, a fragmentary half-skull (subsequently described as a female of the robust australopithecine lineage), some skeletal parts and some isolated teeth. Preliminary reports were published in *Nature*,[9] but the 'mystery skull' finally achieved taxonomic status in the pages of *Social Biology*, where it was assigned to the *Australopithecus* lineage in 1972.[10]

The next major discovery from East Turkana was the famous 1470 skull. The first scraps of it were found on 27 August 1972 by Bernard Ngeneo. Richard Leakey and Dr Bernard Wood, an anatomist with the research project, joined the search and within days they had collected and assembled enough pieces to satisfy themselves that Ngeneo's find was the oldest, most complete hominid skull with a relatively large brain case ever found. Many believe that large brain equals *Homo*; therefore 1470 was the Oldest Man. An extensive area surrounding the discovery site was carefully sieved to ensure that all pieces that might belong to the skull were recovered. Richard's wife, Dr Meave Leakey, zoologist, continued the reconstruction. Later she was joined by Dr Alan Walker, another of the three anatomists on the project, and together they built a respectably complete skull out of about 150 pieces of the pile that had been recovered. There was a great deal left over. The reconstruction confirmed the first predictions – undeniably 1470 was a large-brained hominid. But Alan Walker saw affinities with the gracile australopithecines that he found equally undeniable. Large brain, yes; *Homo*, no. As far as Walker was concerned, 1470 was a large-brained representative of the *Australopithecus* line.[11]

Richard Leakey did not agree, nor did Bernard Wood. They acknowledged the distinctive australopithecine attributes of the specimen. But 1470, Leakey announced to *National Geographic* readers, represented the 'earliest suggestion of the genus *Homo*'.[12]

Richard showed the skull to his father shortly before he died. The

meeting was by way of a reunion that Richard remembers fondly. Relations between father and son had been strained for some time. 'He (Louis) was a sick old man at the end of his career,' Richard has said,[13] 'and he found my successes very difficult. I was not old enough or mature enough to respond to that adequately.' By unspoken agreement, they preferred not to meet. 1470 brought them together again and, indeed, showed that in science as in spirit there was never much separating them.

Louis was tremendously excited by the skull. He believed it confirmed his views on the antiquity of true man, vindicated his Kanam finds and dismissed *Australopithecus* from the human line once and for all. If 1470 really was, as Richard believed, about 2.6 million years old, then, together with a robust australopithecine Richard had found at the same level in 1969, it seemed to prove that at least two hominid lines had existed at East Turkana well before the days of Zinj and *habilis* at Olduvai. Louis was certain there would be more. 1470 was one thing, he told Richard, the robust australopithecines are another, *Homo erectus* is yet something else and there will be others, he said, and you will find them.

But some of Leakey's contemporaries, notably Alan Walker, could not accept 1470 as *Homo*. This difference of opinion gives rise to two crucial questions. Firstly: if both the large brain of *Homo* and demonstrable affinities with *Australopithecus* are recognizable in a skull two million years old, does this not suggest that the two lineages are more closely linked than the Leakey theory of two distinct lines evolved from a very distant common ancestor allows? Perhaps there was only one line after all, along which *Australopithecus* evolved into *Homo* with 1470 representing an intermediate stage. Or secondly: if *Homo* and *Australopithecus* were indeed two separate lineages, as Leakey says, and assuming human evolution was gradual and proceeded at a regular pace, then does not 1470's blend of distinctive *Homo* and *Australopithecus* features imply that the two genera had diverged from a common ancestor a relatively short time before, as the believers in mankind's more recent ancestry have proclaimed?

1470 is an outstanding specimen, and some modern theorists might prefer to regard the opposing interpretations of its features as inadequacies of hypothesis rather than inadequacies of evidence.[14] Certainly the significance of the differing interpretations is diminished when the specimen is assessed in terms of a new approach to the study of fossil man which suggests that evolution may not have been a simple process of gradual change from ancestral form to descendent, to be substantiated by the discovery of fossils marking distinct transitional stages, as everyone had supposed. According to the new theorists,[15] evolution is more likely

The 1470 skull

to have been 'punctuated' with changes occurring rapidly in the course of just a few generations (possibly in response to sudden environmental change), interspersed with long periods of little or no change, so that the fossil record could be expected to show 'quantum leaps' of development from stage to stage with no evidence of change in between. The concepts of 'Missing Link' and 'Oldest Man' have less relevance in such a scheme.

There can be little doubt that in an earlier scientific era 1470 would have been presented as the archetypal 'Missing Link' and would have encountered few who disputed its credentials. And it is certainly true that by September 1973, when Richard Leakey called a meeting in Nairobi to discuss the formal scientific description of the fossil, he had already introduced 1470 to the world as the 'Oldest Man', bolstering his personal belief in mankind's unique antiquity.

Foremost among those attending the Nairobi meeting were the three anatomists: Bernard Wood, Alan Walker and Michael Day. In private conversation scientists have described the meeting as one distinguished by emotion and lack of harmony; the fact that different participants give different accounts of the proceedings must lend credence to this. The following is a synthesis.

As the anatomist most involved with the reconstruction of the skull, Alan Walker had undertaken and already completed the detailed, technical description of the specimen when the meeting was convened. He opened the discussions with a proposal that the title and preamble of the published paper should mention the australopithecine affinities he saw in the skull. Although all acknowledged that these existed (and the anatomists could all have made a case for them), Leakey and Wood insisted that the large brain was pre-eminent. 1470 was *Homo*, they said. Day remained non-committal.

In the ensuing debate Walker detailed the australopithecine affinities[16] and insisted that they merited nomenclatural acknowledgement regardless of brain size. Furthermore, the skull had been distorted during fossilization, he said, and the configuration of the right side of the vault squashed into a deceptively *Homo*-like form. But for Leakey and Wood, brain size was all that counted. As the debate warmed to argument with no concession from either side, Walker resorted to persuasion of a more personal nature. If the published description of 1470 was to include *Homo* attribution, he said, then his name must be removed from the paper. This was no mean threat, given Walker's academic standing and contributions to the science, but it did not bring the capitulation he sought. Quite the contrary in fact, for the threat drew from across the table the flippant and injudicious remark that his withdrawal might be welcomed. At this Walker picked up the fossil and left the room.

After his departure, Richard Leakey decided to resolve the conflict in the following manner: if Walker stayed away then 1470 would be attributed to *Homo* without qualification; if he returned then Walker's views would be accommodated, to some degree, in the paper. Walker did return, and the paper was published with his name beneath the innocuous title: 'New Hominids from East Rudolf, Kenya'.[17] The preamble refers to the preliminary accounts in which Leakey – personally – had attributed the specimen to *Homo*, while making it clear that detailed comparative studies (which would determine what the skull should be called) were not yet complete. This aspect of the study was subsequently assigned to Bernard Wood.[18]

The worldwide admiration and congratulation that greeted the twenty-eight-year-old Richard Leakey and his two-and-a-half-million-year-old 1470 were subsequently marred by just one thing – an authoritative suggestion that the skull was not as old as Leakey claimed – that it might, in fact, be only 1.8 million years old and therefore no older than *Homo habilis* from Olduvai Gorge. The suggestion was founded on paleontological evidence,[19] espoused by others and, by September 1973, Richard Leakey was beginning to realize that interpreting the significance of 1470 seemed to depend more upon accurate determinations of its geological, stratigraphical and geochronological status than upon its anatomical detail.

It is particularly difficult to achieve absolute accuracy when dating hominid fossil levels. This is partly because the deposits in which hominid fossils are found are, in geological terms, relatively young. They are therefore nearer the surface and much more likely to be contaminated with extraneous material of a quite different origin – and age.

The intrinsic problems of dating young deposits were further compounded at East Turkana by the manner in which the fossil beds had been formed – and re-formed. The ash and pumice originally came from volcanoes and fissures; it variously settled in the ancient lake, was eroded, or was transported by streams and rivers. The lake level rose and fell; geological faulting uplifted some parts, caused others to subside. The sequence of deposition (the stratigraphy) is nowhere easy to determine, and relating the stratigraphy of one area to that in another is even more difficult.

All in all then, giving an accurate absolute date for the East Turkana fossils is fraught with problems: there is room for error at every turn. Nowhere is this better demonstrated than in the case of the KBS tuff (KBS stands for Kay Behrensmeyer Site, the spot where the tools were found), a layer of solidified volcanic ash designated as a 'marker' in the stratigraphic determinations and a reference point against which many of the important fossils are dated, including 1470.

Fitch and Miller's tests on the first samples of the KBS tuff that Leakey sent to Cambridge actually gave an average age of 221 million years.[20] Such an age was impossible – clearly the sample must have been contaminated – so Leakey sent more samples. From these the scientists selected crystals that seemed fresher than others[21] and produced an age of 2.4 million years. (Later they adjusted this to 2.6 million plus or minus 260,000 years.)[22] But Fitch and Miller's work on the KBS tuff did not stop there. They subsequently tested many more samples (including some they had collected themselves) and their results range from a minimum of 290,000 years to a maximum of 19.5 million.

The scientists are not embarrassed by this apparent imprecision. They are perfecting a complicated technique and developing another that they hope will give greater accuracy. They expect discrepancies and endeavour to identify the cause – that is how experimental science proceeds. The trouble is, paleoanthropology is an interpretative science that depends upon expensive research, and publicity-conscious paleoanthropologists find the 'Oldest Man' a most valuable asset in their quest for funds. So when a fossil appears to have achieved that status, the potassium/argon date upon which it is based tends to receive far greater emphasis than the experimental techniques justify.

The potassium/argon process undoubtedly is an important aid to the study of fossil man, but it is not a final arbiter. Its validity is very much contingent upon others factors – geology, stratigraphy, chemistry, for example. And furthermore, it is only one of several ways by which the antiquity of fossils can be assessed, and its concordance with other assessments is fundamental to the validity of any particular potassium/argon date. Where it conflicts there is likely to be something wrong.

The KBS date conflicted with certain paleontological evidence, which cast doubt upon the 'Oldest Man' status of 1470. And naturally enough perhaps, the East Turkana research team was at first more concerned with defending the antiquity of the fossil than with objectively investigating the question of its age. Paleomagnetic determinations (relating the shifts of the earth's magnetic field as revealed by the magnetic properties of the rocks to a geochronological scale) were instigated[23] as counterargument and 1470 thereby acquired an age of close to three million years. But those of more open mind remained unconvinced. Opposition grew, especially among paleontologists familiar with the faunal evidence of the region. Eventually it became irresistible and the younger age of

1470 and the KBS tuff was reluctantly accepted – primarily because it conformed with the evidence of some fossil pigs.

In 1668 Robert Hooke, an English mathematician with an interest in how the world functioned, had suggested that fossils could be used to define a geological timetable 'and state the invervals of the times wherein . . . catastrophies and mutations have happened'.[24] In the early years of the nineteenth century William Smith, an English surveyor, confirmed Hooke's idea and in 1817 set down a basic tenet of paleontology with the observation that rocks containing the same kind of fossils are likely to be the same age. In 1973, Basil Cooke, a professor of geology in Canada, presented a report[25] on the fossil pigs of the Turkana basin which suggested, in effect, that if the 2.6 million year – or more – age proposed for the KBS tuff was correct, then the fundamentals of paleontology must be revised.

Cooke had studied the pig fossils from the Omo and East Turkana. The sites are only about 150 kilometres apart; the fossil fauna is generally similar, so it would be reasonable to expect that the sequence of fossils found in the beds at one site would be the same as the sequence found at the other. And indeed it was: Cooke was able to trace an identical line of evolutionary development in the pigs at both Omo and East Turkana. Now, according to William Smith and the precepts of paleontology, it should follow that identical ages could be attributed to the beds in which the identical fossils had been found.

But when he came to place the evolving pig lineages side by side on the scale of their radiometric dating, Cooke found that identical fossils seemed to differ substantially in age. For instance, the data on one of the pigs, *Mesochoerus*, suggested that the KBS tuff at East Turkana should be about the same age as the bed known as Member F at Omo, whereas the radiometric date said it was 600,000 years older. 'The discrepancy is considerable and cannot be ignored,' wrote Cooke.[26]

The implications of the discrepancy were serious. If the KBS tuff was 600,000 years younger than had been deduced from the Fitch and Miller age determinations, then everything dated in relation to it was that much younger too. The tools, for instance, were no older than those found at Olduvai, and 1470 was no longer the earliest specimen of the genus *Homo* but simply an extremely well preserved contemporary of *Homo habilis*.

Some responded to Cooke's findings, naturally enough with the suggestion that the Omo dating must be wrong. However, this was hard to support, since the Omo sequence is particularly well defined. Furthermore, both the potassium/argon dates and the fossil fauna (including the pigs) agree with the ages given for Olduvai Gorge, which are exemplary.

Leakey and his supporters soon realized that if their belief in the unique antiquity of 1470 and other finds associated with the KBS tuff was to stand, then the pigs had to be accommodated. Pig-proof helmets were an early suggestion that raised a laugh. Some mirth also greeted the more seriously intended suggestion that although the fossil pigs at first seemed 'an embarrassing discrepancy between geophysics and paleontology', they might turn out to be 'an exciting glimpse of the existence of prehistoric mosaics of spatial and ecological differentiation between the faunas of adjacent but environmentally contrasting regions'.[27]

In plain language the proposal here was that perhaps the Omo and East Turkana pigs had evolved quite independently and at different rates. Having inherited the identical evolutionary impetus from their common ancestor, the two populations were somehow completely isolated from one another and, for some reason, proceeded along their identical paths of evolutionary development at quite different rates. Thus, the idea went, the East Turkana pigs could have reached the *Mesochoerus* stage 600,000 years before their cousins 150 kilometres away at the Omo. This process would conveniently account for the age difference between identical specimens, but the barrier that kept the pigs apart for so long and evolving at such different rates was not so easily envisaged. The problem exercised the imaginations of several very earnest scientists. Islands were proposed, both acquatic and ecological, which arose very suddenly and trapped the East Turkana pigs in unique conditions that hastened their evolutionary development.

Though these attempts to explain the pigs' age discrepancy were not as frivolous as they may seem, Richard Leakey quickly realized that something more substantial was required. The 2.6 million year date for the KBS tuff had meanwhile received another blow from Dr Garniss Curtis at the University of California, Berkeley, a pioneer of the potassium/argon process whose tests on KBS samples confirmed Cooke's pronouncements and contested the findings of Fitch and Miller. Curtis dated the KBS tuff at 1.8 million years.[28]

While noting that critics of the East Turkana research team's age estimates were willing to believe a single report from Curtis before a whole series from Fitch and Miller, and were prepared to accept the word of one geologist, Basil Cooke, before that of an entire multi-disciplinary research team, Richard Leakey countered the attack on the dates he and his collaborators preferred with another, grander study of the fossil pigs of Africa. He hoped the results would prove Cooke wrong, he has said,[29] and the study was instigated with that objective in mind, but even it its results did dismiss the 2.6 million year or more estimate for the KBS tuff, he preferred to be proved wrong by his own efforts rather than by someone else's, he explains.[30]

The new study was undertaken by John Harris and Tim White (paleontologist and physical anthropologist respectively) and amounted to a complete review of all the fossil pigs from fifty African sites south of the Sahara.[31] They reduced the number of genera from twenty-three to seven and the number of species from seventy-seven to sixteen. They recognized the evolutionary trends shown especially well in some species, and confirmed the value of these fossils in correlating geological sequences such as Hooke, Smith and Cooke would have approved.

Then they applied their findings to the evidence of the Omo, East Turkana and Olduvai. The results confirmed all Cooke's conclusions. In their view as well as his, the pigs convincingly showed that the KBS tuff was 600,000 years older than the paleontological evidence implied. With particular reference to the implications of their findings on the study of fossil hominids, said Harris and White,[32] the pigs showed that 1470 was 'essentially' the same age as *Homo habilis* at Olduvai.

In the light of more age determinations from a number of laboratories involving a variety of methods, Richard Leakey now concedes that earlier pronouncements on the age of 1470 (and the other fossils dated by the KBS tuff) were wrong. He suggests 1.8 million years as the age of the tuff itself, and something between 1.8 and 2 million years as the age of 1470, which was found below it. But if the earlier estimates were wrong, what caused the error? Richard Leakey blames the dating procedures employed by Fitch and Miller;[33] Dr Fitch, on the other hand, wonders if the material his team dated was actually representative of the KBS tuff.[34] Repeated tests on the samples have confirmed the older dates, he says, suggesting to him that they may have been collected from a tuff thought to be part of the KBS, but actually part of an older level. Leakey and others deny this possibility, arguing that the KBS tuff is unmistakable.

This difference of opinion at least affirms that dating discrepancies are as likely to reflect errors of geology as of geochronology; and it under-lines, once again, the observation that accurate geological and strati-graphic determinations are crucial to the interpretation of fossil evidence. More fundamentally, the dating controversy shows that modern paleo-anthropologists are no less likely to cling to erroneous data that supports their preconceptions than were earlier investigators. Dubois and the 'Missing Link', Leakey and the 'Oldest Man' – both dismissed objective assessment in favour of the notions they wanted to believe.

The relevance of 1470 in the study of fossil man transcends the con-troversy about its age, and the significance of the East Turkana fossil

OVERLEAF *Four skulls illustrating Richard Leakey's view that three hominid lineages existed at East Turkana. They are:* Homo erectus (*left*), gracile Australopithecus (*2nd left*) *and* robus Australopithecus (*right, male – unbroken – and female*)

collection far exceeds the significance of the interpretations that Richard
Leakey imposes upon them. In ten years the research team has assembled
an extensive and diverse assortment of hominid (and other) fossils from a
known timespan – skulls, jaws, teeth, limb bones.[35] Many of the fossils
have already been described and discussed in various publications, but a
considerable amount of information remains to be gleaned from the
collection. Experts are presently compiling a series of monographs in
which the fossils and their significance will be comprehensively defined.[36]
As they appear these publications will become the basis of reference and
appraisal upon which the East Turkana project's contribution to science
may be judged. Five, ten, or even twenty years may pass before this
information is fully presented and assimilated.

Meanwhile, however, Richard Leakey himself has chosen to describe
1470 as a representative of the species *Homo habilis*. In November 1977
he appeared on the cover of *TIME* magazine.[37] Crouched beside him
in the photograph is an African member of his staff, discreetly naked but
for a rubber mask that is intended to resemble the physiognomy of *Homo
habilis*. In cover picture and content, the *TIME* story reveals the extent of
Richard Leakey's debt both to 1470 and to his father's beliefs. 1470
proves, says Leakey, that *Homo habilis* co-existed with *Australopithecus*
and was not its descendant. He believes three hominid lineages can be
distinguished among the East Turkana fossils: the robust australopithecines, the gracile australopithecines and *Homo* – the first two subsequently
suffering extinction, and the last two having diverged from their common
ancestor about six or seven million years ago.[38]

But to what extent does the East Turkana evidence substantiate
Richard Leakey's beliefs? If the measure is the degree to which Leakey's
interpretation of the evidence renders all others invalid, then the answer
must be not very much. Other authorities believe that the specimens
Leakey calls gracile australopithecines could just as well be females of the
Homo line, for instance; and the australopithecine attributes of 1470
could indicate much closer affinity between *Homo* and *Australopithecus*
than Leakey allows. So it seems that although Leakey uses the evidence
to support his belief in mankind's distant ancestry among several lines of
hominid evolution, the East Turkana fossils could support other beliefs
equally well. They could even support the directly opposing belief that
mankind is the direct descendent of *Australopithecus* on a single line of
hominid evolution. In this case it would be said that 1470, Richard
Leakey's most famous fossil, was not the 'Oldest Man' after all, but a
'link' between the *Australopithecus* and *Homo* stages of human evolution. This indeed is the view propounded by Donald Johanson.

Chapter Eleven

Australopithecus afarensis

(1978)

THE TALENTS and ambitions of Dr Donald Johanson, arguably today's leading proponent of the belief that mankind has but recently evolved from *Australopithecus*, contributed substantially to the success of international expeditions that between 1973 and 1977 found 250 hominid fossils in deposits exposed along the ravines and tributary valleys of the Hadar river in the Afar region of north eastern Ethiopia. More fossils might have been found in following years, but Ethiopia's internal strife so far has made further exploration impossible.

The Afar fossils are all about three million years old and the extraordinary variety of bones and teeth is said to represent a minimum of thirty-five and a maximum of sixty-five individuals. The most famous is called 'Lucy' and comprises roughly forty per cent of a complete skeleton. Another large collection of bones from a single site, known by its accession number 333 and sometimes referred to as 'The Family', includes a minimum of thirteen adults and juveniles. This is the first discovery of fossils that might represent a 'population' of early man.

In the first announcements of these remarkable discoveries, Johanson and his colleagues suggested there were three species of hominid among the Afar fossils: a small one which they thought might be *Australopithecus africanus*, a large one which could have been *Australopithecus robustus* and a third which they thought might represent *Homo*.[1] And of course *Homo* at three million years would also represent the 'Oldest Man'.

The fossil deposits of the Afar region were first noted by the French geologist Maurice Taieb in 1967, while he was working there on research for his doctoral dissertation. The Afar, a fractured depression in the earth's crust, is of great interest to geologists because it links the African Rift Valley to the rift systems of the Red Sea and the Gulf of Aden. It is known as a geological hotspot, and has supplied important information

on plate tectonics and the origins of the continents.

Part of the Afar depression is below sea level. Here and there hot sulphur springs bubble as active reminders of the earth's internal stirrings which about four million years ago caused lava to erupt from surface fissures and flooded basalt across the Afar. The basalt subsequently became the floor of a lake basin which in turn filled with the clays, sands, gravels and silts brought down by rivers and streams from the surrounding highlands. These sediments settled and consolidated on the lake beds at a rate of about one centimetre every ten years, filling the entire basin in the relatively short period of barely one million years, and presenting Taieb with a rugged terrain to explore in 1967. By then, of course, the sediments had been tilted and broken by geological faulting, and rivers had sliced through them. One such river is the Hadar which, as it carried the seasonal flood from the highland down to the larger Awash river, has gouged a meandering channel up to 140 metres deep through the sediments, exposing in its banks and ravines the fossilized remains of the many creatures that had lived and died on the shores on the ancient lake.

In 1971 Taieb and Johanson worked together on a joint French-American venture exploring the fossil deposits traversed by the Omo river in Southern Ethiopia. They talked of the Afar, and in 1972 Taieb took Johanson there to assess the paleontological potential of the region. It was a brief trip, squeezed between their commitments to that year's Omo expedition but, nonetheless, Johanson and Taieb found substantial quantities of splendidly preserved fossils of extinct animals suggesting the beds were up to three, and perhaps even four million years old – predating Olduvai Gorge and East Turkana and therefore a likely repository of fossils representing the earlier stages of mankind's evolution. Johanson realized immediately that the Afar presented a unique opportunity in the search for human origins. 'It was like a dream within reach,' he has said. He drew up plans with Taieb for a major research expedition to explore the region in 1973.

Don Johanson was born in Chicago in 1943; his parents were immigrants from Sweden. In 1966 he completed his undergraduate course with a distinction in anthropology and embarked upon a study of chimpanzee teeth for a master's degree. Simultaneously he began teaching anthropology and set his mind upon the search for early man as an ultimate ambition. 'But the fossil man game is like being an astronaut,' he recalls, 'there aren't many of them. Actually finding the fossils is only for very few, and when you're a graduate student in Chicago the prospect seems as far away as Jupiter.' And indeed, while Maurice Taieb was discovering the fossil beds of the Afar in 1967, Don Johanson was in Alaska, helping

Donald Johanson with co-workers and the entire Afar collection

to measure teeth for someone else's anthropological study. But fossils and human evolution drew closer. He undertook an *Odontological Study of the Chimpanzee with some Implications for Hominid Evolution* for his Ph.D and in 1970 was invited to join the Chicago group on that summer's Omo Research Expedition.

Johanson's job on the Omo expedition in 1970 (and again in 1971 and 1972) was paleontological excavation. He and his co-workers cleared up to eight metres of overburden from over 500 square metres of fossil-bearing deposits. Most of the excavations were inspired by the discovery of hominid fragments on the surface, but none fulfilled the initial promise. Of the 11,781 vertebrate fossils the Chicago team recorded,[2] fewer than forty were hominid. There was one mandible, one lower armbone, four matching skull fragments and twenty-four isolated teeth. Most of the Omo fossils, in fact, were of baboons, crocodiles and ruminants. Nonetheless, Johanson gained valuable experience in the Omo – and a valuable introduction to Maurice Taieb.

The first International Afar Research Expedition (IARE) under the joint leadership of Yves Coppens, Donald Johanson and Maurice Taieb began work in the late summer of 1973. At first it seemed destined to follow the familiar pattern – weeks of mapping geology and stratigraphy; collection and cataloguing of nearly 6000 fossils of some forty different vertebrate species – but no hominids, not even a single tooth. Until 30 October when, late in the afternoon as his party was completing the survey of a small gully, Johanson found four pieces of hominid leg bones, two of which belonged together and formed a perfect knee joint. The fossils came from deposits over three million years old. The individual of whom they formed a part had been a small adult, but unquestionably he or she had been fully capable of walking upright. Johanson had found the earliest conclusive evidence of mankind's bipedalism.

The promise of this discovery was confirmed the following year (1974). Within a week of the IARE establishing its camp on the banks of the Awash, Alemeyhu Asfaw (seconded from the Ethiopian Antiquities Department) found a fragment of hominid jawbone with two teeth still in place. The next day Alemeyhu found another, more complete specimen, and then another. And the day after that the site foreman, Melissa, found yet another. 'Unbelievable,' Johanson later reported, 'in three days, four hominid specimens, representing four individuals.'[3] The most remarkable of these was a palate with all sixteen teeth still in place. It was remarkable not only because of its splendid preservation, but also because of its combination of primitive and modern features. The front teeth were large relative to the back teeth, as in modern man; but there was a gap between the canines and the incisors, as in the apes, the teeth rows were parallel rather than curved and the palate was shallow – all primitive features reminiscent of the chimpanzee, in Johanson's view. He believed that such a combination of ape- and man-like features had not been encountered before and arranged to announce the discovery at a press conference in Abbis Ababa.

The fossils were introduced to representatives of the world press as 'an unparalleled breakthrough in the search for the origins of man's evolution. In a prepared statement the IARE team claimed: 'We have in a matter of merely two days extended our knowledge of the genus *Homo* by nearly 1.5 million years. All previous theories of the origins of the lineage which leads to modern man must now be totally revised. The genus *Homo* was walking, eating meat and probably using tools to kill animals' three to four million years ago and probably already had 'some kind of social cooperation and some sort of communication system', the statement declared.[4]

The Addis announcement read rather more into the evidence of one and a half palates, two half mandibles and a knee joint than most authorities were willing to accept; and the IARE's claim that they had discovered the Oldest Man was soon countered by Richard Leakey, who pointed out that evidence of a relatively large brain was required before fossils could be assigned to the genus *Homo*.

Johanson returned to the field. Around midday on 24 December he noticed a fragment of armbone poking from a slope he was casually exploring with a colleague, Tom Gray. At first sight it could have been a monkey bone but, though small, it lacked the characteristic bony flange of the comparable part of a monkey. 'My pulse was quickening,' Johanson writes, 'suddenly I found myself saying, "It's hominid" '; there were more fragments higher up on the slope and then: 'the realization struck us both that we might have found a skeleton. An extraordinary skeleton . . . The searing heat was forgotten. Tom and I yelled, hugged each other, and danced, mad as any Englishman in the midday sun.'[5]

The slope was sieved extensively during the following three weeks. Many more pieces of hominid bones were recovered, including skull fragments (but not enough to reconstruct a brain case), a mandible, most of a left and right arm, several vertebrae, a number of rib fragments, the sacrum, the left pelvic bone, the left thighbone and some pieces of the right lower leg. In all, about forty per cent of an entire skeleton. The form of the pelvic bones showed that the individual had been female, and erupted wisdom teeth suggested she had been about twenty years old, but the size of the thighbone made it clear that she had been very small –

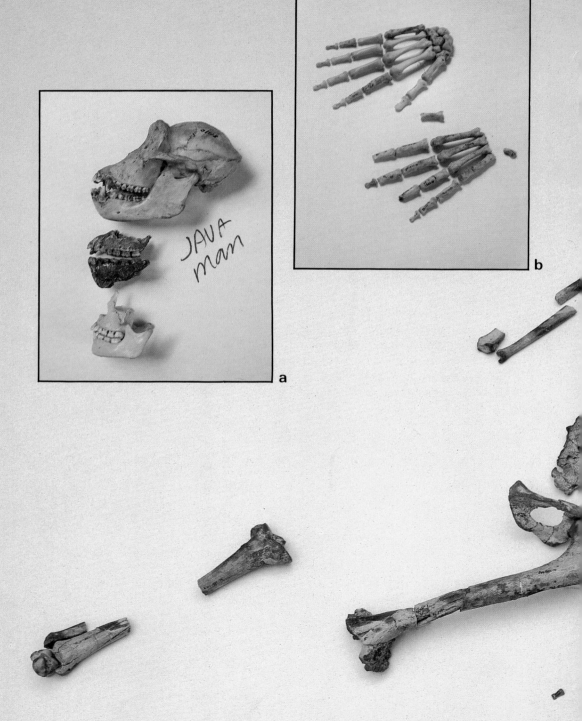

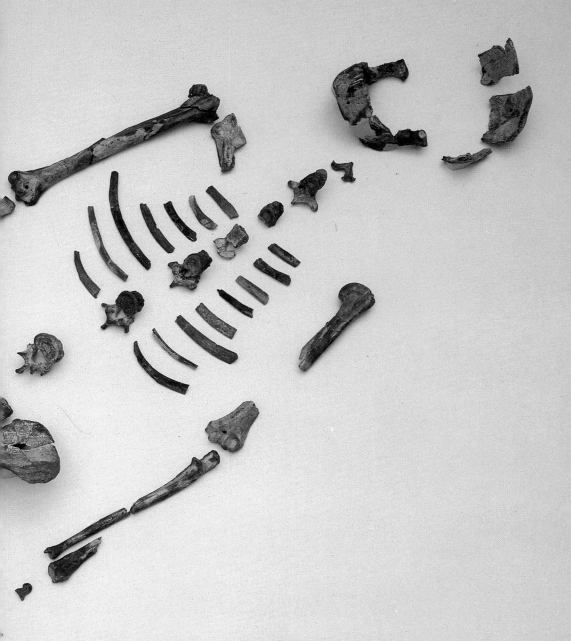

Lucy. INSET A): *Afar fossils (centre) show that the
3 million years old hominid face more closely resembled the
chimpanzee (above) than the modern human (below).*
INSET B): *these fossil handbones and modern human handbones
show that the Afar hominids were probably as dextrous as we are.*

no more than 122 centimetres tall, and perhaps as little as 107 centimetres.

The Afar skeleton features in the IARE field collection specimen list as: A.L. 288-1 Partial Skeleton. But this formal title only extends to the academic journals; everywhere else – in conversation and in print – the specimen is known as Lucy, from the Beatles' song 'Lucy in the Sky with Diamonds' which the camp tape recorder frequently broadcast across the Afar deposits. The song was first released in the 1960s just as pop and drugs began to pervade the public consciousness. Pop music mythology claims the Beatles wrote 'Lucy in the Sky with Diamonds' as an evocation of the highs they occasionally experienced: the initial letters of the title are said to refer to LSD. Johanson and the IARE could be said to have achieved a peak of paleoanthropological endeavour with their discoveries, so the name Lucy is not altogether inappropriate. But the name the Ethiopian workmen chose is a more respectful: 'Denkenesh – you are wonderful.'

Lucy was the star of a press conference held in Addis Ababa at the end of the 1974 season. But Johanson was cautious on the question of her attribution, saying only that she was either 'a small *Homo* or a small australopithecine', which inspired the *Washington Post*'s reporter the comment that Johanson's team 'refused deliberately to say that the skeleton belonged to the genus *Homo* . . . They are trying to avoid further controversy with Richard Leakey . . . who has contested their claims to have found specimens of early man in the absence of crania'.[6]

Given the success of the IARE in 1973 and 1974, the following year might have been expected to be an anti-climax; but in fact 1975 was no less successful. 'I felt I was moving through a dream,' Johanson recalls, 'each day produced more remains', including 'some of the oldest remains of the genus *Homo* ever unearthed. And not just a few fragments, but pieces enough to identify men, women and children – perhaps a family – who had died together three million years ago. The find was unprecedented – the earliest group of associated individuals ever found.'[7]

In all, the trove comprised 197 hominid fossils – jaws, teeth, leg bones, scores of hand and foot bones, vertebrae, ribs, adult skull fragments and part of an infant's skull. It was a disproportionate collection, but a minimum of thirteen individuals, young and old of both sexes, appeared to have been buried together at the site. Maurice Taieb speculated that they had died together too, perhaps caught in a flash flood while sleeping in a riverbed. This explanation has been repeated by Johanson on several occasions,[8] but it is not popular with other experts. Richard Leakey suggests the band may have succumbed to a particularly virulent disease;[9] Dr Alan Walker proposes a carnivore assemblage wherein the bones were remnants of a leopard's meals, perhaps, dropped from a tree into a waterhole below where they sank into the mud and were fossilized. But however the bones arrived where the IARE found them, Johanson was certain they represented the genus *Homo*, were over three million years old, and were conclusive evidence, therefore, of the 'Oldest Man'.

In a *National Geographic* article entitled *Ethiopia yields first 'family' of man*, Donald Johanson describes the Afar fossil hominids as 'discoveries that are writing new chapters in the annals of early man research'. He resigns Lucy to her australopithecine affinities, but quite unequivocally assigns the 'family' fossils to the genus *Homo*. And upon what evidence was his judgement based? Well, there was the dental evidence already noted, and in general the bones were larger than Lucy's, says Johanson, and there were features among them that were very much like *Homo*. The foot bones, for instance, closely resembled those of modern man, and the hand bones could be combined with modern bones to reconstruct a completely modern hand. Unhappily there were no skulls to provide the evidence of a relatively large brain that critics might call for; but among the Afar fossils Johanson did find a lower jaw that he was certain would fit 1470[10] – Leakey's claimant to the title of Oldest Man.

In 1974, while the IARE were still gathering their evidence of *Homo* in the Afar, apparent confirmation of the attribution came from a distant and perhaps unexpected source. During a Christmas picnic that year, Mary Leakey and her son, Philip, found a number of hominid fossils at Laetoli, the fossil beds near Olduvai she and Louis had visited many years before. The new fossils were from deposits over 3.5 million years old; they included several isolated teeth, a juvenile mandible and one adult mandible that bore a striking resemblance to the specimens found at Afar, 2000 kilometres away, and at least half a million years younger.

At an early opportunity Mary Leakey and Donald Johanson met to compare the Afar and Laetoli specimens side by side. Given the distance separating the fossils in both space and time their overall similarity was astonishing. Mary Leakey and Johanson agreed that among the larger specimens, *Homo* affinities were dominant. In her *Nature* report[11] on the Laetoli discoveries, Mary Leakey writes: 'preliminary assessment . . . suggests placement of the Laetoli specimens among the earliest dated members of this genus'. Some critics preferred to emphasize the specimens' australopithecine affinities (which undeniably are present), but Mary Leakey argues that since *Australopithecus* became extinct while *Homo* survives, any fossils with distinct *Homo* features must be assigned to the surviving lineage – *Homo*. The inference, of course, is that the Laetoli specimens represent the 'oldest man'.

Because Mary Leakey considers herself an archaeologist and not qualified to write the formal description of fossils for publication, she asked Tim
White, a physical anthropologist who had worked at Laetoli, to undertake
the task. White knew Johanson, who was then similarly engaged with
the description of the Afar material. Because of the general similarity
between the two collections some discussion between White and Johanson was obviously helpful to both, and perhaps rendered it inevitable
that the Laetoli and Afar fossils were subsequently grouped together in a
publication[12] which assigned all the material to a new hominid species.

When she invited White to describe the Laetoli material, Mary Leakey
was confident there were two species to be named. The Laetoli specimens
were all *Homo* in her view, and even her critics seemed to agree that the
large and small specimens from Afar must represent two distinct species.
However, when Johanson, White and their French associate, Yves
Coppens, began to analyse the fossils and compare them with other
collections they found themselves forced to reject conclusions that had
previously seemed obvious in favour of 'exciting new possibilities', as
Johanson has written in a popular report.[13] To cite one among several
points: although Lucy was small enough to be a representative of the
Australopithecus africanus, equally small individuals among the 'family'
would stand out as anomalies if she were. Clearly it was unlikely that two

ABOVE *A juvenile mandible found at Laetoli by Mary Leakey
in 1974. Note the emergent permanent teeth.*

distinct species would have existed within the confines of one family group. The anomaly disappeared, however, when Johanson, White and Coppens concluded from their analytical studies that only one species had existed at Afar and at Laetoli. The individuals from both sites were morphologically identical, they said, and the size variation was due entirely to sexual dimorphism – very large males and very small females – within a single species. But the degree of sexual dimorphism seemed quite exceptional, remarked other commentators; how could it be explained?

In living primates sexual dimorphism is least among the smallest species and most among the largest – which is the gorilla. The Afar hominids were demonstrably smaller than the larger living primates, yet their sexual dimorphism as proposed by Johanson and White appeared to exceed that of the gorilla – a point raised at an informal seminar in Nairobi when White presented the conclusions of the IARE studies to members of the East Turkana Research Project.

'If the degree of sexual dimorphism is outside the modern range, then you must justify your reasoning,' Dr Alan Walker, anatomist, observed.

'It's simplest to have only one species in the family collection, so . . .' began Dr White in reply.

'Numerical simplicity is not necessarily the truth,' interjected Dr Walker.

'Have you done sufficient study and measurements to convince us?' asked Richard Leakey.

'Our scheme elucidates . . .' continued Dr White.

'Obscures!' put in Dr Andrew Hill, paleontologist.

'We recognize a significant . . .' persisted Dr White.

'How do you know it's significant if you haven't quantified.'

'From my experience!'

'You need to be just a little more precise . . .'

'It's my feeling that you are guilty of imposing what you think is right upon the fossils,' said Richard Leakey.

'It might be nice to put the numbers down,' suggested Dr Walker.

'Sure!' retorted Dr White, 'there'll be someone with red-hot water-cooled calipers to provide the measurements you want, but we're trying to understand the evolution and biology – not just catalogue the fossils.'

'Well, we think the chances are that you've got it wrong,' said Richard Leakey.'[14]

In their understanding of the evolutionary significance of the Afar and Laetoli fossils, Johanson and White concluded that the blend of *Homo* and *Australopithecus* they found within the single species must imply that it had been ancestral to both – so, what should it be called? At the generic level they might have been inclined to call it *Homo*, given Johanson's oft-stated predisposition and Mary Leakey's preference. But there was no evidence of the relatively large brain that distinguishes the genus *Homo*, while the fossils did have many characteristics in common with the gracile australopithecines.

The evidence, they concluded, demanded attribution to the genus *Australopithecus*. At the specific level, they felt several features (the more primitive teeth, for instance) merited distinction from the known species of *Australopithecus*, so they created a new one for their fossils – *Australopithecus afarensis*.[15] As type specimen of the new species Johanson and White chose the adult mandible from Laetoli (which, though less well preserved than a similar specimen from Afar, had already been described and published[16] by White), and thus *Australopithecus afarensis* acquired a maximum age of about 3.7 million years.

The evolutionary scheme that Johanson and White presented with the new species is a single, straight and slender stem with *Australopithecus afarensis* at the bottom and *Homo sapiens* at the top. One short truncated branch is provided along which *Australopithecus africanus* evolved from the main stem into *Australopithecus robustus* and subsequent extinction. Johanson and White believe that *Australopithecus* was the only hominid line for a very long time, from which the *africanus* stock diverged about 2.5 million years ago, while the genus *Homo* arose even more recently with the advent of *Homo habilis* about 1.9 million years ago. The new scheme, though simple, is all-embracing. Within it, *Australopithecus afarensis* becomes not just the ancestor of mankind and *Australopithecus*, but also of virtually every hominid fossil ever found. *Homo* and *Australopithecus*; *africanus* and *robustus*; *habilis*, *erectus* and *sapiens*, all owe their origin to *Australopithecus afarensis*. Including, of course, the most important example of large-brained *Homo habilis*: 1470.

'Yippee,' wrote White to Johanson with the final draft of their *afarensis* manuscript, 'tell them to start up their armchairs and fasten their seat-belts. We're on our way!' This exhortation referred to members of the scientific community who White felt were likely to question the validity of the new species.

Australopithecus afarensis was the first new hominid species to be created around original fossils since Louis Leakey had named *Homo habilis* fourteen years before; Johanson and White gave careful thought to the question of where and how it should be announced. For a while Johanson favoured a carefully coordinated press campaign, but in the end he reserved the announcement for the occasion of a Nobel Symposium on Early Man held in Sweden under the auspices of the Royal Swedish Academy during May 1978, and *Australopithecus afarensis* remained a close secret until Johanson read his paper. The new species was hardly better known when he had finished. The paper was long and not easily followed; its import probably escaped most of the audience. The invited authorities on early man noticed *afarensis*, of course, but their response was not clamorous. As the assembly adjourned for tea Richard Leakey remarked that he did not like it very much, and Phillip Tobias suggested that perhaps sub-specific distinction would have been adequate – something like *Australopithecus africanus tanzanensis* ... Subsequently, however, response to the new species was considerable and sustained. Comment was favourable at the popular level – where *afarensis* has inspired a book, a television 'special', as well as several articles – but less favourable within the science.

Apart from quibbles about taxonomy and the flouting of convention[17] that seem to greet every new species, the scientific criticism centred around two points: firstly, the validity of grouping the Afar and Laetoli material together as one species – were there not at least two species among them? ask critics. And secondly, the question of whether or not the material was distinctive enough to justify a new species – could it not have been assigned to an existing species of *Homo* or *Australopithecus*?

After due consideration Phillip Tobias, for one, concluded that *Australopithecus afarensis* was invalid on both counts.[18] At least fifteen cranial, mandibular and dental features that Johanson *et al* had cited as diagnostic of the new species were also present in *Australopithecus africanus*, he told a meeting of the Royal Society in March 1980, and therefore were not diagnostic at all. *Australopithecus afarensis* should be formally suppressed, Tobias demanded, and the fossils re-named with no more than sub-specific distinction based on geographic distribution: *Australopithecus africanus ethiopicus* for the Afar fossils, and *Australopithecus africanus tanzanensis* for the Laetoli specimens. In the ensuing discussion, however, Tobias was reminded that the International Code of Zoological Nomenclature prohibited such suppression. Once in existence, *Australopithecus afarensis* could not be simply wished away.

Mary Leakey's reaction to the new species was restrained on the whole. She did not agree with it, and when told that the published announcement would include her name among its authors she demanded that it be removed. She reiterated her conviction that the Laetoli fossils and the large specimens from Afar should be assigned to *Homo*, but commended Tobias' 'expostulation' at the Royal Society despite his affection for *Australopithecus*. In her own address she expressed deep regret that 'the Laetoli fellow was now doomed to be called *Australopithecus afarensis*'.

Richard Leakey did not agree with the new species either. With Alan Walker he attacked the Johanson and White scheme on phylogenetic grounds,[19] and in his personal capacity insisted that Johanson had been correct in his very first interpretation of the fossils and should not have changed his mind.[20] There were two distinct species among the Afar and Laetoli collections, he said, one of them an ancestor of *Homo* and the other an ancestor of *Australopithecus*. Which in Leakey's view proved that the two hominid lineages had co-existed in the Afar basin three million years ago, just as they had at East Turkana one and a half million years ago. Richard Leakey, in fact, regarded the evidence of Johanson's Afar fossils as proof of his belief that *Homo* and *Australopithecus* are no more closely related than cousins who shared an ancestor in the very distant past – some six or seven million years ago.[21]

Just as Leakey's fossils from East Turkana could support Johanson's belief that mankind had recently evolved from *Australopithecus*, so Johanson's fossils from the Afar could support Leakey's belief that *Homo* and *Australopithecus* had been distinct lineages for a very long time. Each, it appears, had found the evidence to substantiate the other's theory. The fact that the evidence could sustain alternative interpretations raises another point: where could the science stand today if, for argument's sake, Leakey had worked at Afar as well as East Turkana? Or if Johanson had likewise worked at both sites? With the same fossils to hand, one or other of them presumably would claim his beliefs doubly affirmed, and the quantitative value of the fossils from two widely separated sites might persuade many that the evidence substantiated those beliefs.

For the time being, the ambiguous nature of fossil evidence obliges paleoanthropologists to pursue the truth mainly by hypothesis and speculation. And in a science powered by individual ambitions and so susceptible to preconceived beliefs, interpretations are bound to differ whenever the evidence is sufficiently ambiguous. The *afarensis* affair, and the opposing views of Leakey and Johanson concerning the status of *Australopithecus*, are classic examples. There have been – and presumably will be – many more such differing interpretations; and they persist until some new evidence or new procedure resolves the ambiguity.

Jaws, palates and teeth from the Afar

Chapter Twelve

Footprints

WHATEVER ITS ambiguities, the evidence from Afar, East Turkana and Laetoli tidily confirmed the hypothesis that hominids had stood up and walked erect long before the brain achieved any great size.[1] Just when brain expansion began, and what its precise significance was during the early stages of man's evolution from the ancestor he shares with the apes, were matters of speculation, though the majority had long believed that bipedalism came first. Now this was confirmed. The new evidence showed that while the brain of *Australopithecus afarensis* was barely larger than that of an ape of comparable body size (a chimpanzee, for example), the creature was fully capable of walking upright. Thus, if *Australopithecus afarensis* represented the ancestor of man, the habitual bipedal gait assuredly had preceded brain expansion in man's divergence from the common ancestor. It would seem that contrary to the assertions of Sir Grafton Elliot Smith and others, it was not the brain, but the feet which had led the way after all.

Of course, since the theory of evolution was first propounded it has often been claimed that man's bipedal gait was an early acquisition. In the eighteenth century Jacob Bontius, a Dutch doctor living in Java, even credited the orang utan with this peculiarly human trait. These creatures, he observed, 'generally walk upright and behave much like other people'. And, as we have seen, the name *Pithecanthropus erectus* reflects Dubois' belief that the Java Man he discovered in 1891 had stood erect. Similarly, in 1925 Raymond Dart deduced from the evidence of the Taung skull that *Australopithecus* was capable of erect posture and bipedal gait; and in the 1930s and 1940s Robert Broom found fossils which, he claimed, fully confirmed Dart's deduction. Peking Man and his relations from Java were eventually named *Homo erectus*. In 1960 Louis Leakey claimed that *Zinjanthropus* possibly held his head 'even more erect than in man's carriage today'[2] and in 1964 the *Homo habilis* foot bones from Olduvai Gorge were said to possess 'most of the specializations associated with the plantigrade propulsive feet of modern man'.[3]

But while these assertions may have reflected a common belief that the early ancestors of mankind had been able to stand erect and move about on two legs, the belief was not unqualified. A curious reluctance to believe in the *perfection* of early man's bipedal gait persisted for a long time. For many years the misinterpretation of Neanderthal Man's arthritis, for example, contributed to the idea that although early man may have walked upright, he could do so only in a shambling bow-legged fashion. This view was reinforced by the pronouncements of Boule and Elliot Smith, and without evidence to contradict the eminent gentlemen such notions became points of faith to their followers. Even the skeletal remains found by Robert Broom brought no complete change of attitude. The trouble with Broom's fossils was that although their overall appearance indicated an upright stance and bipedal gait, the detail was uncertain, lost in the peculiarities and the distortions of the fragmented fossils. And where the evidence was uncertain, even scientists appeared predisposed to believe that the mode of locomotion was not entirely human. In reviewing the evidence of the South African fossils the anatomist Wilfred le Gros Clark, for instance, concluded that erect bipedalism in the australopithecines 'had not been developed to the perfection shown in *Homo sapiens*'.[4]

The *Homo habilis* leg and foot bones were much more complete than the evidence Broom had offered, but even they were said to be less than adequate to propel their owner in a fully modern human manner. The structure of the *habilis* foot fell somewhere between that of man and gorilla in its weight-bearing capabilities, the preliminary report said, and certain peculiarities of the ankle bone in particular suggested that 'the unique striding gait of *Homo sapiens* had not yet been achieved'.[5] The size and shape – the form – of the Olduvai ankle bone was subsequently compared with 131 other human, ape and fossil ankle bones in an exhaustive study which took the measurements of seven angles and indexes of functional significance, combined them in a computer and analysed the results. This study[6] was a notable example of the then popular canonical analysis, a multivariate statistical technique exploiting recent advances in computer technology. Its results precisely confirmed the earlier conclusions based solely on personal experience and contemplation of the evidence: 'whilst the Olduvai Hominid 8 foot is the foot of a biped,' the new report said, 'the striding gait of modern man had not yet been achieved'. Meanwhile, another anatomist was analysing the 'functional implications' of the *habilis* leg bones. The tibia and fibula (the lower leg bones) were preserved and, although the upper parts were missing, the evidence of the remainder – the 'robusticity factor' for example – suggested that the adaptation to bipedalism was well advanced at the ankle, but less so at the knee. This study also concluded that 'while the fossil form was clearly a habitually bipedal plantigrade primate, its gait may well have differed considerably from that of modern man.'[7]

These conclusions on the bipedal status of Homo habilis echo views expressed by Wilfred le Gros Clark, who believed that as the ancestor of mankind had evolved from quadruped to biped, the adaptation would have commenced at the foot and ended at the hip[8] – so that fossils representing an intermediate stage of mankind's evolution could be expected to demonstrate intermediate adaptation to bipedalism. And Homo habilis, therefore, could be expected to have stood with ankles 'somewhat flexed, suggesting a rather bent-kneed posture' as one authority surmised.[9]

But if early man did not employ the bipedal plantigrade propulsive gait of modern man, how did he walk? The fossils themselves could not provide the answer to this question for, although measurement and comparative analysis could indicate competence in certain known functions, they could not define a completely unknown function – even where scientists may have believed the fossils were capable of performing one.

Pondering the nature of this unknown function, Professor Sherwood Washburn has suggested that perhaps the ancestors of mankind *ran* on two legs before they were able to walk easily that way, and subsequently acquired the efficient bipedal striding gait only in response to a need to cover long distances.[10] And Richard Leakey has envisaged that 'several methods of bipedalism' besides the modern variety must have evolved. He does not define them however, and confines them to Australopithecus[11] who, he believes, employed 'a locomotor pattern unique and distinctive' to himself during the lower Pleistocene times while the true ancestors of mankind were already as fully upright and bipedal as Homo sapiens.[12]

In the absence of conclusive evidence speculation on the nature of early man's gait proliferated, but it was halted by new evidence of an unusual but wholly appropriate kind – evidence of function rather than form: fossil footprints rather than fossil feet or legs. These earliest known footprints of man were discovered in 1977 during the course of Mary Leakey's expedition to Laetoli in search of more fossils. Natural erosion had exposed a trail of five prints set in a cement-like volcanic tuff laid down at least 3.6 million years ago. The trail was not as clear and conclusive as it might have been. Only two prints were fully exposed and some experts argued that they were not hominid prints at all. Mary Leakey herself was '75% certain' they represented the tracks of mankind's

Footprints fossilized in a 3.6 million-year-old surface at Laetoli. First recognized in 1977, two prints (lower centre) were believed to be hominid. Elephant, and small mammal prints also can be distinguished.

earliest ancestor; but by emphasizing the non-human quality of the ancestor's stance and stride, announcements of her discovery demonstrated a continuing reluctance to accept the antiquity of bipedalism. TIME, for example, reported that the creature 'probably walked with what Leakey calls "a slow rolling gait", like a chimpanzee's.'[13]

But while one group of experts sought to deduce the gait of early man from the logic of evolutionary theory, and another from the evidence of fossils, yet a third approached the subject from a related but essentially different direction – biomechanics, a discipline which attempts to assess the limits and potential of the skeletal frame and musculature and define the mechanical requirements of movement and locomotion. And here the work of an American anatomist and anthropologist, Owen Lovejoy, is especially relevant.

Early in his career Lovejoy worked on the excavation of an Amerindian (American Indian) burial site about 1000 years old, and the study of the skeletons that were recovered there has been an important component of his researches ever since. The collection is unique. It represents over 1300 individuals and spans burials during a period of between 200 and 250 years. The remains of males and females of all ages are preserved, including several foetuses, one of which fits on the palm of the hand. Some skeletons demonstrate strange physical deformities, others appear to exceed the 'normal' limits of the human form. In all, the collection presents a convincing example of the extraordinary degree of variation to which the human skeletal frame is susceptible; in particular it shows very clearly that living bone is a plastic material which can be moulded to suit the demands of behaviour and anatomy. Where anatomy is normal and behaviour is not unusually demanding, the skeletal frame functions in a consistent manner, subject only to the variations of size and muscular development. But disease or broken or distorted bones may force the skeletal frame to function quite differently; and the bones may assume unusual shapes as they grow and are moulded to suit the abnormal function. Thus, although the style and mechanics of man's movement and locomotion are potentially consistent throughout the species, the detail may vary considerably and morphological variations in the form of the bones are not necessarily indicative of functional variation. Nor are they necessarily indicative of taxonomic distinction. The Amerindian collection on which Lovejoy works undoubtedly represents a population belonging to the species *Homo sapiens*, yet it includes many unusual bones that probably would have been assigned to a different species, or even a different genus, if they had been discovered as individual fossils.

This apparent contradiction between conclusion and known fact lies close to Lovejoy's belief that shape and form are not enough to reconstruct the pattern of function. Isolated features of the components vary much more in their shape and size, he says, than does the function they perform. Feet, ankles, shin bones, knees, thigh bones, hip joints, and pelvises may vary enormously, together and individually, but whether the variation actually prevents the body they support from walking with the bipedal propulsive plantigrade gait of *Homo sapiens* is another question. And to find the answer Lovejoy and his associates have sought to place the fossil evidence of the early hominids' lower limbs in their biomechanical perspective, seeking to discover not how closely they resemble the *form* of modern man, but rather to what extent they were capable of performing the *function* of walking like him.

The answer, to summarize the published results,[14] is that the early hominids were probably better adapted to bipedalism than modern man. The biomechanical pattern of their lower limb skeleton differs in one significant respect: the articular ball of the hip joint in *Australopithecus* exerts only half the pressure on the joint that was the average for the *Homo sapiens* sample. This is a considerable mechanical advantage reflecting the manner in which body weight and the stresses of bipedal locomotion are distributed in the australopithecine pelvis. The distance of the hip joint from the centre of gravity is the most important feature, and in *Australopithecus* the distance is such that it permits a smaller femoral head (the ball of the hip joint) than in *Homo*, and a longer femoral neck (the extension at the top of the thigh bone which carries the femoral head) which in turn provides a more efficient lever arm for the muscles that operate the hip joint. Both the small femoral head and the longer femoral neck of *Australopithecus* have been cited as evidence that the physical form of *Australopithecus* was not fully adapted to the upright bipedal gait. Lovejoy's work now shows that these features were integral components of a pelvic structure that was stronger and functionally more efficient than the pelvis of modern man. But if our ancestors really were more advantageously adapted to bipedalism, how did we lose the advantage? According to Lovejoy the regression of bipedal efficiency was inevitably combined with the advance of the other most critical factor in mankind's evolution – the development of a large brain.

As the brain and the innovative processes it inspired (the manufacture of stone tools perhaps) brought survival advantages to those best able to use it, enlargement of the brain through successive generations was constrained only by the size of the pelvic opening – the birth canal. Clearly there would have been immediate natural selection against the combination of large-brained infant and small birth canal (both mother and child would have died during birth), and in favour of females with large birth canals through which large-brained offspring could pass into the world. For a time the progressive enlargement of the brain could have been accommodated by a progressive broadening of the hips, but there is a limit to the total pelvic breadth that can be maintained in a biped of any given stature, beyond which rapid locomotion becomes awkward and striding efficiency is lost, says Lovejoy.[15] So as babies with increasingly large heads were conceived, their birth was most satisfactory – both in terms of maternal ease and species evolution – where the size of the birth canal had increased while the overall breadth of the pelvis remained unchanged. This adjustment could only be achieved by the shortening of the femoral neck, thus disturbing the structural and mechanical efficiency of the pelvis, doubling the weight stress on the articular ball of the hip joint and rendering modern man less favourably adapted to bipedalism than his ancestors.

The large brain may have become the survival tool of the species, but far from leading the way to our present status as many surmised, its development actually appears to have compromised our earlier and more fundamental evolutionary asset – the habitual upright stance and striding bipedal gait. The compromise is evident in several aspects of modern life: the greater incidence of hip joint failure in women than men demonstrates their closer proximity to the limits of pelvic structural and functional capability. By comparison with the foetal development of other mammals the human infant is born six months earlier than it should be so that the relatively large head may pass through the birth canal. Even so, the head is severely squashed during birth, and the bones of the skull may overlap as it is squeezed through the pelvic opening. And of course many difficult births, especially among those achieved by Caesarian section or with the aid of forceps, are instances of the evolutionary conflict between brain size and bipedalism that natural selection would resolve more drastically in the absence of modern medical practice.

Lovejoy investigated the biomechanics of the lower limb in the early 1970s, at a time when the available fossil evidence was limited to specimens from South Africa and Olduvai Gorge. His hypothesis was essentially complete by 1973 when, in March, Richard Leakey announced the discovery at East Turkana of an almost complete fossil left leg[16] and, in October, Donald Johanson found the knee joint at Afar. The anatomical evidence of the 1.8 million-year-old East Turkana fossils and the three million-year-old specimen from Afar supported Lovejoy's biomechanical deductions, but it was equivocal. The evidence undoubtedly proved that hominids had walked erect at those times, but Richard Leakey, for

The hominid trail uncovered by Mary Leakey at Laetoli in 1978–9 offered proof that mankind has walked bipedally for at least 3.6 million years.

instance, claimed the East Turkana specimens were proof that only the ancestor of man 'walked erect as his normal mode of locomotion'. *Australopithecus* had walked differently, he said, its longer femoral neck implying that although the creature was capable of walking upright, it did so only for short periods.[17] Leakey's assertion of course underlines the inadequacy of fossil *form* as conclusive evidence of bipedalism. Proof of Lovejoy's assertion concerning biomechanical *function* was ultimately supplied by the fossil footprints discovered by Mary Leakey's Laetoli expedition – not so much by the trail already mentioned, as by another uncovered in 1978 which inspired Mary Leakey to ask on one occasion: 'Now who needs fossil bones to substantiate bipedalism? They're superfluous. Absolutely superfluous.'

The preservation of fossil prints at Laetoli has been attributed to an unusual and possibly unique combination of climatic, volcanic and

mineralogic conditions.[18] Not less than 3.6 million years ago a series of
light ash eruptions from a volcano called Sadiman coincided with a
series of rain showers, probably at the onset of the rainy season. The
eruptions contained a significant amount of natrocarbonatite, which
yielded carbonate on contact with the rain. This substance then cemented
the ash layer quite solidly as it dried in the sun. Evidently a profusion of
animals crossed the ash layers while they were still wet, leaving their
tracks to be preserved and then protected by further showers of ash and
rain. The succession of showers created at least six distinct surfaces on
which prints are preserved; all together they are no more than 15.6 centimetres thick. Raindrops are clearly defined on some surfaces, hare prints
are present on virtually all of them, guinea fowl prints are numerous, so
too are small antelopes and gazelles. In all, over twenty different animals
have been identified, including giraffe, elephant, rhinoceros, pig, hyena,
baboon, the three-toed horse and, of course, bipedal hominids.

The fossil footprints at Laetoli were not recognized until the end of
Mary Leakey's 1976 expedition, even though scientists and research
workers had regularly walked across some of them on their way to and
from the fossil beds during two full seasons. But, of course, those expeditions were inspired by the hominid fossil discoveries mentioned in
chapter 11, and the participants were intent on looking for fossils and
defining the geology and stratigraphy of the region. The fossil beds were
dated at between 3.59 and 3.77 million years during that time; a good
collection of vertebrate fossils was assembled, but hominids were few.
Some mandibular fragments and isolated teeth were found in 1975, and
fragments of a juvenile skeleton in 1976 – but that was all. After a
promising start it seemed as though the Laetoli potential was exhausted.
The deposit in which the fossils are preserved is extremely hard, and
specimens that do erode from it are often fragmented by the sun and rain –
especially the delicate hominid fossils. But, as already noted, the beds
were uniquely suited to the preservation of footprints.

In a manner which matches the fortuity, if not the consequence, of
Archimedes' bath and Newton's apple, the fossil footprints were
eventually noticed one evening in September 1976 by Dr Andrew Hill,
paleontologist, who fell while avoiding a ball of elephant dung hurled
at him by Dr David Western, ecologist. The two gentlemen were paying a
visit to the Laetoli camp at the end of the season; their walk that sunny
evening took them along a dried river bed in which an expanse of solidified
fine-grained volcanic tuff was exposed. Elephants apparently frequented
the area, and the ecologist's familiarity with the evidence of their passing
thus lent a new angle to the paleontologist's eye. While on his knees

Dr Hill noticed a curious spattering of tiny indentations in the flat grey surface. These were later identified as raindrop prints but, having attracted his attention that day, they led Dr Hill to examine the surface and other indentations very closely. Among them he recognized a quite unmistakable series of animal tracks.

Thereafter, Dr Hill's fortuitous fall imposed a new outlook upon the Laetoli expeditions. During the final weeks of the 1976 season, footprints of birds and mammals ranging from elephant and rhinoceros to carnivores and hares were identified. In 1977 and 1978 seven sites were found where the footprint-bearing surfaces were well exposed by natural erosion and weathering. Mammal and bird prints occurred everywhere, including the first inconclusive hominid trail (which actually was close to where Dr Hill had suffered his fall), and another, undeniably hominid trail which was uncovered in 1978 and 1979.

The latter discovery comprised not just one, but two trails. The first evidence of them was found in July 1978 when a geologist, Dr Paul Abell, noticed a hominid heel print at the broken edge of an erosion gully. Skilful excavations that season and the following year uncovered two trails nearly fifty metres long, transected by other mammalian trails, fractured by subsidence here and there, but traceable throughout. The trails are parallel and about twenty-five centimetres apart – too close for the individuals to have been walking abreast. In any case, there is a noticeable difference in the clarity and condition of the two trails which suggests that the individuals had crossed the ash at different times as it was drying. The prints of one trail are smaller and more splayed than the other; at one point the smaller individual seems to have paused and made a half turn to the left. Where the trail is exceptionally well preserved, yet another series of hominid prints seems to be set in those of the larger trail, as though a third individual had walked in the other's footsteps.

The Laetoli footprints are entirely human. Unlike the form of the ape footprint, they show a well-developed arch to the foot and no divergence of the big toe. The size of the feet and stride suggests the larger individual stood about 140 centimetres tall, and the smaller about 120 centimetres. They were slight figures in the ancient landscape, but whether they be called *Australopithecus* or *Homo*, there can be no doubt that the Laetoli hominids had already acquired the habitual, upright, bipedal, free-striding gait of modern man three million six hundred thousand years ago. The hypothesis of bipedal precedence was confirmed. No one could argue against the Laetoli evidence of function quite as easily as they had against the evidence of fossil form. But while the footprints thus confirmed one hypothesis, by the nature of paleoanthropological enquiry they

OVERLEAF *Two individuals made the Laetoli hominid trails (and there is a suggestion that a third had walked in the footsteps of the larger individual), while an extinct form of horse (hipparion) made the trail running from lower right to upper left.*

immediately began to spawn more, as scientists used the new evidence to explain other outstanding problems. One such hypothesis, published by Dr R. J. Clarke,[19] concerns the kind of fossils paleoanthropologists should expect to find as they trace the human lineage five, ten, fifteen million years back towards its divergence from the ancestor man has in common with the apes.

The human-like characteristics of the Laetoli footprints imply that hominids acquired the bipedal gait considerably more than 3.6 million years ago, says Clarke. Yet the Afar fossils show that a small-brained hominid with some ape-like cranial features was still living three million years ago. So that if bipedalism had developed while wholly ape-like features were retained, the very earliest ancestors of mankind are likely to have been creatures whose skulls would merit classification as apes while their feet could have belonged to a hominid, says Dr Clarke. And if so, sorting the ape and the human ancestor from among the fossil remains of primates that existed as the human and ape lineages diverged is likely to be very difficult. As perhaps is demonstrated by the controversy surrounding the status of *Ramapithecus*, suggests Dr Clarke.[20]

Remains of the ramapithecids have been found in deposits seven to at least fourteen million years old in India, Pakistan, Kenya, Turkey and Greece (see map pp. 266–7). For many years the remains known to science consisted of a few jaw fragments and a few teeth. Some scientists claimed that *Ramapithecus* was an ancestor of man on the grounds that the teeth and jaws were more hominid- than ape-like;[21] other scientists disagreed. In 1977, some fragmentary skeletal remains were found in Pakistan but they did not clarify the issue. The bones seemed more suited to an arboreal existence[22] than to either the knuckle-walking habit of the African apes or to the bipedalism of man. And then, in 1979, a ramapithecid skull was found in Pakistan, comprising jaws, face, part of the forehead and jaw joint. The back teeth were no less man-like than the previously known specimens, but the canines and incisors were more ape-like, and the skull could sustain at least two interpretations of its status. There was a strong resemblance to the orang utan, for example, suggesting some evolutionary link in that direction. But relevant affinities with *Australopithecus* and *Homo* were also discernible, suggesting the creature could have been ancestral to man.

On present evidence the ramapithecids are an enigma. Dr David Pilbeam concludes that although *Ramapithecus* could represent the ancestor of man alone, the truth is unlikely to be so simple. The ramapithecids could equally well represent the ancestor of all the modern apes (African and Asian) and humans, he says, or they could be ancestral to just the African apes and humans, or to just the apes alone.[23]

So it now seems that although scientists had long believed that the clues to the evolution of man will be found most readily in the fossil skulls and teeth of his ancestors, the tenet does not apply to the earliest stages of human evolution. The evidence of *Ramapithecus* implies that it will be extremely difficult to identify the human ancestor from skulls and teeth alone. And Dr Clarke's hypothesis suggests that on the evidence of the Laetoli footprints, paleoanthropologists 'should be looking not to the head but to the feet and legs for the earliest indications of hominid status.'[24]

The 3.6 million year old footprints at Laetoli have also called into question another long-cherished belief – namely that of the role culture has played in the evolution of man. Ever since Darwin commentators have supposed that once man's hands were free to develop manipulative skills, stone tools would have been an immediate consequence of bipedalism (immediate on the evolutionary scale, that is). It was said that tools were probably a critical factor in the initial divergence of the hominid line from the ancestral stock of man and ape. Yet although hominids were bipedal and free to develop manipulative skills at Laetoli 3.6 million years ago not a single artefact or introduced stone has been found anywhere among the eighty square kilometre deposits. The earliest tools known to date are about two million years old. Hominids, it seems, were walking erect with their hands free for at least 1.6 million years before the advent of stone tools. For the greater part of our evolutionary history the human ancestor was no more advantageously endowed to cope with the vagaries of nature than any other creature.

We can conclude from this that for millions of years the combination of zoological inheritance and environmental circumstance was quite enough to ensure the survival of those small, lightly-built animals of erect posture. Then some among their number perceived the value of the cutting edge and discovered how to reproduce the rare accident that created it. They began making stone tools. That event marked the beginning of culture – no less a product of inheritance and circumstance than any other development in the three thousand million years that life has existed on earth, but one that distinguishes man from every other creature and has brought radical change to the world in just two million years. As culture has burgeoned man has increasingly manipulated the environment to his own ends, and become ever more dependent upon the brain that made it possible. Now the cognitive brain is the survival tool of the species. It also permits – among its many gifts – the contemplation of our origins.

OVERLEAF *Fossil deposits, Makapansgat, Transvaal*

Acknowledgements

Two people have inspired this book. The first is Mary Leakey, who advised and encouraged me when I was first planning it. The concept has changed a little since then, but throughout the two and a half years I have been working on the book, Mary has been a constant source of valuable information and advice. She read the first draft, and contributed significantly to the improvement of the second. Her help, kindness and hospitality, at Olduvai Gorge and at Laetoli, are very much appreciated.

The second source of inspiration has been my wife, Brigitte, who sought and collected papers both obscure and recent, translated some technical French and German, maintained an extremely efficient system of filing and retrieving information and occasionally displayed more confidence than I secretly thought the project deserved. Such special support has been invaluable.

I am no less indebted to the organizations and individuals listed below, without whose assistance and cooperation the research and photography could not have been contemplated. I imposed myself upon some institutions for several weeks, on some individuals for no more than a cup of tea – but every contact contributed to the book in some way, and I am especially grateful for the kind patience with which my enquiries were treated. I have tried hard to be accurate, and to ensure that my own opinion, where expressed, is clearly distinguishable from that of the relevant authority. If I have failed in any instance the responsibility is entirely mine, and I offer sincere apologies.

American Museum of Natural History, New York.
Bernard Price Institute, Johannesburg.
British Museum (Natural History), London.
University of California: Department of Anthropology, Berkeley; Department of Geology and Geophysics, Berkeley.
Cleveland Museum of Natural History, Laboratory of Physical Anthropology.
Dubois Collection, Rijksmuseum von Natuurlijke Historie, Leiden.
Geologisch-Paläontologisches Institut der Universität, Heidelberg.
The International Afar Research Expedition.
National Museums, Kenya.
Koobi Fora Research Project, Kenya.
Laetoli Research Project, Tanzania.

The London Library.
National Geographic Society, Washington.
Olduvai Gorge Research Project, Tanzania.
Laboratoire de l'Anthropologie, Musée de l'Homme, Paris.
Rheinisches Landesmuseum, Bonn.
The Royal Society, London.
The Royal Swedish Academy of Sciences.
National Museum, Tanzania.
TILLMIAP, Nairobi.
Transvaal Museum, Pretoria.
Paleontological Institute, Uppsala.
Senckenberg-Museum, Frankfurt am Main.
University of the Witwatersrand Medical School: Department of Anatomy.

Dr P. Abell
Dr J. Aronson
Dr K. Behrensmeyer
Professor Birger Bohlin
Karl Bolt
Dr C. K. Brain
Professor L. Brongersma
Dr M. Bush
Dr R. Chicicon
Dr R. J. Clarke
Professor Y. & Jacqueline Coppens
Dr Harvey Croze
Dr A. Cruikshank
Professor G. H. Curtis
Professor Raymond Dart
Professor M. H. Day
Hilary Davies
Dr R. Drake
Ms Carmean-Dubois
Jean M. F. Dubois
Peter Faugust
Dr Ian Findlater
Dr F. J. Fitch
Hod French
Gatenby-Davies family
Dr Alan Gentry
Bob Ginna
Dr C. Gow
Dr T. Gray
Dr J. M. Harris
Professor S. H. Haughton

John Hawkins
Hawthorne family
Dr P. van Helsdingen
Dr Andrew Hill
Dr R. L. Holloway
The Hominid Gang
Mr C. R. Hooijer
Adrian House
Alun Hughes
Dr Hans Joachim
Dr Don Johanson
Peter Jones
Dr Trevor Jones
Mac Kamoya
W. H. Kimbel
Dr James Kitching
Professor Dr Dr h.c. G. H. R. von Koenigswald
Professor Lars-König Königsson
Dr Reinhart Kraatz
Professor Björn Kurtén
Dr Meave Leakey
Philip & Valerie Leakey
Richard Leakey
Bonnie Lipschutz
Professor Owen Lovejoy
Drs Brian & Judy Maguire
Dr Henry McHenry
Professor Car-Axel Moberg
Dr Theya Molleson
Dr Mike Norton-Griffiths

Emma Nzuki
Dr K. P. Oakley
Professor Alan Ogot
Melvin M. Payne
Professor David Pilbeam
Hazel Potgieter
Rick Potts
Dr Louise Robbins
Dr Pat Shipman
Dr Elwyn Simons
Mary Griswold Smith
Bill & Ginny Smith
Chris & Sylvia Smith
Solveig Stuenes
Dr Ian Tattersall

Teutsch family
J. Thackeray
Professor Phillip Tobias
Dr Eric Trinkaus
Dr Elizabeth Vrba
Professor Alan Walker
Priscilla Ward
Dr Steve Ward
Professor Sherwood Washburn
Ron Watkins
Dr Tim White
James & On-Ke Wilde
Dr Bernard Wood
Professor Otto Zdansky

All photographs were taken by the author unless otherwise stated, and by courtesy of the following:

Frontispiece, 26: Rheinisches Landesmuseum, Bonn; **31** (Engraving of George Busk): The Royal Society, London; **31** (specimen): Trustees of the British Museum (Natural History); **35**: Musée de l'Homme, Paris; **43, 45, 49, 51, 53**: Dubois Collection, Rijksmuseum von Natuurlijke Historie, Leiden; **58** (photograph of Sir Arthur Keith): The Royal Society, London; **58** (specimen): Trustees of the British Museum (Natural History); **62** (drawing): Illustrated London News Picture Library; **62** (specimens and letters): Trustees of the British Museum (Natural History); **67** (photograph): Illustrated London News Picture Library; **67** (specimen), **79**: Trustees of the British Museum (Natural History); **86**: Department of Anatomy, University of the Witwatersrand Medical School, Johannesburg; **90**: Raymond Dart personal papers; **95** (specimen): Department of Anatomy, University of the Witwatersrand Medical School, Johannesburg; **95** (publication): Bernard Price Institute, Johannesburg; **98**: Prof. Dr. Dr. h.c. G. H. R. von Koenigswald; **106, 108**: Paleontological Institute, Uppsala; **111**: Professor Birger Bohlin, Uppsala; **115**: National Museums, Kenya; **119**: Robert Broom Collection, Transvaal Museum, Pretoria; **126, 127, 131, 133**: Transvaal Museum, Pretoria; **135**: C. K. Brain and Transvaal Museum, Pretoria; **142**: Photograph by Emory Kristof, © National Geographic Society, Washington D.C.; **146** (photograph): Dr M. D. Leakey; **146** (specimens): Trustees of the British Museum (Natural History); **154**: National Museum, Tanzania; **159**: Professor G. H. Curtis, Department of Geology and Geophysics, University of California, Berkeley; **163**: Peter Jones, Oxford; **170**: Dr M. D. Leakey, Olduvai Gorge Research

Project; **173**: Cambridge University Press, *Olduvai Gorge* vol. 3, Dr M. D. Leakey; **175, 179, 183, 186, 190, 191**: Dr M. D. Leakey, Olduvai Gorge Research Project; **195, 198, 202, 210**: R. E. F. Leakey, National Museums, Kenya; **214, 218**: Dr D. C. Johanson, Cleveland Museum of Natural History on behalf of The National Museum of Ethiopia; **222**: Dr M. D. Leakey, Laetoli Research Project, Tanzania; **227**: Dr D. C. Johanson, Cleveland Museum of Natural History on behalf of The National Museum of Ethiopia; **231, 235, 238**: Dr M. D. Leakey, Laetoli Research Project, Tanzania.

Bibliography

CHAPTER ONE

1 EISELEY, L. 1958 New York: *Darwin's Century*: 86.

2 BRITISH MUSEUM 1814 London: *Philosophical Transactions*.

3 BLAKE, C. C. 1862 London: On the Crania of the most Ancient Races of Men, *The Geologist*, 5: 207.

4 ANON. 1864 London: Notes on the Antiquity of Man, *Anthropological Review*: 71.

5 LYELL, C. 1863 London: *The Antiquity of Man*: 183.

6 EISELEY, L. 1958 New York: *Darwin's Century*: 133.

7 CHAMBERS, R. 1844 London: *Vestiges of the Natural History of Creation*: 231.

8 *ibid*: 208.

9 *ibid*: 281.

10 DARWIN, C. 1888 London: *The Origin of Species*, Historical Sketch: xviii.

11 OWEN, R. 1848 London: On the Archetype and Homologies of the Vertebrate Skeleton, *Encyclopaedia Britannica*, 8th edition, 16: 498–503.

12 OWEN, R. 1855 London: Of the Anthropoid Apes and their relation to Man, *Proceedings of the Royal Institution of Great Britain 1854–1858*, 3: 26–41.

13 SCHAAFHAUSEN, D. 1858 Bonn: On the Crania of the most Ancient Races of Man. Müller's Archiv 1858 page 453; translated by G. Busk 1861 with remarks and original figures, taken from a cast of the Neanderthal Cranium, *Natural History Review*, April 1861: 155–75.

14 *Medical Times and Gazette*, 28 June 1862.

15 a) as 13.
    b) BLAKE, C. C. 1864 London: On the alleged peculiar characters and assumed antiquity of the human cranium from the Neanderthal, *Journal of the Anthropological Society*, 2: 139–57.

16 MAYER, F. 1864 Leipzig: Ueber die fossilen Ueberreste eines menschlichen Schädels und Skeletes in einer Felsenhöhle des Düssel – oder Neander – Thales, *Arch. Anst. Physiol.* 1864: 1–26.

17 HUXLEY, T. H. 1864 London: Further remarks upon the human remains from the Neanderthal, *Natural History Review*, 1: 429–46
    HUXLEY, T. H. 1863 London: *Man's Place in Nature*; Ann Arbor edition, 1959 Michigan.

18 KING, W. 1864 London. The reputed fossil man of the Neanderthal, *Quarterly Journal of Science*, 1: 88–97.

19 BUSK, G. 1864 Bath: report on British Association Meeting, *Bath Chronicle*, 22 September 1864.

20 BUSK, G. 1864 London: Pithecoid Priscan Man from Gibraltar, *The Reader*, 23 July 1864.

21 as 19.

22 FALCONER, H. 1864 London: letter to Busk of 27 August 1864, quoted by Keith, A. 1911 London: The Early History of the Gibraltar Cranium, *Nature*, 87: 313.

23 VIRCHOW, R. 1872 Berlin: Untersuchung des Neanderthal-Schädels, *Zoo. Ethn.*, 4: 157–65.

24 BOULE, M. 1921 Paris: *Les Hommes Fossiles*; 1923 Edinburgh: *Fossil Men*.

25 BOULE, M. 1911–13 Paris: L'Homme fossile de La Chapelle-aux-Saints, *Annales de Paleontologie*, 6, 7, 8.

26 SMITH, G. E. 1924 London: *The Evolution of Man*: 109.

27 CAVE, A. J. E. & STRAUS, W. L. Jnr. 1957: Pathology and Posture of Neanderthal Man, *Quarterly Review of Biology*, 32: 348–63.

28 WOLPOFF, M. H. 1971 London: The Single Species Hypothesis, *Man*, 6: 601:14.

29 BRACE, C. L. 1964: The Fate of the 'Classic' Neanderthals: a consideration of hominid catastrophism, *Current Anthropology*, 5: 3–43.

30 LEAKEY, R. E. F. & LEWIN, R. 1977 London: *Origins*: 125.

31 CLARK, W. E. le GROS, 1964 Chicago: *The Fossil Evidence for Human Evolution*.

CHAPTER TWO

1 DARWIN, C. 1871 London: *The Descent of Man*; second edition 1882, introduction: 3.

2 a) HAECKEL, E. 1868 Berlin: *Natürliche Schöpfungsgeschichte*;
   b) 1876 London: *The History of Creation*: 28.

3 as 2(b): 307.

4 as 2(b): 326–7.

5 as 2(b): 325.

6 HAECKEL, E. 1906 London: *Last Words on Evolution*: 77.

7 HAECKEL, E. 1899 London: *The Last Link*: 77.

8 DUBOIS, E. 1891 Batavia: Paleontologische onderzoekingen op Java. *Verslagen van het Mijnwezen*, fourth quarter 1891.

9 DUBOIS, E. 1891 Batavia: *Verslagen van het Mijnwezen*, fourth quarter 1891: 13.

10 DUBOIS, E. 1892 Batavia: *Verslagen van het Mijnwezen*, third quarter 1892: 11.

11 DUBOIS, E. 1894 Batavia: *Pithecanthropus erectus, eine menschenähnliche Uebergangsform aus Java.*

12 DUBOIS, J. M. F. Unpublished manuscript, *Trinil: A Biography of Professor Dr Eugene Dubois, the discoverer of Pithecanthropus erectus*: 65.

13 as 7: 22.

14 KEITH, A. 1942 London: *The Rationalist Annual*.

15 DUBOIS, E. 1898 Cambridge: The brain-cast of Pithecanthropus erectus, *Proceedings of the International Congress of Zoology, 1898*: 79–96.

16 DUBOIS, E. 1920 Amsterdam: The proto-Australian fossil man of Wadjak, Java, *Koninklijke Akademie van Wetenschappen; proceedings*, 13: 1013–51.

17 DUBOIS, E. 1935 Amsterdam. On the gibbon-like appearance of Pithecanthropus erectus, *Koninklijke Akademie van Wetenschappen; proceedings*, 38: 578–85.

18 DUBOIS, E. 1933 Amsterdam: The shape and size of the brain in Sinanthropus and in Pithecanthropus, *Koninklijke Akademie van Wetenschappen; proceedings*, 36: 415–23.

19 as 17.

20 DUBOIS, E. 1940 Amsterdam: The fossil human remains discovered in Java by Dr G. R. H. von Koenigswald and attributed by him to Pithecanthropus erectus, in reality remains of Homo sapiens soloensis, *Konkinklijke Akademie van Wetenschappen; proceedings*, 43: 494–6, 842–51, 1268–75.

21 KOENIGSWALD, G. H. R. von. 1938 Amsterdam: Ein neuer Pithecanthropus-Schädel, *Konkinklijke Akademie van Wetenschappen; proceedings*, 41: 185–92.

22 KOENIGSWALD, G. H. R. von & WEIDENREICH, F. 1939 London: The relationship between Pithecanthropus and Sinanthropus, *Nature*, 144: 926–9.

23 MAYR, E. 1950: Taxonomic categories in fossil hominids, *Cold Spring Harbour Symposia on Quantitative Biology*, 15: 109–18.

24 DUBOIS, E. 1940 Amsterdam: *Konkinklijke Akademie van Wetenschappen; proceedings*, 43: 1275.

25 as 14.

CHAPTER THREE

1 KEITH, A. 1950 London: *An Autobiography*: 122.

2 KEITH, A. 1894 London: *Journal of Anatomy*, 28: 149–335.

3 as 1: 170.

4 as 1: 317.

5 DARWIN, C. 1871 London: *The Descent of Man*; 1922 printing: 80.

6 KEITH, A. 1912 London: *The Human Body*: 78.

7 SMITH, G. E. 1912 Dundee: Presidential Address, Anthropology Section, *Report of the British Association, 1912*: 575–98.

8 WOODWARD, A. S. 1885 Macclesfield: Modern Ideas of the Creation, *Macclesfield Courier and Herald*, 28 March 1885.

9 WOODWARD, A. S. 1913 Birmingham: Missing Links among extinct animals, *Report of the British Association*, 1913: 783.

10 KEITH, A. 1925 London: *The Antiquity of Man*; second edition: 258.

11 *ibid*: 258.

12 *ibid*: 265.

13 a) MOIR, J. REID. 1912: The Occurrence of a Human Skeleton in a Glacial Deposit at Ipswich, *Proceedings of the Prehistory Society of East Anglia*, 1: 194.

  b) KEITH, A. 1915 London: *The Antiquity of Man*.

  c) ANON. 1912 London: The Earliest Known Englishman, *Illustrated London News*, 140: 442, 446–7.

14 KEITH, A. 1912 Dundee: Modern problems relating to the antiquity of Man, *Report of the British Association*, 1912: 758.

15 as 7: 577.

16 WOODWARD, A. S. W. 1916 London: Charles Dawson – An Obituary, *Geological Magazine* (6) 3: 477–9.

17 DAWSON, C. & WOODWARD, A. S. 1913 London: On the discovery of a Palaeolithic human skull and mandible in a flint-bearing gravel overlying the Wealden (Hastings Beds) at Piltdown, Fletching, Sussex, *Quarterly Journal of the Geological Society*, 69: 117–44.

18 WOODWARD, A. S. 1948 London: *The Earliest Englishman*: 11.

19 WEINER, J. S. 1955 London: *The Piltdown Forgery*: 120.

20 SMITH, G. E. 1913 London: Preliminary report on the cranial cast [Piltdown skull], *Quarterly Journal of the Geological Society*, 69: 145–7.

21 as 17: 134–5.

22 as 20: 147.

23 as 1: 324.

24 KEITH, A. 1913 London: The Human skull etc. from Piltdown, discussion, *Quarterly Journal of the Geological Society*, 69: 148.

25 KEITH, A. 1913 London: Reported in *The Times*, 11 August 1913.

26 as 9: 786.

27 KEITH, A. 1913 London: The Piltdown Skull and Brain Cast, *Nature*, 92: 197.

28 *ibid*: 198–9.

29 *ibid*: 267.

30 SMITH, G. E. 1924 London: *The Evolution of Man*: 184.

31 as 27:292.

32 as 1: 327.

33 a) KEITH, A. 1914 London: The Reconstruction of fossil human skulls, *Journal of the Royal Anthropological Institute*, 44: 12.

  b) as 13(b): 537–78.

34 WOODWARD, A. S. 1917 London: Fourth note on the Piltdown gravel, with evidence of a second skull of Eoanthropus dawsoni, *Quarterly Journal of the Geological Society*, 73: 1–10.

35 *ibid*: 8.

36 KEITH, A. 1917 London: Second Skull from Piltdown Gravel, discussion, *Quarterly Journal of the Geological Society*, 73: 10.

37 WATERSTON, D. 1913 London: The Human skull etc. from Piltdown; discussion, *Quarterly Journal of the Geological Society*, 69: 150.

38 WATERSTON, D. 1913 London: The Piltdown Mandible, *Nature*, 92: 319.

39 MILLER, G. S. 1915 Washington: The jaw of Piltdown man, *Smithsonian Miscellaneous Collections*, 65: 1–31.

40 BOULE, M. 1923 Edinburgh: *Fossil Men*: 171 & 471.

41 SMITH, G. E. 1924 London: *Essays on the Evolution of Man*: 73.

42 as 40: 472.

43 KEITH, A. 1948 London: In a foreword to Woodward A. S., *The Earliest Englishman*.

44 HRDLICKA, A. 1930 Washington: The skeletal remains of early man, *Smithsonian Miscellaneous Collections*, 83: 65–90.

45 OSBORN, H. F. 1927 Princeton N.J.: *Man Rises to Parnassus*: 53.

46 LEAKEY, L. S. B. 1934 London: *Adam's Ancestors*: 221.

47 White, H. J. O. 1926 London: The Geology of the Country near Lewes, with map by Edmunds, F. H., *Memoir Geological Survey of England and Wales*. Expl. sheet 319.

48 MARSTON, A. 1937 London: The Swanscombe Skull, *Journal of the Royal Anthropological Institute*, 67: 394.

49 MIDDLETON, J. 1844 London: On flourine in bones, its source, and its application to the determination of the geological age of fossil bones, *Proceedings of the Geological Society*, 4: 431–3.

50 CARNOT, A. 1893 Paris: Recherches sur la composition générale et la teneur en fluor des os modernes et des os fossiles de différent âges, *Ann. Min. (9, Mém.)* 3: 155–95.

51 OAKLEY, K. P. & MONTAGU, M. F. A. 1949 London: A re-consideration of the Galley Hill skeleton, *Bulletin of the British Museum (Natural History)*, Geology, 1, 2: 27–46.

52 OAKLEY, K. P. & HOSKINS, C. R. 1950 London: New evidence on the antiquity of Piltdown man, *Nature*, 165: 379–2.

53 as 19: 26–35.

54 LYNE, C. W. 1916 London: The significance of the radiographs of the Piltdown teeth. *Proceedings of the Royal Society of Medicine*, 9 (3 Odont. Sect.): 33–62.

55 *The Times*, 1953 London: Parliamentary report 27 November 1953.

56 KRAMER, L. M. J. 1953 London: Letter to *The Times*, 28 November 1953.

CHAPTER FOUR

1 DART, R. 1978 Johannesburg: Personal communication. Interview with author.

2 DART, R. 1959 London: *Adventures with the Missing Link*: 26.

3 HAUGHTON, S. H. 1920 Cape Town: On the Occurence (sic) of a species of Baboon in Deposits near Taungs, Abstract in *Transactions of the Royal Society of South Africa*, 12, 1925: lxviii.

4 a) PARTRIDGE, T. C. 1973 London: Geomorphological Dating of Cave Opening at Makapansgat, Sterkfontein, Swartkrans and Taung, *Nature*, 246: 75 9.

    b) BRAIN, C. K. 1975 Amsterdam: An introduction to the South African australopithecine bone accumulations, *Archaezoological Studies* (editor Clason, A. T.): 109–19.

5 TERRY, R. 1974 Johannesburg: Raymond A. Dart Taung 1924–1974, *The Museum of Man and Science*.

6 *The Star*, 1925 Johannesburg: News Report, 4 February 1925.

7 as 2:16.

8 DART, R. 1925 London: *Australopithecus africanus*: The Man-Ape of South Africa. *Nature*, 115: 195–9.

9 KEITH, A., SMITH, G. E., WOODWARD, A. S. & DUCKWORTH, W. J. H. 1925 London: The Fossil Anthropoid from Taungs, *Nature*, 115: 234–6.

10 BROOM, R. 1950 London: *Finding the Missing Link*: 86.

11 as 2: 40.

12 CLARK, W. E. le GROS, 1967 New York: *Man-Apes or Ape-Men?*: 26

13 KEITH, A. 1925 London: The Taungs Skull, *Nature*, 116: 11.

14 *ibid*: 11.

15 *ibid*: 462.

16 as 2: 62.

17 as 12.

18 ABEL, W. 1931: Kritische Untersuchungen über *Australopithecus africanus* Dart, *Morphol. Jahrb.* 65 (4): 539–640.

19 as 2: 146.

20 as 2: 56.

21 DART, R. 1978 Johannesburg: Personal communication. Interview with author.

CHAPTER FIVE

1 ANDERSSON, J. G. 1934 London: *Children of the Yellow Earth*; Foreword: xx.

2 ZDANSKY, O. 1978 Uppsala: Personal communication. Interview with author.

3 as 1: 101.

4 as 2.

5 ANDREWS, R. C. 1932 New York: Natural History of Central Asia.

A narrative of the explorations of the Central Asiatic Expeditions in
Mongolia and China 1921–30. 12 volumes, Volume One, *The New
Conquest of China*: Introduction.

6 ANDREWS, R. C. 1932 New York: *The New Conquest of China*: 572.

7 *ibid*: 208.

8 ZDANSKY, O. 1923 Peking: Über ein Säugerknochenlager in Chou K'ou
Tien, *Geological Survey of China Bulletin*, 5: 83–9.

9 ZDANSKY, O. 1928 Peking: Die Säugetiere der Quartärfauna von Chou
K'ou Tien, *Palaeontologia Sinica*, Series C, 5 (4).

10 *Manchester Guardian*, 1926: News report, 17 November 1926.

11 BLACK, D. 1926 London: Tertiary man in Asia: The Chou Kou Tien
discovery, *Nature*, 118: 733–4.

12 *ibid* 1926 Washington: *Science*, 64: 586–7.

13 ZDANSKY, O. 1927 Peking: Preliminary notice on two teeth of a hominid
from a cave in Chihli (China), *Geological Society of China Bulletin*, 5:
281–4.

14 BOHLIN, B. 1978 Uppsala: Personal communication. Interview with
author.

15 BLACK, D. 1927 London: Further hominid remains of Lower Quaternary
age from the Chou Kou Tien deposit, *Nature*, 120: 954.

16 OSBORN, H. F. 1922 New York: Quoted in: Hesperopithecus, the First
Anthropoid Primate found in America, *American Museum Novitates*,
37: 1–5.

17 WOODWARD, A. S. 1922 London: Letter to *The Times*.

18 OSBORN, H. F. 1925 New York: *American Museum of Natural History
Bulletin*, February 1925, quoted in *The Times*, London, 25 February 1928.

19 *The Times*, 1928 London: *Hesperopithecus Dethroned*, Leader comment,
25 February 1928.

20 SMITH, G. E. 1929 Manchester: report in the *Manchester Guardian*,
16 September 1929.

21 HOOD, D. 1964 Toronto: *Davidson Black A Biography*: 93.

22 BLACK, D. 1929: Quoted in: Hood, D. 1964 Toronto, *Davidson Black A
Biography*: 100.

23 PEI, W. C. 1929 Peking: An Account of the Discovery of an Adult Sinanthropus Skull in the Chou-K'ou-tien Deposit, *Geological Society of China
Bulletin*, 8 (3).

24 KOENIGSWALD, G. H. R. von & WEIDENREICH, F. 1939 London:
The relationship between Pithecanthropus and Sinanthropus, *Nature*,
144: 926–9.

25 DAY, M. H. 1977 London: *Guide to Fossil Man*: 316–8.

26 SHAPIRO, H. L. 1974 London: *Peking Man*: chapter one.

27 WOO, J. K. 1978 Uppsala: Personal communication.

CHAPTER SIX

1 HALDANE, J. B. S., Quoted in: Terry, R. 1974 Johannesburg: *Raymond A. Dart – Taung 1924–1974*: 12.

2 FINDLAY, G. 1972 Cape Town: *Dr Robert Broom, F.R.S.*: 101.

3 *ibid*: 43.

4 a) BROOM, R. 1933 London: *The Coming of Man – Was it Accident or Design?*

b) BROOM, R. 1950 London: *Finding the Missing Link*: chapter ten.

5 BROOM, R. 1939 Johannesburg: On Evolution, *The Star*, 18 August 1939.

6 BROOM, R. 1885 Edinburgh: On the volume of mixed liquids, *Royal Society of Edinburgh, proceedings*; 13: 172–4.

7 a) BROOM, R. 1915 London: On the organ of Jacobson and its relations in the 'Insectivora' Part I. Tupaia and Gymnura, *Zoological Society of London, proceedings*; 157–62.

b) Part II. Talpa, Centetes, and Chrysochloris, *Zoological Society of London, proceedings*; 347–54.

8 Quoted in 2: 57.

9 BROOM, R. 1925: Quoted in 2: 52.

10 DART, R. 1959 London: *Adventures with the Missing Link*: 37.

11 BROOM, R. 1925 London: Some notes on the Taungs skull, *Nature*, 115: 569–71.

12 as 4(b): 39.

13 BROOM, R. 1946 Quoted in: Wells, L. H. 1966 Johannesburg: The Robert Broom Memorial Lecture, *South African Journal of Science*, September 1967: 365.

14 BROOM, R. Quoted in 2: 54.

15 JONES, T. 1978 Pretoria: Personal communication. Interview with author.

16 WELLS, L. H. 1966 Johannesburg: The Robert Broom Memorial Lecture, *South African Journal of Science*, September 1967: 364.

17 BROOM, R. 1936 London: A new fossil anthropoid skull from South Africa, *Nature*, 138: 486–8.

18 BROOM, R. 1936 London: On a new ancestral link between ape and man, *Illustrated London News*, 189: 476–7.

19 as 4(b): 50.

20 BROOM, R. 1938 London: More discoveries of Australopithecus, *Nature*, 141: 828–9.

21 BROOM, R. 1938 London: The missing link is no longer missing, *Illustrated News*, 193: 310–1.

22 as 4(b): 55.

23 a) BROOM, R. 1942 London: The hand of the ape-man Paranthropus robustus, *Nature*, 513–4.

b) An ankle-bone of the ape-man Paranthropus robustus, *Nature*, 152: 689–690.

24 BROOM, R. (with Schepers, G. W. H.), 1946 Pretoria: The South African fossil ape-men. The Australopithecinae. Part I. The occurrence and general structure of the South African ape-men, *Transvaal Museum Memoir*, 2: 7–144.

25 *ibid:* 142.

26 CLARK, W. E. le GROS, 1946 London: *Nature*, 157: 863–5.

27 as 4(b): 63.

28 KEITH, A. 1948 London: *A New Theory of Human Evolution*: 210.

29 *ibid:* 159.

30 *ibid:* 234.

31 *ibid:* 206.

32 *ibid:* 229.

33 BROOM, R. (with Robinson J. T. & Schepers, G. W. H.), 1950 Pretoria: Sterkfontein ape-man, Plesianthropus, *Transvaal Museum Memoir*, 4.

34 ASHTON, E. H. & ZUCKERMAN, S. 1950 London: Some quantitative dental characters of fossil anthropoids. *Philosophical Transactions of the Royal Society*, B, 234: 485.

35 Quoted in 2: 86.

36 CLARK, W. E. le GROS, 1967 New York, London:
     a) *Man-apes or Ape-men?* 35.
     b) Hominid characters of the australopithecine dentition, *Journal of the Royal Anthropological Institute*, 80: 37.

37 YATES, F. & HEALY, M. J. R. 1951 London: Statistical methods in anthropology, *Nature*, 168: 1116.

38 ZUCKERMAN, S. 1966 Edinburgh: Myths and methods in anatomy, *Journal of the Royal College of Surgeons of Edinburgh*, 11: 87–114.

39 ARDREY, R. 1961 London: *African Genesis*: 322.

CHAPTER SEVEN

1 LEAKEY, L. S. B. 1969 California: Public Lecture. Recording in possession of Leakey, M. D.

2 LEAKEY, L. S. B. 1937 London: *White African*: 55.

3 *ibid:* 56.

4 *ibid:* 76, 132.

5 *The Times*, 1914 London: News report, 19 April 1914.

6 RECK, H. 1914 London: Quoted in: A Man of 150,000 years ago? *Illustrated London News*, 4 April 1914: 563.

7 LEAKEY, M. D. 1979 Olduvai: Personal communication. Interview with author.

8 as 2: 252.

9 LEAKEY, L. S. B., HOPWOOD, A. T. & RECK, H. 1931 London: Age

of the Oldoway Bone Beds, Tanganyika, *Nature*, 128: 724.

10 LEAKEY, L. S. B. 1931 London: Article in *The Times*, 3 December 1931.

11 LEAKEY, L. S. B. 1932 London: Article in *The Times*, 9 March 1932.

12 LEAKEY, L. S. B. 1932 London: Article in *The Times*, 19 April 1932.

13 KEITH, A. 1931 London: *New discoveries relating to the antiquity of man.*

14 ROYAL ANTHROPOLOGICAL INSTITUTE, 1933 Cambridge: Early human remains in East Africa, *Man*, 33:66.

15 WOODWARD, A. S. 1933 Cambridge: Early human remains in East Africa, *Man*, 33: 210.

16 LEAKEY, L. S. B., RECK, H., BOSWELL, P. G. H., HOPWOOD, A. T. & SOLOMON, J. D. 1933 London: The Oldoway Human Skeleton, *Nature*, 131: 397–8.

17 BOSWELL, P. G. H. 1935 London: Human remains from Kanam and Kanjera, Kenya Colony, *Nature*, 135: 371.

18 LEAKEY, L. S. B. 1936 London: Fossil Human Remains from Kanam and Kanjera, Kenya Colony, *Nature*, 138: 643.

19 LEAKEY, L. S. B. 1951 Cambridge: Olduvai Gorge: A Report on the Evolution of the Hand-axe Culture in Beds I–IV.

19 LEAKEY, L. S. B. 1951 Cambridge: *Olduvai Gorge: A Report on the Evolution of the Hand-axe Culture in Beds I–IV.*

20 COLE, S. 1975 London: *Leakey's Luck*: 117–25.

21 Quoted in LEAKEY, M. D. 1971 Cambridge: *Olduvai Gorge*, Vol 3: 199.

22 LEAKEY, L. S. B. 1965 Cambridge: *Olduvai Gorge 1951–1961*. Vol I: 76.

23 LEAKEY, L. S. B. 1954 London: The Giant Animals of Prehistoric Tanganyika, and the Hunting Grounds of Chellean Man. . . . *Illustrated London News*, 244: 1047–51.

24 LEAKEY, L. S. B. 1958 London: Recent Discoveries at Olduvai Gorge, Tanganyika, *Nature*, 181: 1099–1103.

25 LEAKEY, L. S. B. 1958 London: A Giant Child Among the Giant Animals of Olduvai? A Huge Fossil Milk Molar Which Suggests That Chellean Man in Tanganyika May Have Been Gigantic, *Illustrated London News*, 232: 1104–5.

26 ROBINSON, J. T. 1959 London: An Alternative Interpretation of the supposed Giant Deciduous Hominid tooth from Olduvai, *Nature*, 185: 407.

27 LEAKEY, L. S. B. 1959 London: *Nature*, 185: 408.

28 LEAKEY, M. D. 1979 London: *Olduvai Gorge: My Search for Early Man*: 75.

29 OAKLEY, K. P. 1956 London: The Earliest Toolmakers, *Antiquity*, 30: 4–8.

30 DART, R. 1955 London: The first australopithecine fragment from the Makapansgat pebble culture stratum, *Nature*, 176: 170.

31 as 24: 31.

32 LEAKEY, L. S. B. 1959 London: A new fossil skull from Olduvai, *Nature*, 184: 491–3.

33 LEAKEY, L. S. B. 1960 London: From the Taung Skull to "Nutcracker Man": Africa as the Cradle of Mankind and the Primates. . . . *Illustrated London News*, 236: 44.

34 LEAKEY, L. S. B. 1960 Washington: Finding the World's Earliest Man, *The National Geographic Magazine*, 118: 420–35.

35 ROBINSON, J. T. 1960 London: The affinities of the new Olduvai australopithecine, *Nature*, 186: 456–7.

36 WASHBURN, S. 1960 New York: Tools and Human evolution, *Scientific American*, 203 (3): 3–15.

37 LEAKEY, L. S. B. 1959 London: quoted in *The Times* report, 4 September 1959.

38 as 7.

39 LEAKEY, L. S. B., EVERNDEN, J. F. & CURTIS, G. H. 1961 London: Age of Bed I, Olduvai Gorge, Tanganyika, *Nature*, 191: 478–9.

40 PAYNE, M. 1978 Washington: Personal communication. Interview with author.

41 TOBIAS, P. V. 1967 Cambridge: *Olduvai Gorge, 2, The Cranium and Maxillary Dentition of Australopithecus (Zinjanthropus) boisei.*

CHAPTER EIGHT

1 FRERE, J. 1800 London: *Archaeologia*, 13: 204.

2 OAKLEY, K. P. & LEAKEY, M. D. 1937 London: Report on excavations at Jaywick Sands, Essex (1934), *Prehistoric Society, proceedings, 1937, 3*: 217–60.

3 LEAKEY, M. D. 1971 Cambridge: *Olduvai Gorge, volume 3, Excavations in Beds I and II.*

4 HAY, R. L. 1976 Berkeley: *Geology of the Olduvai Gorge.*

5 LEAKEY, M. D. 1979 London: *Olduvai Gorge: My Search for Early Man*: 86.

6 *ibid*: 51.

7 LEAKEY, M. D. 1967 Chicago: Preliminary Survey of the Cultural Material from Beds I and II, Olduvai Gorge, Tanzania, in: Bishop, W. W. & Clark, J. D. (editors) 1967 Chicago: *Background to Evolution in Africa*: 417.

8 LEAKEY, L. S. B. 1951 Cambridge: *Olduvai Gorge: A Report on the Evolution of the Hand-axe Culture in Beds I–IV*: 34.

9 JONES, P. R. 1979 Washington: Effects of Raw Material on Biface Manufacture, *Science*, 204: 835–6.

CHAPTER NINE

1 CAMPBELL, B. 1964 London: Just another 'man-ape'? *Discovery*, 25 (June issue): 37–8.
2 NAPIER, J. R. 1962 London: Fossil Hand Bones from Olduvai Gorge, *Nature*, 196: 409–11.
3 DAY, M. H. & NAPIER, J. R. 1964 London: Fossil Foot Bones, *Nature*, 201: 969–70.
4 DAVIS, P. R. 1964 London: Hominid Fossils from Bed I, Olduvai Gorge, Tanganyika – A Tibia and Fibula, *Nature*, 201: 967–70.
5 LEAKEY, L. S. B. 1961 London: New Finds at Olduvai Gorge, *Nature*, 189: 649–50.
6 TOBIAS, P. V. 1964 London: The Olduvai Bed I Hominine with special reference to its cranial capacity, *Nature*, 202: 3–4.
7 LEAKEY, L. S. B., TOBIAS, P. V. & NAPIER, J. R. 1964 London: A New Species of the Genus *Homo* from Olduvai Gorge, *Nature*, 202: 7–9.
8 LEAKEY, M. D. 1971 London: Discovery of Postcranial Remains of *Homo erectus* and associated artefacts in Bed IV at Olduvai Gorge, Tanzania, *Nature*, 232: 380–3.
9 as 7: 7–9.
10 CLARK, W. E. le GROS, 1955 Chicago: *The Fossil Evidence for Human Evolution*: 86.
11 a) OXNARD, C. E. 1972 Chicago: Functional morphology of primates: some mathematical and physical methods. In: Tuttle, R. (editor) 1972 Chicago: *The Functional and Evolutionary Biology of Primates*.
  b) DAY, M. H. 1976 California: Hominid Postcranial Material from Bed I, Olduvai Gorge. In: Isaac, G. Ll. & McCown, E. R. (editors) 1976 California: HUMAN ORIGINS: *Louis Leakey and the East African Evidence*.
12 as 1: 37–8.
13 a) ROBINSON, J. T. 1965 London: Homo 'habilis' and the australo-pithecines, *Nature*, 205: 121–4.
  b) CLARK, W. E. le GROS, 1964 London: The evolution of man, *Discovery*, 25 (July issue): 37.
14 as 1: 37.
15 TOBIAS, P. V. & NAPIER, J. R. 1964 London: Letter to *The Times*, 29 May 1964.
16 OAKLEY, K. P. 1964 London: The evolution of man, *Discovery*, 25 (August issue): 49.
17 PILBEAM, D. 1972 New York: *The Ascent of Man*: 135.

CHAPTER TEN

1 PILBEAM, D. 1977 New York: Quoted in: Puzzling Out Man's Ascent, *Time*, 7 November 1977: 53, 54.

2 LEAKEY, R. E. F. 1979 London: Personal communication. Interview with author.

3 *ibid.*

4 LEAKEY, R. E. F. 1970 Washington: In search of man's past at Lake Rudolf, *National Geographic*, 137: 723.

5 *ibid*: 725.

6 FITCH, F. J. & MILLER, J. A. 1970 London: Radioisotopic age determinations of Lake Rudolf artefact site, *Nature*, 226: 226–8.

7 LEAKEY, R. E. F. 1970 London: Fauna and artefacts from a new Plio-Pleistocene locality near Lake Rudolf in Kenya, *Nature*, 226: 223–4.

8 as 8: 731–2.

9 LEAKEY, R. E. F. 1971 London: Further evidence of Lower Pleistocene hominids from East Rudolf, North Kenya, *Nature*, 231: 241–5.
   LEAKEY, R. E. F. 1972 London: Further evidence of Lower Pleistocene hominids from East Rudolf, North Kenya, 1971, *Nature*, 237: 264–9.

10 LEAKEY, R. E. F. 1972: New evidence for the evolution of man, *Social Biology*, 19: 99–114.

11 WALKER, A. W. 1978 Cambridge, Mass.: Personal communication. Interview with author.

12 LEAKEY, R. E. F. 1973 Washington: Skull 1470, *National Geographic*, 143: 819–29.

13 LEAKEY, R. E. F. 1977 New York: Quoted as in 1: 53.

14 TATTERSALL, I. & ELDREDGE, N. 1977 New Haven: Fact, Theory, and Fantasy in Human Paleontology, *American Scientist*, 65: 204–11.

15 ELDREDGE, N. & TATTERSALL, I. 1975 Basel: Evolutionary models, phylogenetic reconstruction, and another look at hominid phylogeny. In: Szalay, F. S. (editor) 1975 Basel: *Approaches to Primate Paleobiology*.

16 WALKER, A. C. 1973 Nairobi: Remains attributable to Australopithecus in the East Rudolf succession, In: Coppens, Y., Howell, F. C., Isaac, G. Ll. & Leakey, R. E. F. (editors) 1976 Chicago: *Earliest Man and Environments in the Lake Rudolf Basin*: 484–9.

17 DAY, M. H., LEAKEY, R. E. F., WALKER, A. C. & WOOD, B. A. 1975 Philadelphia: New Hominids from East Rudolf, Kenya, I, *American Journal of Physical Anthropology*, 42: 461–76.

18 WOOD, B. A. 1981 Oxford: The cranial hominid remains from Koobi Fora. In preparation for: Leakey, R. E. F. & Isaac, G. Ll. (editors): *Koobi Fora Research Project monograph series*.

19 COOKE, H. B. S. 1973 Nairobi: Suidae from Plio-Pleistocene strata of the Rudolf Basin. In: *Earliest Man and Environments in the Lake Rudolf Basin*, (see 16): 251–63.

20 FITCH, F. J. & MILLER, J. A. 1973 Nairobi: Conventional potassium-argon and argon-40/argon-39 dating of volcanic rocks from East Rudolf. In: *Earliest Man and Environments in the Lake Rudolf Basin*, (see 16): 132.

21 HALL, E. T. 1974 London: Old bones – but how old? *The Sunday Telegraph*, 3 September 1974.

22 as 6: 226–8.

23 BROCK, A. & ISAAC, G. Ll. 1974 London: Paleomagnetic stratigraphy and chronology of the hominid-bearing sediments East of Lake Rudolf, Kenya, *Nature*, 247: 344–8.

24 HOOKE, R. 1668 London: Discourse of Earthquakes (1705); quoted in: Edwards, W. N. 1976 London: *The Early History of Paleontology*: 31.

25 as 19:.

26 as 19: 261.

27 ISAAC, G. Ll. 1976 Chicago: In: *Earliest Man and Environments in the Lake Rudolf Basin*, (see 18): 6.

28 CURTIS, G. H., DRAKE, R., CERLING, T. E. & HAMPEL, J. E. 1975 London: Age of KBS tuff in Koobi Fora Formation, East Rudolf, Kenya, *Nature*, 358: 395–8.

29 as 2.

30 as 2.

31 WHITE, T. D. & HARRIS, J. M. 1977 Washington: Suid evolution and correlation of African hominid localities, *Science*, 198: 13–21.

32 as 31: 20.

33 as 2.

34 FITCH, F. J. 1979 London: Personal communication. Interview with author.

35 LEAKEY, M. G. & LEAKEY, R. E. F. (editors) 1978 Oxford: The fossil hominids and an introduction to their context. Volume 1 of: Leakey, R. E. F. & Isaac, G. Ll. (editors) 1978– Oxford: *Koobi Fora Research Project monograph series*.

36 a) DAY, M. H. 1981 Oxford: The post-cranial hominid remains from Koobi Fora. In preparation for: Leakey, R. E. F. & Isaac, G. Ll. (editors) *Koobi Fora Research Project monograph series*.

b) WALKER, A. C. 1981 Oxford: Biological adaptations in the Koobi Fora hominids. In preparation for: *Koobi Fora Research Project monograph series* (see above).

c) as 18.

37 *Time* 1977 New York: Puzzling out man's ascent, 7 November 1977.

38 a) as 2.

b) WALKER, A. C. & LEAKEY, R. E. F. 1978 New York: The Hominids of East Turkana, *Scientific American*, 239 (August issue): 54–66.

CHAPTER ELEVEN

1 JOHANSON, D. C. & TAIEB, M. 1976 London: Plio-Pleistocene hominid discoveries in Hadar, Ethiopia, *Nature*, 260: 293–7.

2 JOHANSON, D. C., SPLINGAER, M. & BOAZ, N. T. 1973 Nairobi: Paleontological excavations in the Shungura Formation, Lower Omo Basin, 1969–73. In: Coppens, Y., Howell, F. C., Isaac, G. Ll. & Leakey, R. E. F. (editors) 1976 Chicago: *Earliest Man and Environments in the Lake Rudolf Basin*: 402–20.

3 JOHANSON, D. C. 1976 Washington: Ethiopia yields first "Family" of early man, *National Geographic*, December 1976: 801.

4 JOHANSON, D. C. 1974 Addis Ababa: Quoted in: Ottoway, D. B. 1974 Paris, 3-million-year-old human fossils found, *Herald Tribune*, 28 October 1974.

5 as 3: 793.

6 OTTAWAY, D. B. 1974 Paris: Oldest partial skeleton of 'Man' is found, *Herald Tribune*, 27 December 1974.

7 as 3: 791–811.

8 JOHANSON, D. C. 1979 Chicago: Our roots go deeper, In: *Science Year 1979*; Worldbook Childcraft International Inc.

9 LEAKEY, R. E. F. & LEWIN, R. 1977 London: *Origins*: 90.

10 as 3: 809.

11 LEAKEY, M. D., HAY, R. L., CURTIS, G. H., DRAKE, R. E., JACKES, M. K. & WHITE, T. D. 1976 London: Fossil hominids from the Laetolil Beds, *Nature*, 262:460–6.

12 a) JOHANSON, D. C., WHITE, T. D. & COPPENS, Y. 1978 Cleveland: A new species of the genus *Australopithecus* (Primates: Hominidae) from the Pliocene of Eastern Africa, *Kirtlandia*, 28: 1–14.

   b) JOHANSON, D. C. & WHITE, T. D. 1979 Washington: A systematic assessment of early African hominids, *Science*, 203: 321–30.

13 as 8.

14 READER, J. A. 1978 Nairobi: White, T. D. presents Australopithecus afarensis, Notes on TILLMIAP seminar and discussion, 28 June 1978.

15 JOHANSON, D. C., WHITE, T. D. & COPPENS, Y. 1978 Cleveland: A new species of the genus Australopithecus (Primates: Hominidae) from the Pliocene of Eastern Africa, *Kirtlandia*, 28: 1–14.

16 WHITE, T. D. 1977 Philadelphia: New fossil hominids from Laetolil, Tanzania, *American Journal of Physical Anthropology*, 46: 197–230.

17 DAY, M. H., LEAKEY, M. D. & OLSON, T. R. 1980 Washington: On the status of Australopithecus afarensis, *Science*, 207: 1102–3.

18 TOBIAS, P. V. T. 1980 London: *The emergence of man in Africa and beyond*. Paper read at a meeting of the Royal Society in conjunction with the British Academy, 12 March 1980.

19 LEAKEY, R. E. F. & WALKER, A. 1980 Washington: On the status of Australopithecus afarensis, *Science*, 207: 1103.

20 LEAKEY, R. E. F. 1979 Pittsburgh: Quoted in: Rensberger, B. 1979 New York: Rival anthropologists divide on 'Pre-human' find, *New York Times*, 18 February 1979.

21 LEAKEY, R. E. F. 1979 London: Personal communication. Interview with author.

CHAPTER TWELVE

1 LEAKEY, M. D. & HAY, R. L. 1979 London: Pliocene footprints in the Laetolil Beds at Laetoli, northern Tanzania, *Nature*, 278: 317–323.

2 LEAKEY, L. S. B. 1960 Washington: Finding the world's earliest man, *National Geographic*, 118: 434.

3 LEAKEY, L. S. B., TOBIAS, P. V. & NAPIER, J. R. 1964 London: A new species of genus *Homo* from Olduvai Gorge, *Nature*, 202: 7–9.

4 CLARK, W. E. le GROS 1964 Chicago: *The fossil evidence for human evolution*: 162.

5 DAY, M. H. & NAPIER, J. R. 1964 London: Fossil foot bones, *Nature*, 201: 969–970.

6 DAY, M. H. & WOOD, B. A. 1968 London: Functional affinities of the Olduvai Hominid 8 talus, *Man* (new series), 3: 440–455.

7 DAVIS, P. R. 1964 London: Hominid fossils from Bed I, Olduvai Gorge, Tanganyika – A tibia and fibula, *Nature*, 201: 967–970.

8 CLARK, W. E. le GROS 1967 New York: *Man-apes or Ape-Men?*: 43.

9 PILBEAM, D. 1972 New York: *The Ascent of Man*: 140.

10 WASHBURN, S. L. 1960 New York: Tools and human evolution, *Scientific American*, 203: (3) 3–15.

11 LEAKEY, R. E. F. 1978 Nairobi: Personal communication. Interview with author.

12 LEAKEY, R. E. F. 1972 London: Man and sub-men on Lake Rudolf, *New Scientist*, 56: 386–7.

13 *Time*, 1978 New York: *Leakey's find – Tracks of an ancient ancestor*, 6 March 1978.

14 a) LOVEJOY, C. O., HEIPLE, K. G. & BURSTEIN, A. H. 1973 Philadelphia: The gait of Australopithecus, *American Journal of Physical Anthropology*, 38: 757–80.

b) LOVEJOY, C. O. 1973 Philadelphia: The gait of australopithecines, *Yearbook of Physical Anthropology*, 17: 147–61.

c) LOVEJOY, C. O. 1975 The Hague: Biomechanical perspectives on the lower limb of early hominids. In: Tuttle, R. H. (editor) 1976 The Hague: *Primate Morphology and Evolution*: 291–326.

15 as 14(a): 777.

16 a) LEAKEY, R. E. F. 1973 London: Further evidence of Lower Pleistocene hominids from East Rudolf, North Kenya, 1972, *Nature*, 242: 170–3.

   b) LEAKEY, R. E. F. 1973 London: Evidence for an advanced Plio-Pleistocene hominid from East Rudolf, Kenya, *Nature*, 242: 447–50.

17 LEAKEY, R. E. F. 1973 Washington: Skull 1470, *National Geographic*, 143: 819–29.

18 as 1: 317–23.

19 CLARKE, R. J. 1979 Pretoria: Early hominid footprints from Tanzania, *South African Journal of Science*, 75; 148–9.

20 *ibid*: 149.

21 PILBEAM, D. 1972 New York: *The Ascent of Man*: 91–9.

22 PILBEAM, D., MEYER, G. E., BADGLEY, C., ROSE, M. D., PICKFORD, M. H. L., BEHRENSMEYER, A. K. & SHAH, S. M. I. 1977 London: New hominoid primates from the Siwaliks of Pakistan and their bearing on hominoid evolution, *Nature*, 270: 689–95.

23 PILBEAM, D. 1980 London: Personal communication.

24 as 19: 149.

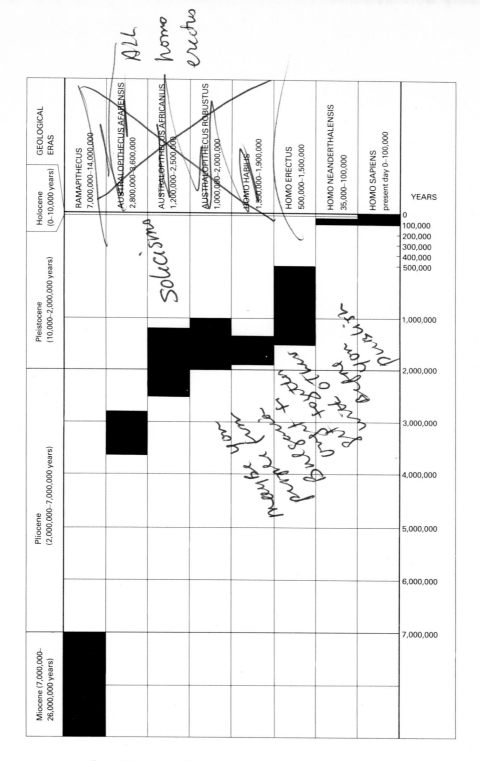

CHRONOLOGICAL TABLE

Neander Valley
Piltdown Common ●
Heidelberg
Les Eyzies ●
La Chapelle-aux-Saints ●

Gibraltar ●

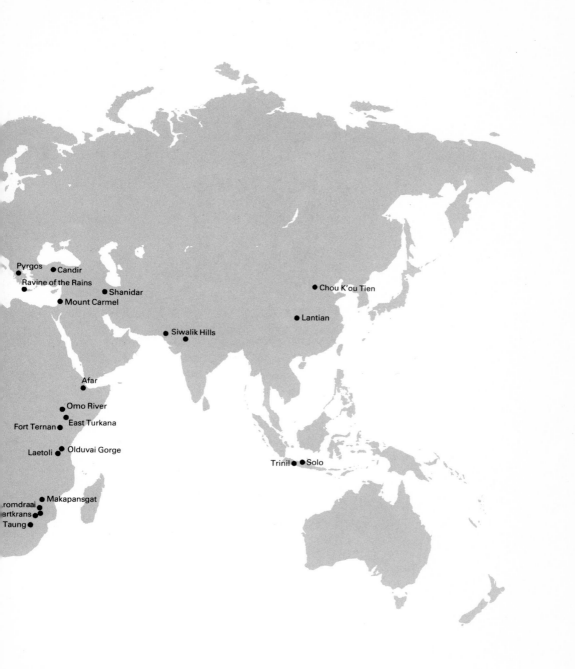

Pyrgos
● Candir
Ravine of the Rains
● Shanidar
● Mount Carmel

● Chou K'ou Tien

● Lantian

● Siwalik Hills

Afar

● Omo River
Fort Ternan ● ● East Turkana

Laetoli ● ● Olduvai Gorge

Trinil ● ● Solo

romdraai ● ● Makapansgat
artkrans ●
Taung ●

HOMINOID FOSSIL SITES

Index